AF606064

Morphology Now

SUNY Series in Linguistics

Mark Aronoff, Editor

MORPHOLOGY NOW

Edited by
Mark Aronoff

State University of New York Press

Published by
State University of New York Press, Albany

Printed in the United States of America

For information, address State University of New York
Press, State University Plaza, Albany, N.Y., 12246

Production by E. Moore
Marketing by Fran Keneston

Library of Congress Cataloging-in-Publication Data

Morphology now / Mark Aronoff, editor.
p. cm.—(SUNY series in linguistics)
Includes bibliographical references and index.
ISBN 0-7914-0815-9.—ISBN 0-7914-0816-7 (pbk.)
1. Grammar, Comparative and general—Morphology. I. Series.
P241.M67 1991
415—dc20 90-22725
CIP

10 9 8 7 6 5 4 3 2 1

CONTENTS

INTRODUCTION

The papers in this volume originated in a workshop on morphology that I organized at the Linguistic Society of America Summer Institute that was held at the University of Arizona in Tucson during the summer of 1989. Except for the paper by Jack Hoeksema, all papers were presented and discussed at the workshop.

LSA Summer Institute workshops are usually highly formal affairs, with papers solicited in advance on a closely circumscribed topic within a particular theoretical framework. By contrast, this workshop just grew. At the Arizona institute, there were more that the usual number of morphologists, and it seemed to me, after a few days at the institute, that it would be useful to have a forum where we could meet as a group on a regular basis and discuss current research. I sent round a notice, announcing the workshop and asking for volunteers. To my great pleasure, within a few days we had a full schedule and to my even greater pleasure, all the weekly workshop sessions were very well attended and all the presentations were very well received. When it was over and everyone was getting ready to go home, it struck me that a way should be found to preserve this moment, not simply for reasons of nostalgia, but also because the presentations, despite the lack of an explicit organizing framework, did seem in retrospect to fit together very well indeed. Let me now try to demonstrate this last point.

All the papers in this volume are formulated within the generative tradition. The study of morphology within a generative framework, although it is conventionally rooted in Chomsky's 1970 article "Remarks on Nominalizations," did not really begin until some time later.[1] The first works, such as Remarks and Halle's Prolegomenon, were more in the way of exhortations: There are interesting things going on here in morphology; let's have a look! Only after a few years had passed did research began to appear that dealt directly and unapologetically with morphological phenomena from a generative perspective, and it is only very recently that the generative study of morphology has become a normal part of the field, so that departments advertise positions in morphology and there are regular sessions on morphology at scholarly meetings.

Generative morphology has come of age and this volume is a kind of celebration of this ritual passage. All the papers in the volume assume without question that the field of generative morphology exists and needs no special defense. Furthermore, they all assume, implicitly for the most part, that morphology should be dealt with on its own terms, that it is different from phonology and syntax (what we fashionably call autonomous), although it must inevitably interact with the rest of language. They thus differ as a group from much recent revisionist work done within the generative paradigm, which seeks to subsume morphology under other components, as it was in earlier periods of the generative enterprise.

The skeptic might counter that morphology never needed any defense in the first place, because it had a legitimate place in linguistics long before generative theory was ever dreamed of. Yes, this point is well taken, and the fact that morphology has again assumed its rightful place in the core after decades of exile is testimony to its power. Nonetheless, it is important to understand that the study of morphology within the generative framework, broadly defined, has distinct properties that set it apart from other morphological enterprises.

First, the generative tradition is a theoretical one, so that most work, although it is grounded in fact, is directed toward theoretical ends. The purpose of the generative enterprise is to explain rather than to describe, although description must inevitably accompany (some would say precede) explanation. In this, generative linguistics only follows a long tradition in mainstream American linguistics that stretches in an unbroken line back to Boas, although certain polemicists of the fifties liked to believe that their "descriptive linguistics" lay above theoretical concerns. Each one of the articles in this volume is thus centered around a point of morphological theory. That is not to say that the volume is theoretically unified. In fact, several distinct general linguistic theories are represented here: Autolexical theory (Chelliah), Categorial Grammar (Hoeksema; Raffelsiefen), Functional Grammar (Haspelmath), and Government and Binding (Drijkoningen). The remaining three articles (Aronoff, Kari, de Reuse) are compatible with a number of general frameworks, and none of the articles is so deeply imbedded within a single theory as to be inaccessible to the average well-educated linguist. Altogether, though, this is a collection of theoretical works, each one designed to further the development of morphological (and hence general linguistic) theory.

Second, the best of the generative tradition has always followed the maxim that a language is a system where everything holds together. A grammar may consist of autonomous parts, but they all interact. This is especially true of morphology, which lies at the center of language, so that it is impossible to treat morphology without treating some other aspect of language at the same time. Indeed, perhaps the most difficult task in morphological research is to figure out what aspect of a particular phenomenon is morphological, as opposed to phonological or syntactic or semantic. There are (surprisingly to the novice) no purely morphological phenomena, despite the existence of purely morphological concepts. Thus, all the articles in this volume deal directly or indirectly with the interaction of morphology with other theoretical modules.

Finally, the generative tradition has always emphasized the diverse unity of human language. In this volume, although each article is devoted to either a single language or a small number of related languages, we find many very different kinds of languages, from Sino-Tibetan Manipuri (Chelliah), through Eskimo Central Siberian Yupik (de Reuse) and Athabaskan Ahtna (Kari) to Latin (Aronoff) and modern European languages, and finally to English (although no paper is devotedly solely to that most widely discussed language). Nonetheless, each of the authors assumes that all these sometimes dramatically different systems are a manifestation of a single unified human language faculty, so that the goal of linguistic theory is to reconcile the two, to create a theory that will permit just the diversity that we find.

I hope that the reader will enjoy reading these articles as much as I have enjoyed working on them. For most, they will not have the Proustian effect that they will have on those of us who were there. They will not conjure up the intensity, both intellectual and meteorological, of those summer afternoons in Tucson. Nonetheless, I hope that they will, like the desert sun, generate as much light as they do heat.

MARK ARONOFF

STEMS IN LATIN VERBAL MORPHOLOGY

Mark Aronoff

INTRODUCTION

Robert Beard (1981, 1987) has developed an approach to morphology in which there is a strong separation between the side of morphology that deals with forms and the sides that deal with syntax and semantics. Beard himself, having made the separation, has dealt mostly with the latter two. In this work, I will explore the consequences of separationism for the form side of things. In particular, I will examine the role of stems, defined purely as units of form.

I will adopt the traditional definition of a stem as "that part of a complete wordform which remains when an affix is removed"[1] and explore the consequences of treating stems as pure forms from the general perspective of modern lexeme-based theories of morphology such as those of Anderson (ms.), Aronoff (1976), Beard, Hoeksema (1985), Matthews (1972), or Zwicky (1989).

1. PRISCIANIC FORMATION

I will begin with Matthews, since that is where modern lexeme-based morphology originates. Matthews devotes a great deal of attention to what he calls Priscianic or parasitic formation, in which one member of a paradigm seems not to be formed on the lexical root[2] of the paradigm but instead on the stem of another member of the paradigm.[3] The best-known case of a putative Priscianic formation, and the one to which Matthews devotes most of his attention, is the Latin future active participle. This participle is invariably marked by the suffix *-uur-*, and, since it is an adjective morphologically, it agrees in gender, number, and case with its modified head noun or subject,[4] as in the following examples:[5]

[1] **a.**

cum hooc	equit-e	pugn-aa-t-uur-ii
with this.ABL.SG	cavalry-ABL.SG	fight-Th-T-FP-NOM.PL

es-tis
be-2pl.PR.IND.ACT
'you are about to fight with this cavalry' [Livy]

b.

qu-oos	Cn. Pompeeius	fac-t-uur-us	est
which.ACC.PL	Pompey	do-T-FP-NOM.SG	is

'which Pompey is to do' [Cicero]

Two things are noteworthy about the future active participle. First, it is not formed directly on the verb root, but instead on the stem of the perfect (passive) participle (PP), as shown in table 1:[6]

The perfect participle marker is usually the suffix *-t:* attached directly to the verb theme (the root followed by the theme vowel), as in *am-aa-t-* 'love PP', *aud-ii-t-* 'hear PP', or attached directly to the verb root, as in *duc-t-* 'lead PP'. The perfect participle, like the future participle, is an adjective morphologically and therefore always carries a marker for gender, number, and case of its head noun or subject in the form of a suffix following the perfect participle suffix.[7] Often, however, there is some irregularity, either in the perfect participle suffix, which may be *s* instead of *t*,[8] or in the form of the verb to which the perfect participle suffix is attached. In these cases, the perfect participle must be listed.

Table 1
Perfect and Future Participles

Present Infinitive Active	*Perfect Participle*	*Future Participle*	*Gloss*
laudaa-re	laudaat-	laudaat-uur-	'praise'
monee-re	monit-	monit-uur-	'warn'
duce-re	duct-	duct-uur-	'lead'
audii-re	audiit-	audiit-uur-	'hear'
cape-re	capt-	capt-uur-	'take'
vehe-re	vect-	vect-uur-	'carry'
haeree-re	haes-	haes-uur-	'stick'
preme-re	press-	press-uur-	'press'
fer-re	lat-	lat-uur-	'bear'
loqu-ii	locut-	locut-uur-	'speak'
experii-rii	expert-	expert-uur-	'try'

Generally, if the perfect participle is irregular, the future participle stem is identical to it, as shown in table 2 below. There are only a handful of exceptions to this statement.[9] This covariance has led grammarians to an analysis whereby the future participle is formed by suffixing *-uur* to the stem of the perfect participle.[10] However, this analysis has an unfortunate side effect, which is the second interesting property of the future participle: the perfect participle is usually passive,[11] but the future participle is always active. Indeed, although there exists a future passive participle (the *gerundive*), it is formed on the present stem of the verb and not on any future or passive stem.

If we derive the future participle from the perfect participle, then what do we do with the passive meaning of the perfect participle? Matthews says that the future participle is based on the perfect participle solely in terms of its form and not in terms of its meaning. The future participle is in this way parasitic on the perfect participle and hence his term *parasitic* for a formation of this sort, where one item is built on another solely in terms of their forms and not in terms of their meanings. Mel'cuk (1989) discusses this discrepancy between semantic and formal effects very clearly. According to him, assuming that the *-t-* suffix marks the perfect participle, the suffix of the future participle is an additive sign that contains an additive signifier (*-uur-*), but a replacive signified: it replaces the original meaning of the *-t-* with its own future active meaning.

2. LEXEME-BASED MORPHOLOGY

Other analyses of the phenomenon may be possible within other frameworks. For the moment, I would like to provide an analysis within the word-based framework of Aronoff (1976) that is also compatible with more recent related theories.

To some, it might seem odd to attempt any analysis of Latin morphology from a word-based point of view, since Latin is a paradigm example of a language with what Bloomfield calls stem-inflection and which he contrasts with word-inflection (1933, 225). More generally, Bloomfield contrasts a

Table 2
Perfect and Future Participles of Irregular Verbs

Infinitive	*Perfect Participle*	*Future Participle*	*Gloss*
fer-re	laat-	laatuur-	'bear'
siste-re	stat-	statuur-	'place'
esse	—	futuur-	'be'
posse	—	—	'be able'
velle	—	—	'wish'

language like English, which "may be said to have *word-inflection, word-derivation,* and *word-composition*" with German, which "is an example of *stem-inflection, stem-derivation,* and *stem-composition*" (ibid.). Even more generally, one may extend Bloomfield's terminology and speak of word-based versus stem-based morphology, so that a language in which realization rules are usually defined on stems that occur as free phonological words will have word-based morphology and those whose realization rules are usually defined on stems that do not occur as phonologically free words will have stem-based morphology.

If we speak in this way (and I do not think we should), then Latin morphology is obviously "stem-based" while English is "word-based." In such a terminological world, a word-based theory of morphology or word formation such as that of Aronoff (1976) would be inapplicable to Latin or to any other highly inflective language.

But this conclusion follows from a misinterpretation of the use of the term *word* in Aronoff (1976). There is a systematic ambiguity in that work, as pointed out in its preface, among the various meanings of the term *word.* In particular, the sense with the meaning of 'lexeme' is not distinguished from the other common senses, especially those of Matthews's *word form* or *phonological word* and his *word* or *grammatical word.* However, on page 9, in a discussion of what has come to be called the weak lexicalist hypothesis, I noted that "in general, throughout the rest of this work, *word* should be taken to mean 'word sans inflection', or *lexeme* in the sense of Matthews (1974)."[12] The theory of word-based morphology or word formation is therefore a theory of lexeme-based morphology or word formation, and the word-based hypothesis is a claim about the semantics and syntax of word formation and morphology, as much as or perhaps more than a claim about affixation. Thus, although English may differ from Latin in whether an affix attaches to a morphologically free or bound form, this difference is orthogonal to the question of whether morphology and word formation are word(lexeme)-based.[13]

3. STEMS AS FORMS WITHOUT MEANING

Having laid this misunderstanding to rest (for the duration of this paper, at least), we may now return to the Latin data. My claim is that there is no need for a parasitic formation, but that, instead, both participles are formed on the same stem and that this stem is neither active nor passive semantically. In fact, when the nature of stems is properly understood, the semantic question becomes irrelevant, because, being purely a form, this Latin stem has no semantic value at all. The evidence for my claim is largely negative: there is no reason to believe that the future participle is derived in any way from the perfect participle. In fact, there are a number of morphological functions, both inflectional and derivational, that are based on this same stem, with little evidence that any one of them is basic to another.

3.1. Form versus Meaning

Beginning with the future participle and perfect participle, what evidence is there for deriving one from the other? Certainly there is no semantic evidence. Morphologically, though, since the perfect participle is marked only by the *t* and the future participle by *-t-uur-*, it seems reasonable to claim that the perfect participle is basic. There are, however, several arguments against this simple solution. Most obviously, there are verbs that lack a perfect participle (being intransitive), but nevertheless have a future participle, as in the following examples:

[2]	caleoo, calituur-	'burn, be hot'
	doleoo, dolituur-	'suffer pain'
	iaceoo, iactuur-	'lie'
	recidoo, recaasuur-	'fall back'
	eesurioo, eesurituur-	'be hungry'

Kuhner and Holzweissig (1912) say that these future participles are constructed by analogy to other verbs that have a perfect participle, but that claim is unprovable. There are also cases like *discoo, discituurus* where Kuhner and Holzweissig can find no analogous forms. In the absence of a perfect participle, it is difficult to see how these future participles can be derived unless this stem, which I will call the 3 stem, has some independent status.[14]

3.2. The Supine

The second and most commonly remarked obstacle to deriving future participles from perfect participles (the semantic problem being the first) is the form called in traditional Latin grammar the supine noun, which is also marked by the 3 stem alone.[15] The supine is syntactically a kind of infinitive with a very limited distribution. It occurs in only two case forms, the accusative and the ablative singular. In the accusative, it is used mainly as the verb of a purpose clause after verbs of motion, as in the following examples:

[3] ab-i-it pisc-aa-t-um
away-go-3.SG.PERF.IND.ACT. fish-Th-T-ACC.SG.
'he/she has gone fishing' [Plautus]
ses-s-um it praetor
sit-T-ACC.SG. go.3SG.PRES.IND.ACT. praetor
'the praetor is going to sit down' [Cicero]

In the ablative, the supine occurs after adjectives as a kind of specifier. In this use, it is almost always bare, as in [4]:

[4]	sii hoc	faas	est	dic-t-uu
	if this.ACC.SG.	allowed	is	say-T-ABL.SG.
	'if it is permissible to say this'			[Cicero]

From its two forms (*-um* and *-uu*), we may conclude that the supine is morphologically a fourth declension masculine noun.[16] The perfect participle, by contrast, may be classified as a first/second declension adjective, judging solely by its morphology.[17] We may represent the forms schematically as in figure 1.[18]

It is clear from figure 1 that there is no way, judging from form alone, to choose either one of the supine or the perfect participle as underlying the other (in Bloomfield's sense of *underlying*), or to choose either one as underlying the future participle, since they are identical in all constant aspects of their forms (up to and including the *-t-*).[19] In fact, the grammar books are just about evenly divided as to whether they derive the future participle from the perfect participle or the supine. Older grammars (e.g., Allen and Greenough 1894) tend to speak in terms of the supine, while newer grammars tend to derive the future participle from the perfect participle; some modern school grammars (e.g., Wheelock 1960) do not even mention the supine.

Which brings us to one possible argument in favor of choosing the perfect participle over the supine: frequency. The supine is infrequent in the classical period (enough so that an elementary textbook can get by without mentioning it), and many common verbs are not attested in the supine. Hence the choice of the perfect participle in the more modern elementary grammars. But this argument, though pedagogically sound, has no theoretical validity.[20]

I conclude that the existence of the supine form casts doubt on any analysis that derives the future participle from either the perfect participle or the supine. That is why, so as not to prejudice the case, I refer to what is

Figure 1
Schematic Form of Supine and Perfect Participle

Supine Schema

$[[\text{ROOT OR DERIVED STEM}_i]_V + (\text{THEME VOWEL})_j + t]_N + [\text{4 decl. masc. sg. case}]$

Perfect Participle Schema

$[[\text{ROOT OR DERIVED STEM}_i]_V + (\text{THEME VOWEL})_j + t]_A + [\text{1/2 decl. num. case gen.}]$

common to all three forms as the 3 stem, rather than using either of the traditional terms (*past participle* or *supine stem*). I have chosen the numeral 3 to designate this stem because it is the third stem that Latin verbs have, and because, unlike the other two stems, it cannot be associated reliably with a category like *present* or *perfect*.

3.3. The 3 Stem

Besides the three form types discussed so far, the 3 stem of verbs appears regularly with three derived noun suffixes and three derived verb types. The noun suffixes are the *-or*[21] (feminine *-rix*)[22] agentive suffix and two abstract nominal suffixes, *ioo*(*n*) and *-uur-*. The verb types are the desiderative *-ur-ii-*, the intensive (no overt suffix, but with theme vowel always *aa*), and the iterative *-it-* (also with theme vowel *aa*).[23] Examples of each are given in table 3.[24]

Each item is given in citation form,[25] and for each item the citation form of the base verb and the 3 stem are given in parentheses. Of special note are doubly derived forms, in which one 3 stem derivative is built on another, as in table 4.

We now have a total of nine reasonably productive form types built on the 3 stem of verbs. The obvious question to ask is whether any one of these types can be said to be systematically based on another, in a word formation sense. Semantically, the answer is decidedly no, except in one case. There are a number of *-uur-* nouns that correspond systematically to *-or* nouns with the special sense 'office held by X-or' (e.g., *censuura* 'office of the censor' and *quaestuura* 'office of the quaestor'). But not all *-uur* nouns follow this pattern, so we are probably dealing here with morphological potentiation (Williams 1982) rather than with semantics pure and simple. In the case of the doubly derived 3 stems in table 4, the noun types are simply deverbal and not restricted semantically by the 3 stem of the base. I conclude that a fairly exhaustive search reveals a good number of 3 stem types but no semantic or morphological evidence that any one of them is basic to any other. I will therefore adopt the null hypothesis—that all 3 stem types are based on the category *verb* (as their semantics dictates) and built on a particular form of the verb, the 3 stem.[26] We therefore must distinguish the syntactic category of a lexeme (on which a Word Formation Rule (WFR) is based) from its morphological form (on which a word form is built).

4. LEXEME, STEM, AND RELATED NOTIONS

I will now show how such an analysis can be represented within a lexeme-based framework. What we need, and what the framework provides, is a distinction between the aspect of morphology that deals purely with the mor-

Table 3
Form Types Derived from t Stems

Derived Word	*Base Verb*	*Gloss*
	-or *Nouns*	
cantor	(canoo, cant-)	'singer'
vector	(vehoo, vect-)	'carrier'
petiitor	(petoo,petiit-)	'candidate'
victor	(vincoo,vict-)	'winner'
tonsor	(tondeoo,tons-)	'hair cutter'
	-io(n) *Nouns*	
cogitaatio	(cogitoo,cogitaat-)	'thought'
conventio	(convenioo,convent-)	'meeting'
muunitio	(muunioo,muunit-)	'fortification'
deepulsio	(deepelloo,deepuls-)	'defense'
	-uur- *Nouns*	
scriptuura	(scriiboo,script-)	'writing'
tonsuura	(tondeoo,tons-)	'shearing'
pictuura	(pingoo,pict-)	'painting'
	Desiderative Verbs	
eesurioo	(edoo,ees-)	'be hungry'
empturioo	(emoo,empt-)	'want to buy'
parturioo	(parioo,part-)	'be in labor'
	Intensive Verbs	
iactoo	(iacioo,iact-)	'fling'
voluutoo	(volvoo,voluut-)	'tumble about'
tractoo	(trahoo,tract-)	'drag'
	Iterative Verbs	
scriptitoo	(scriiboo,script-)	'write often'
viisitoo	(videoo,viis-)	'see often'
iactitoo	(iacioo,iact-)	'bandy'

Table 4
Doubly Derived t Stem Forms

Derived Noun	*Gloss*	*Derived Verb*	*Gloss*	*Base Verb*	*Gloss*
haesitaatio	'indecision'	⟨haesitoo	'stammer'	⟨haereoo	'stick'
iactaatio	'tossing'	⟨iactoo	'fling'	⟨iacioo	'throw'
cantaator	'singer'	⟨cantoo	'sing'	⟨canoo	'sing'

phological determination of forms, or morphological spell-out (which, following Zwicky 1986, I will call morphological realization)[27], and a more inclusive notion of morphology, which includes both this morphophonological aspect of morphology (what I have termed elsewhere the morphophonological operation of a WFR) and a more abstract syntactic notion that I have called, somewhat infelicitously "the syntacticosemantic specification of the base [and derivative]" (Aronoff 1976, 48). This distinction, if it is to be coherent, depends on a particular (though reasonably orthodox) view of what a lexeme is and of how lexemes and stems are related.

4.1. Lexeme

A lexeme is a (potential or actual) decontextualized vocabulary word, a member of a major lexical category: noun (N), verb (V), or adjective/adverb (A).[28] As a vocabulary word standing outside any syntactic context, a lexeme is inherently unspecified for those syntactically, semantically, and pragmatically determined categories that are marked by inflection, although it contains within itself sufficient information for realizing those categories morphophonologically.

A lexeme is abstract in at least three ways. First, a lexeme is not a form or a set of forms, but rather a sign or a set of signs—form, distribution, and meaning bound arbitrarily together by the social contract of language (Mel'cuk ms). It is natural, in our materialist world, to think of a lexeme as a form or to rely more on form than on meaning. That is because of the tangible imbalance between the (relatively) concrete form of a word and the abstract nature of distribution and meaning. It is easier to grasp a form, to be sure of its reality, and to study it, than it is to grasp a meaning. Consider the simple fact that even linguists normally use a form of an expression when we want to mention its meaning and that so-called abstract entities, like the performative and causative verbs of Generative Semantics, are so difficult to control in large part because they have no detectable form. But a lexeme is not just a form, although a major strategy of American linguistics since Boas has been to trust form over meaning.

In my view (Aronoff 1983), and here I depart from some, the lexeme is also abstract in that it is not necessary to assume, for any given member of a major lexical category, that it be lexical (in the sense of this term that is more or less equivalent in meaning to *arbitrary*)[29] or listed in a lexicon. All vocabulary words that are members of a major lexical category, regardless of whether they are actual or potential, are lexemes. The set of potential (regularly derived and compounded) lexemes for any given language is therefore infinite. That at least some lexemes exist only potentially is the second abstract property of lexemes. Being a lexeme and being in a (Bloomfieldian) lexicon are thus separate matters.[30]

Not only is being in a lexicon or dictionary not a necessary condition for being a lexeme, it is not a sufficient condition either, so that idiomatic phrases, although they are lexical (inasmuch as one would list them in an ideal dictionary), are not lexemes, because they are not words. Here I agree with Matthews (1974, 35), but not with Lyons (1977), who explicitly includes idioms among lexemes and uses the term *word-lexeme* for Matthews's lexeme.

One aspect of the dictionary metaphor that does prove to be useful is the notion that a lexeme has status as a vocabulary item outside any syntactic context, in the way that a dictionary entry "exists" outside context, even though in actual use it will only occur in the syntactic and pragmatic context of an utterance. This third and final major abstract property of lexemes is especially important in inflective languages like Latin. So, for example, a Latin noun must always have a particular case and number when used in a sentence, both in its meaning and in its form. But the lexeme ("in the lexicon" as some linguists say, remembering all along that not all lexemes are in the lexicon) has no case and no number. Similarly for verbs, the lexemes for which exist in Latin outside the tense, aspect, mood, voice, person, and number—which must all be specified in any actual use.[31]

To recapitulate, a lexeme is a (potential or actual) member of a major lexical category, having both form and meaning but being neither, and existing outside any particular syntactic context. Having provided this informal characterization of what a lexeme is, I will now turn to stems and try to clarify especially what the difference is between a lexeme and a stem.

4.2. Stem and Related Notions

While a lexeme consists of form, meaning, and the usually arbitrary association between them, I will reserve the term *stem* for only the form part of this trinity. A stem, in my use of this term, is a form. In particular, it is the domain of a realization rule, that form of a lexeme to which a given affix is attached or on which a given nonaffixal realization rule operates.[32] It is especially important to realize, however, that we cannot simply equate the two notions 'stem' and 'form of a lexeme'. There are several reasons for this. First, as I will show in detail later on, a lexeme may have more than one stem, not all of them necessarily listed. Second, there are several other well-established notions having to do with 'form of a lexeme' that must be distinguished from 'stem'. Three of these, 'base', 'root', and 'lexical representation', are traditional and useful. The last, 'citation form', needs clarification and is not, I would contend, linguistically significant. Although in the end I am interested only in stems, nonetheless it is useful to touch on all of the others, if only to clarify the first by way of contrast.

Matthews notes that "in many discussions 'root' and 'stem' . . . also 'base' . . . are used in equivalent senses" (1972, 165, n. 4). The first two differ from the last in that, while stems and roots are purely forms, the base (in my own use, as defined in Aronoff 1976) is an entire lexeme or syntacticosemantically defined set of lexemes. Thus, the base of the WFR that derives abstract nouns of the form X-*ation* in English is the set of verbs, and the base of the single abstract noun *pulverization* is the verb lexeme *pulverize,* not simply the form of this verb lexeme.

Turning to the notion of 'root', although *root* and *stem* both designate forms of lexemes, the most important difference between them is that a root is defined with respect to a lexeme, while a stem is always defined with respect to a realization rule. One might say that 'root' thus abstracts away from all morphology.[33] The most important thing about roots, in the sense for which I wish to reserve the term, is that they be morphologically unanalyzable. A root is what is left when all morphological structure has been wrung out of a form. This is the sense of the term in Semitic grammar.

Let me now turn to the notion '*citation form*'. Here I will cite Lyons's definition, which seems entirely satisfactory: "By the citation-form of a lexeme is meant the form of the lexeme that is conventionally employed to refer to it in standard dictionaries and grammars of the language" (1977, 19). The term thus refers to the form of a lexeme that is conventionally used in mentioning it. As such, 'citation form' is a metalinguistic notion not necessarily meant to be of significance in a theory of language. Here the word *conventionally* is important. Different traditions use different forms for citation. In Classical Greek and Latin dictionaries, it is always the first person singular present indicative active for verbs, while in Semitic languages it is the third person masculine singular perfect form. In Sanskrit, it is the root. In most other languages, it is the infinitive for verbs. Sometimes, when there is no established scholarly tradition for a particular language, different dictionaries may use different citation forms. For example, as Robert Hoberman points out to me, one dictionary of Modern Aramaic uses the infinitive, while another uses what Hoberman (1989) calls the J stem. For nouns, the nominative singular form is the one most commonly used for citation purposes.

The choice of a citation form is (at least originally) governed by a pedagogical principle. The idea is to pick a single full surface form of a lexeme (hence pronounceable in isolation) from which the rest of that lexeme's paradigm may be deduced and which conversely may be retrieved from any form of that lexeme. This allows learners, in theory, to have an entire paradigm at their command by memorizing only one form and a small set of algorithmic principles. It also makes the use of a dictionary possible, since the dictionary user—native or nonnative speaker—must know what form of a lexeme to look up in searching for a definition in a dictionary. The citation form thus also normally serves as the address of the lexeme in the dictionary.[34] In actual fact, a single full surface form is not always sufficient for predicting an entire paradigm, even in regular cases, nor is the system always reversible (allowing for the recovery of the citation form from any other form of the lexeme). Hence the use in Latin dictionaries of three or four principal parts for verbs and two forms (nominative and genitive singular) for many types of nouns.

Within linguistic theory, the idea of there being, for any given lexeme, a single form in the mental lexicon from which an entire paradigm may be deduced, which is furthermore the address of the lexeme whose paradigm is being generated—the idea, in short, of a 'lexical representation' (Aronoff 1978) has been tremendously important. The lexical representation, however, differs from the citation form inasmuch as it is (or may be) an abstract form, both phonologically and morphologically, that never actually occurs as a surface form of the lexeme.

5. STEMS AND THE PERMANENT LEXICON

The term *stem* has been used for all the notions that I have now distinguished by the terms *lexeme, base, root, citation form,* and *lexical representation*—not all of which are of interest to morphological theory. One property, however, sets stems apart from all those other entities: a given lexeme may have more than one stem, different stems being demanded for different realization rules. Traditional Latin grammar, for example, recognizes three stems for every verb; Semitic grammar recognizes two for simple (qal) verbs. Some recent theorists have accepted the possibility of multiple stems, but they have attempted to link this possibility to an entirely tangential entity, the Bloomfieldian lexicon, which I will call the permanent lexicon, following Allen (1978). Their idea is that a lexeme may have more than one stem just in case these stems are irregular and hence listed in the permanent lexicon. The most influential use of this idea is in Lieber (1980). Because Lieber deals specifically with Latin verb stems in developing her framework, I will discuss her work in some detail.

The clearest cases of needing more than one stem for a given lexeme come from suppletion. No one would say that *went,* the past tense form of the English verb *go,* is derived from the same stem as the present tense forms. We therefore conclude that, for this verb, at least two stems must be listed, *go* and *went.* The question that naturally arises to the theoretically minded is whether this is the only circumstance under which a lexeme may have more than one stem. A common fallacy is to assume that it is. The fallacy is based on a confusion (discussed at length in Aronoff 1988) between two largely unrelated senses of the term *lexical.* In one sense, *lexical* means 'arbitrary', while in the other major sense it means 'having to do with words'. In the case of stems, the confusion of the two senses leads one to conclude that, if a lexeme (which is lexical in the 'having to do with words' sense of the term) demonstrably has more than one stem, then all these stems must also be lexical in the 'arbitrary' (hence listed) sense of the term *lexical*.

Let us see how this works in Lieber's analysis. According to Lieber, "the permanent lexicon consists of a set of all those terminal elements which cannot be decomposed into smaller parts" (1980, 38).[35] A class of rules, which Lieber calls morpholexical rules, operates on this set. Lieber defines morpholexical rule informally as "a relation defined between pairs of lexical items which are listed in the permanent lexicon" (p. 39). Furthermore, the members of this pair are related to one another in a special way: they are what Lieber calls stem variants or morpheme variants. In other words, it is not the case that just any two lexical items may be related by morpholexical rules, since morpholexical rules define only the special morphophonological relation of being variants.[36] Lieber thus claims that there is a special set of morphophonological rules that defines only *existing* variant forms of lexical items. Lieber discusses two such sets of rules in detail, one for German (later rejected in favor of another device, String Dependent Rules) and one for Latin verb stems. In analyzing the latter, Lieber takes great pains to show that Latin verbs must have more than one stem (in addition to a root for each verb) and that these stems and roots must be related to one another by means of morpholexical rules. She provides a set of five such rules for present stems (root + theme vowel), a rule for nasal infixing of certain present stems, six rules for forming perfect stems, and two for (perfect) participles. Lieber argues that these rules are all morpholexical, based on the fact that it is not always possible to predict which stem form a given root will select for a given stem type (present, perfect, 3 stem). In every case, Lieber argues that none of these morpholexical rules can be considered to be a productive rule, since it is arbitrary which rule will apply to a given lexical item. The inevitable conclusion is that all Latin verb stems must be listed in the permanent lexicon. Lieber then goes on to show that all the variants that have been argued to be listed are available for further word formation, thus demonstrating (she feels) that word formation operates on existing stems.

But is it really true that we can never predict what stem type a given verb will have—that the stem allomorphs of Latin verbs are unpredictable? In the vast majority of cases, once we know the present stem of a simple verb (its theme vowel), it is possible to predict the other stems. For suffixed verbs, the theme vowel is usually determined by the suffix. Consider the first conjugation (theme vowel *aa*), which is the largest. Allen and Greenough say that this conjugation has about 360 simple members, of which all but 16 are regular, making 96 percent of the members of this class regular (once the theme vowel is given). The number of derived members of this conjugation is very large, inasmuch as both large classes of intensive and iterative verbs are members of it, and all these derived verbs are regular, so that the proportion of perfectly regular verbs of this conjugation is actually much higher.[37]

The fourth conjugation (theme vowel *ii*) is the smallest in number, having about 60 simple members, two thirds of which are regular. This class also includes productively derived desiderative verbs. In the second conjugation (theme vowel *ee*), for which Allen and Greenough give 120 members, 75 percent form their perfect and perfect participle stems regularly. This conjugation is not, however, extendable by any regular WFR. The third conjugation (theme vowel *e* and *i*) is the least predictable, but even here, of approximately 170 simple verbs, more than 35 percent form their perfects in *s*. Thus, of the 700 or so simple Latin verbs, more than 75 percent are regular within their conjugation. This is a far cry from Lieber's characterization of the system as unpredictable, and it does not take into account productive derivation, which would raise the predictability of the system even further. It is therefore disingenuous to conclude that Latin verb stems are essentially unpredictable and that they must be listed in the permanent lexicon.

Latin therefore provides no evidence for a necessary connection between a verb's having more than one stem and those stems being listed in the permanent lexicon. Contrary to what Lieber claims, the majority of verb stems are regular and hence most likely nonlexical (in the arbitrary sense of the term). Listedness is therefore not a necessary criterion for being a stem. Nor, conversely, is a stem's being listed in the permanent lexicon a sufficient criterion for a stem's serving as an input to further derivation. As Lieber notes (p. 90), there are no cases in Latin of derivational affixes building on the perfect active verb stem (regardless of whether the perfect stem is arbitrary or not). Lieber calls this an accidental gap, but it is no more accidental than the lack of derivatives from past tense verbs in English.

I conclude that a given lexeme may have more than one stem and that these stems are not necessarily arbitrary and hence listed in the permanent lexicon (though they may be). We must remember, however, that the stem in the sense I have adopted is a purely morphologically defined entity. If a given realization rule is viewed as a function from a form (of a lexeme) to another form (of a (possibly identical) lexeme), then the first form is the stem, the domain of the morphophonological function. Put simply, the stem is the form on which a particular form is built.

6. EMPTY MORPHS

Morphology encompasses both form and meaning. Within a simple theory, the two are isomorphic. Every form has a meaning, and when we join meanings we join forms. Morpheme-based theories are usually of this simple sort. Lexeme-based theories allow for a more indirect relation between form and meaning,[38] inasmuch as they permit a separation (in Beard's terms) between building a form and building its meaning. In the case at hand, there are nine form types built morphologically on the Latin 3 stem, all of which are based semantically on the basic meaning of the verb. The *t* (or *s*, or whatever distinguishes a particular 3 stem) can not be said to have a meaning that is constant across all nine types (unless we arbitrarily stipulate one meaning as basic and subtract it in forming the other types, as Mel'cuk would do). Either it has nine separate meanings or it has no identifiable independent meaning at all. We can't tell which, and in fact, the choice between the two may be irrelevant. The *t* is what Hockett (1947) calls an empty morph. It occurs in a specific morphological environment but makes no detectable independent contribution to the meaning of the whole form.

It has long been noticed that stem-forming morphs like Latin *t* may be empty. Bloomfield discusses a number of such cases in compounds (1933, 229–31). In Classical Greek, what he calls the compounding-stem "may differ formally from all the inflections of its paradigm," inasmuch as certain nouns have a suffix *o*- that shows up only when they appear as the first member of a compound. In Germanic languages, Bloomfield notes, the first member of a compound often has a suffix that is semantically inappropriate in this particular environment. Botha (1968) has discussed this at length.[39]

6.1. The Theme Vowel

Among the best-known examples of empty morphs are the theme vowels that characterize the various verb conjugations of Latin. As we will see, Latin theme vowels, in addition to being classic examples of empty morphs of a certain kind, also interact with verb stems in a complex manner. I will therefore explore them in some detail. Table 5 presents a close-to-traditional synchronic classification of the verb conjugations according to their theme vowels.[40]

Let us see what happens if we assume that the theme vowels are ordinary meaningful verb suffixes, which is to say that they work in the same way that the English suffix *-ize* works, simply as derivational affixes. What sorts of problems arise under such an assumption?

Table 5
Theme Vowels of Latin Verbs

Conjugation	*Theme Vowel*	*Present Active Infinitive*	*Gloss*
first	aa	am-aa-re	'love'
second	ee	deel-ee-re	'destroy'
fourth	ii	aud-ii-re	'hear'
third	e	leg-e-re	'pick'
third	i	cap-e-re	'take'
third	—	fer-re	'carry'

One problem is that there will be only a handful of underived verbs in the language under this analysis, namely those few (very frequent and otherwise quite irregular in many respects) verbs like *ferre* that have no theme vowel. All other verbs will be formally derived. This is certainly unusual, but not impossible. Bengali and other modern Indo-Aryan languages, for example, have only a handful of simple verbs, the rest being formally compounds.

Another problem is that the putative suffixes will be largely synonymous, marking only the category *verb,* rather than having any additional significance. Again, this is not impossible. English, after all, has several suffixes with this same value (*ize, -ate, -ify*).

A more serious problem is that actual meaningful derivational verb suffixes are quite common in Latin. I have already discussed a few of them in the context of suffixes that select for the 3 stem (see table 3 for examples). Each one of these suffixes forms verbs that have a sense associated with the suffix, each suffix belongs to a particular conjugation, and different suffixes belong to different conjugations. Because all these derivatives each belong to a particular conjugation, under the theme vowel as suffix analysis, each one of these genuine derivational suffixes would have to be analyzed as complex, consisting of the derivational suffix followed by the theme vowel, which must also be a derivational suffix, but now one that derives verbs from "nonoccurring" verbs. This is very peculiar. Table 6 lists verbal derivational suffixes and indicates the theme vowel of each. The table reveals very clearly that the theme vowel is conditioned by the category of the immediately preceding morph: the theme vowel appears after the morph that carries the category *verb,* regardless of whether that morph is a root or an affix.[41] Furthermore, each category-carrying morph selects a particular theme vowel (arbitrarily). The theme vowel is thus a marker of the category *verb* only in the sense that it is determined by the category *verb,* just as final devoicing is a marker of the word boundary. In itself, it has no significance. It is empty. Nonetheless, it is not useless. It has a use in the language, but that use is purely morphophonological: the theme vowel is the conjugation vowel, it serves to determine the conjugation of the verb stem, which inflectional affixes will mark the various

Table 6
Table of Derivational Verb Suffixes

Suffix	*Theme Vowel*	*Meaning*	*Example*	*Gloss*
-ur-	ii	desiderative	eesuriire	'be hungry'
-it-	aa	iterative	viisitaare	'see often'
-sc-	e	inceptive	calescere	'get warm'
-ess-	e	intensive	capessere	'seize'
—	aa	intensive	iactaare	'throw hard'

morphosyntactic properties that the verb bears in a particular instance.[42] The theme vowel is thus never referred to by any syntacticosemantic rule but only by the realization rules that spell out the various syntacticosemantic categories.

6.2. Theme Vowels and Stems

It is usual to associate the choice of a conjugation class or theme vowel with the lexeme rather than with the stem, so that we speak of first or second conjugation verbs. However, the actual situation in Latin is more complex. From our current perspective, it is also an enlightening example of the workings of pure morphology, form without meaning. I will deal with the simplest case first, that of the most regular conjugation, with the theme vowel *aa*. This conjugation has the largest number of actual verbs and the greatest productivity. It is also the ancestor of the most productive conjugation in the Romance languages.

Latin verbs, unless they are defective (about which more later), have three basic stems, traditionally termed present, perfect, and supine, or perfect participle. I am calling this last one the 3 stem. In regular verbs of the *aa* (first) conjugation, it is easy to see that the theme vowel appears in all stems at the underlying phonological level, being deleted only before vowel-initial suffixes. Table 7 contains a sample of relevant regular verb forms of this conjugation. The same is true with regular verbs of the fourth (theme vowel *ii*) conjugation,[43] except that the theme vowel is shortened rather than deleted before vowels, as shown in table 8.

With the other conjugations, however, the theme vowel is not ubiquitous. In the second conjugation, with theme vowel *ee,* the pattern parallel to those of the preceding tables (with the theme vowel in all stems), appears with only five roots,[44] as shown in table 9. These roots, however, share a singular property: they must be analyzed as being vowelless[45] if the seeming theme vowel is truly a theme vowel. Latin verb roots otherwise are not less than a syllable in length. In other words, it is most likely that the *ee* of these roots is

Table 7
Sample First Conjugation Verb Forms and Stems

Surface Form	*Underlying Form*	*Stem*	*Gloss*
armoo	arm-aa-oo	arm-aa	‘I arm’
armaamur	arm-aa-mur	arm-aa	‘we are armed’
armaabunt	arm-aa-b-u-nt	arm-aa	‘they will arm’
armaavistii	arm-aa-u-istii	arm-aa-u	‘you (sg.) armed’
armaatus	arm-aat-us	arm-aa-t	‘armed (m.n.sg.)’

Table 8
Fourth Conjugation Regular Verb Forms and Stems

Surface Form	*Underlying Form*	*Stem*	*Gloss*
audiam	aud-ii-am	aud-ii	'I may hear'
audiireemus	aud-ii-ree-mus	aud-ii	'we might hear'
audiiverat	aud-ii-u-er-at	aud-ii-u	'he had heard'
audiita	aud-ii-t-a	aud-ii-t	'heard (f.n.sg.)'

a root vowel rather than a theme vowel.[46] If we agree that the *ee* of these five verbs is indeed part of the lexical form, then they are not really second conjugation verbs at all, let alone regular. Now, however, there are no second conjugation verbs that have the theme vowel *ee* in either the perfect stem or the 3 stem. The majority of second conjugation verbs are like *mon-ee-* 'warn'. They form their perfect stem with *u* attached to the bare lexical form of the verb (e.g., *mon-u-*). The 3 stem of these verbs is formed with *it* (occasionally just *t*) attached also to the bare lexical form (e.g., *mon-it-*, *doc-t-*). The remainder form their perfect and 3 stems in various ways, but never with a theme vowel. The theme vowel *ee* is thus characteristic of only the present stem of second conjugation verbs, where it occurs without exception. Here, then, is the first clear example of the association of theme vowels directly with particular stems, rather than with the entire lexeme.

The third conjugation is the most heterogeneous of all four. It includes verbs with no theme vowel, those with the theme vowel *e*, and those with *i*. Some have a nasal infix in the present stem. Others have reduplication or vowel lengthening. What unites all these in one conjugation is the selection of particular suffixes by the present stem, to which I will return. In the perfect and 3 stem, however, the members of this class are quite heterogeneous. They form the perfect stem from the verb root in many different ways, including conversion of the root or the present stem, reduplication, root vowel lengthening, ablaut, suffixation of *s*, suffixation of *v* or *u*, and combinations of these. The 3 stems are similarly various. They do, however, share one thing, a

Table 9
Second Conjugation "Regular" Verb Roots

Root	*Present Stem*	*Perfect Stem*	*T Stem*	*Gloss*
(dee)lee	deelee	deelee-v	deelee-t	'wipe out'
flee	flee	flee-v	flee-t	'weep'
nee	nee	nee-v	nee-t	'spin'
viee	viee	viee-v	viee-t	'weave'
-plee	-plee	-plee-v	-plee-t	'fill'

Table 10
Verbs of Mixed Conjugation Type

Present Stem	*Perfect Stem*	*T Stem*	*Gloss*
crepaa	crepu	crepit	'rattle'
iuvaa	iuv	iut	'help'
staa	stet	—	'stand'
reperii	repper	repert	'find'
venii	ven	vent	'come'
sancii	sanx	sanct	'hallow'
sarcii	sars	sart	'patch'
sentii	sens	sens	'feel'
sepelii	sepeliiv	sepult	'bury'
aperii	aperu	apert	'open'
pete	petiiv	petiit	'aim'
cupi	cupiiv	cupiit	'want'

uniform absence of any theme vowel in the perfect and 3 stem, just like the second conjugation. Since the methods of forming the perfect and 3 stems found in the second conjugation are a subset of those found in the third, the two conjugations can be seen to differ only in the formation of the present stem. The category *third conjugation* is therefore valid only for the present stem, just like second conjugation.

A less subtle type of evidence for the relation between conjugation or theme vowel and stems rather than lexemes lies in the fact that there are many verbs whose individual stems "belong to different conjugations." These are almost all verbs of the first or fourth conjugation that lack theme vowels in the perfect or 3 stem. Examples of each type found are given in table 10. In these cases, it is simply impossible to say that a lexeme belongs to a conjugation or selects a theme vowel. Rather, we must say that an individual stem of a lexeme belongs to a particular conjugation, as we did above for second and third conjugation verbs in general.[47] This only reinforces my earlier remark that theme vowels are associated directly with stems of lexemes rather than with entire lexemes.

To what extent, however, can lexemes be said to have theme vowels? The following observations seem to be true:

[5] Almost all verbs have a theme vowel in the present stem, the only exceptions being a small number of high-frequency verbs.
Second and third conjugation verbs never have a theme vowel except in the present stem.
Almost all first and fourth conjugation verbs have a theme vowel in all stems.

It is clear that theme vowels appear reliably only in the present stem. I will now argue that the presence of the theme vowels *aa* and *ii* in first and fourth conjugation nonpresent stems is a secondary phenomenon, with the result that theme vowels are seen to be firmly rooted only in the present stem of verbs.

First we must review the formation of other than present stems. In the second conjugation, the most common method is to add *u* to the verb root of simple verbs for the perfect stem and *it* for the 3 stem. This pattern also appears with simple third conjugation verbs, but more common is the addition of *s* to the root for perfect stems and *t* for 3 stems. Among the other methods of perfect stem formation in the third conjugation is to form the perfect stem not on the verb root but rather on the present stem minus the theme vowel. This may be detected in cases where the present stem has a nasal infix. The nasal is sometimes absent in nonpresent stems, but sometimes it appears either in the perfect or both the perfect and the 3 stem. All the types are exemplified in table 11. The top section of the table contains verbs where the nasal is absent in nonpresent stems; the second section contains those verbs that show the nasal in at least one nonpresent stem; finally, the last section contains roots that vary.

Table 11
Stems of Verbs with Nasal Infixes

Present Stem	*Perfect Stem*	*T Stem*	*Gloss*
frange	freeg	fract	'break'
linque	liiqu	lict	'leave'
line	leev/liiv	lit	'smear'
finde	fiid	fiss	'split'
funde	fuud	fuus	'pour'
(in)cumbe	cubu	cubit	'lie'
rumpe	ruup	rupt	'break'
temne	temps	tempt	'despise'
sine	siiv	sit	'allow'
sperne	spreev	spreet	'spurn'
iunge	iuunx	iuunct	'join'
pinge	piinx	piict	'paint'
lambe	lamb	—	'lick'
ungue	uunx	uunct	'anoint'
pange	pepig	paact	'agree on'
pange	paanx	—	'fasten'
compinge	compeeg	compaact	'confine'
punge	pupug	puunct	'punch'
compunge	compuunx	compuunct	'prick'

The first section of the table shows very nicely the variety of ways in which the nonpresent stems may be formed from the verb root with simple third conjugation verbs. We see clear examples of vowel lengthening, ablaut accompanied by lengthening, and suffixing of *s* and *u* in the perfect. In the 3 stem we see both *t* and *s*, sometimes accompanied by lengthening. In the second section we find the same phenomena, but accompanied by retention of the nasal. The pattern exemplified by *iunge* is the most common.[48] In the third section, we have two good examples of how the same root may show nonpresent stems of different types in different lexemes, sometimes with and sometimes without the nasal.

Overall, the simplest analysis of the table would form those nonpresent stems that retain the nasal on the present stem, while those without the nasal would be formed on the lexical representation.[49] Within a lexeme-based framework, this is easily expressed. A given realization rule always selects as its stem some specified form of the lexeme, which is not necessarily the lexical representation. Normally, this form is specified by a single function across lexemes for a given realization rule, but we see here that this function may be preempted lexically in exceptional instances.[50]

In the second conjugation there are no verbs with a nasal infix, making it impossible to tell, for the second conjugation, whether any nonpresent stems are based on the present stem. Neither do we find nasal infixes in either of the other conjugations. In the first and fourth, however, the theme vowel appears quite regularly in nonpresent stems, almost overwhelmingly, in fact, in the first, which is the most common and most productive conjugation. When the theme vowel is retained, the perfect is always formed by suffixation of *u* and the 3 stem by suffixation of *t*. Since we have already seen that the simplest analysis of the less regular third conjugation patterns permits at least some stems to be formed on the present stem, then we may most easily account for the most common forms by saying that the default method of forming the perfect and 3 stems is by suffixing *u* and *t* to the present stem of the verb. The default method will operate almost without exception on first conjugation verbs and on about two-thirds of fourth conjugation verbs. We also predict that, because it is the default method, it will operate on newly formed verbs unless their morphology specifically triggers another method. This prediction is borne out: newly coined verbs follow this pattern, except those formed with the suffixes *-ess* and *-esc*, both of which select special stems. We can also now accommodate the first and fourth conjugation irregular verbs in table 10. These are seen to be exceptions to the general pattern that first and fourth conjugation verbs follow the default pattern of stem formation.

I conclude that it is reasonable to claim that the theme vowel occurs basically in the present stem for all Latin verbs and that it occurs in other stems specifically when they are built on the present stem. In these other stems, the theme vowel does not necessarily fill any particular function.

Table 12
Sample List of Latin Verb Endings by Theme Vowel

Category Gloss	*Theme Vowel*				
	aa	ee	e	i	ii
active					
pres. ind. 1 sg.	oo	eoo	oo	ioo	ioo
pres. ind. 2 sg.	aas	ees	is	is	iis
pres. ind. 3 sg.	at	et	it	it	it
impf. ind. 1 sg.	aabam	eebam	eebam	ieebam	ieebam
fut. ind. 1 sg.	aaboo	eeboo	am	iam	iam
fut. ind. 2 sg.	aabis	eebis	ees	iees	iees
fut. ind. 3 sg.	aabit	eebit	et	iet	iet
pres. subj. 1 sg.	em	eam	am	iam	iam
pres. subj. 2 sg.	ees	eaas	aas	iaas	iaas
pres. subj. 3 sg.	et	eat	at	iat	iat
imp. sg.	aa	ee	0/e	e	ii
imp. pl.	aate	eete	ite	ite	iite
pres. inf. act.	aare	eere	ere	ere	iire
pres. participle	aans	eens	eens	ieens	ieens
passive					
pres. ind. 1 sg.	or	eor	or	ior	ior
pres. ind. 2 sg.	aaris	eeris	eris	eris	iiris
pres. ind. 3 sg.	aatur	eetur	itur	itur	iitur
impf. ind. 1 sg.	aabar	eebar	eebar	ieebar	ieebar
fut. ind. 1 sg.	aabor	eebor	ar	iar	iar
fut. ind. 2 sg.	aaberis	eeberis	eeris	ieeris	ieeris
fut. ind. 3 sg.	aabitur	eebitur	eetur	ieetur	ieetur
pres. subj. 1 sg.	er	ear	ar	iar	iar
pres. subj. 2 sg.	eeris	eaaris	aaris	iaaris	iaaris
pres. subj. 3 sg.	eetur	eaatur	aatur	iaatur	iaatur
pres. inf. pass.	aarii	eerii	ii	ii	iirii
fut. participle	andus	endus	endus	iendus	iendus

As I have said, the function of the theme vowel is to select the verb endings. In those wordforms that are formed on the present stem, and in those wordforms only, there is a variety of ways in which the morphosyntactic categories are realized morphophonologically. The choice among these is determined by the theme vowel. Table 12 shows how this works. Note that only a representative sample of verb endings is included in the table. Each of the other endings is similar to one of those found in the table. For ease of exposition, I have included the theme vowel along with the endings in a bundle, so that the form given is that of the surface.[51]

There is much to say about this table, especially with regard to syncretism (Carstairs 1987). My concern, however, is only to show that the set of endings for each conjugation is unique, although certain conjugations share more endings than others.[52] The table shows that knowing the theme vowel of a verb will allow one to determine uniquely (and with no exceptions of any kind in the language) the entire paradigm of the forms of that verb that are formed on the present stem. The theme vowel can thus be understood only in purely morphological terms and in their interaction with the morphology of verb stems. Semantically, the theme vowels are empty.[53]

7. SEMANTICS AND THE BASIC STEM TYPES OF LATIN

I will now turn to the semantic role of the three traditionally recognized basic verb stem types[54] of Latin that I have discussed (present, perfect and 3 stem).

Latin paradigms are remarkably rigid, by which I mean that a particular morphosyntactic category is always realized, within a given conjugation, by a particular ending attached to a particular stem type. The imperfect past tense, for example, is always formed by attaching to the present stem of a verb the suffix *b,* preceded by the appropriate conjugation-determined vowel sequence and followed by the imperfect endings. The future is also always formed on the present stem, with the same *b* that we find in the imperfect tense (although the *b* appears with *aa* and *ee* verbs only), and the appropriate endings, which vary this time according to the conjugation of the verb. This same rigidity is found with other stem types: specific categories are always realized by certain endings on certain stem-types.[55] Individual verb stems may be formed irregularly and indeed are irregular in a remarkably large number of cases. Nevertheless, we never find that a given category for a particular exceptional verb is realized by attaching the endings to a different stem type or with different endings from the normal pattern. The only exception is the system of deponent verbs, which are syntactically active (and usually intransitive), but morphologically passive, which is to say that they show passive endings where we would otherwise expect active endings.[56] But even here, the paradigm is rigid, except for the one fact that passive morphology systematically substitutes for active. Furthermore, when we find partially deponent verbs, of which there are a very few, then whether a particular form of a verb is deponent varies entirely by stem type. So, *deevortor* 'turn in' and *reevortor* 'turn back' are deponent only with the present stem but not with the perfect stem, where they show active rather than passive morphology. By contrast, *fiidoo* 'trust' (and its compounds), *audeoo* 'dare', *gaudeoo* 'be happy', and *soleoo* 'be used' are deponent only in the perfect.

Further evidence of the way in which paradigms are organized around stem types comes from so-called *defective verbs,* verbs that lack one or more forms. Most defective verbs, of which there are quite a few, are defective inasmuch as they lack one or more stems, rather than individual forms. Inceptives with the suffix *-sce-* occur only in the present stem, as do desideratives with the suffix *-uurii-*, as well as many individual verbs, such as *lacteoo* 'suck', *tussioo* 'cough', and *gluboo* 'peel'. Some verbs have only the perfect stem, such as *coepii* 'begin' and *meminii* 'remember'. Many verbs lack the 3 stem. In all these defective verbs, what is missing or what occurs is determined by the absence or presence of a stem.[57]

Given the rigidity with which paradigms are organized around stem types, it is reasonable to look at the semantics of these stem types. Indeed, one might expect that the rigidity is due, in part at least, to stem semantics, that a particular ending always goes with a particular stem type because of the semantic relation between the two. I will now show that this is quite surprisingly untrue. A survey of the morphosyntactic categories that are realized on the three verb stem types reveals a constant semantics for one stem-type but much less identifiable semantic value for the other two. It is therefore unlikely that paradigmatic rigidity can be attributed entirely to semantics. Instead, it seems to be at least in part morphological. Table 13 contains a schematic representation of the inflectional morphosyntactic categories that are associated with each of the three verb stem types. I have included only inflection in order to strengthen the possibility of finding a uniform semantics for each stem type, since the inclusion of derivational categories would likely doom the exercise from the start.[58] The general categories of mood, tense,[59] and voice are given in the order in which they are normally realized, although the categories are in actual fact seldom realized by distinct exponents. The table should be read in blocks across as follows: each block represents a set of mood-tense-voice combinations. For example, the first block indicates that combinations of the indicative mood with present, future, or imperfect tenses and active or passive voices exist, all formed on the present stem. In the subjunctive, only present or imperfect is found with active or passive (which is to say that there is no future subjunctive), again all formed on the present stem. Similarly for the remaining blocks. In analyzing the table, we are seeking semantic uniformity for a given stem type in the sense that the stem type should realize a specific morphosyntactic category such as *perfect* or *present*. Ideally, the uniformity should go two ways, so that a given category is also always realized by the same stem type.

Traditional Latin grammar distinguishes two verb aspects, imperfect and perfect, called *infectum* and *perfectum*, associated with the present and perfect stem types, respectively. Also, the perfect stem is found only with active verbs. One might therefore propose that the meaning of the present stem is 'imperfect', while the meaning of the perfect stem is 'perfect active'. The chart reveals that there is indeed a mutual implication between the complex syntactic category *perfect active* and the perfect stem type: all and only perfect active tenses are realized on the perfect stem (deponents aside). Similar rela-

Table 13
Categories Realized on Verb Stem Types

Stem	*Mood*	*Tense*	*Voice*
present	indicative	present future imperfect	active passive
	subjunctive	present imperfect	active passive
	imperative	present	active passive
	infinitive	present	active passive
	participle	present	active
	gerund(ive)	n.a.	n.a.
perfect	indicative	perfect pluperfect future perfect	active
	subjunctive	perfect pluperfect	active
	infinitive	perfect	active
3 stem pp	indicative	perfect pluperfect future perfect	passive
	subjunctive	perfect pluperfect	passive
	infinitive	perfect	passive
3 stem fp	participle	future	active
	infinitive	future	active
t stem supine	infinitive	future	passive

tions for the remaining stem types and the remaining categories cannot, however, be so easily extracted from the table. Thus, although all perfect passive tenses are realized on the 3 stem, not all 3 stem forms are perfect passives, since some nonfinite futures, active and passive, are realized on the 3 stem. These same categories also spoil the symmetry of the present stem, but in the other direction, from meaning to form. We can claim that the present stem goes only with imperfects (if we permit the gerund and gerundive to be imperfect, which they arguably are, being always incomplete in some sense), but then not all imperfects will be realized on the present stem (the nonfinite futures being again exceptional). The following schema seems to express best what is going on:

[6] Perfect active tenses are formed on the perfect stem.
Perfect passive tenses are formed on the 3 stem.
Certain nonfinite futures are formed on the 3 stem.
The remaining (imperfect) categories are formed on the present stem.

This schema has two notable features. First, it only goes one way, from morphosyntactic category to morphological form and not vice versa. Second, the present stem is a kind of default stem, in the sense of Zwicky (1986). It is difficult to see how any more generality could be extracted from the table without doing violence to the data, yet the schema does express, albeit indirectly, precisely the sort of semantic system that we expect to find if we espouse a lexeme-based framework that incorporates stems. Within such a framework, stems do not have meanings. Still, we may say that they are more or less uniform semantically based on the syntacticosemantic categories realized on them. Thus, the perfect stem is semantically uniform because the category *perfect active* is always and only realized on the perfect stem. The other stems are less uniform semantically, because the morphological system of the language uses these stems in a less semantically homogeneous manner.

As I noted above, stems are special entities within the morphological system of a language. Strictly speaking, stems have no semantic value, because, as I have argued at some length, they are only forms of lexemes and not meaningful units. They may therefore not participate in the semantic calculus directly as meaning-bearing units. As I noted briefly above, stems must also be contrasted with affixes, morphs that are introduced by rules as 'markers' of morphosyntactic categories. Affixes, although they do not, strictly speaking, have meaning independent of the rules by which they are introduced, nonetheless are much more easily connected to the semantics of their rules. Thus, we are able to say that the English suffix *s* is a marker of the plural or that it 'means' plural, among other things, without being as misleading about linguistic semantics as we would be in assigning a meaning to the category *Latin present stem*.

Another difference between affixes and stem types is in their abstractness. With affixes, there is a fairly direct connection between meaning and form. But the categories *present stem* or *perfect stem* are neither meaning nor form. On the one hand, they are similar to a morphosyntactic category like *plural* in being realized by realization rules that spell out particular affixed forms as indicators of the present stem or the past stem, for example, by suffixing *u* or *s* to a verb root to form the past stem. On the other hand, unlike plural, they do not reflect directly the semantic or syntactic system. Instead, they are simply part of the abstract and arbitrary morphological machinery of the language. In this respect stems are much closer to theme vowels than to more orthodox morphs.

8. PHONOLOGICALLY SPECIFIC STEMS

Our discussion so far has centered on the three traditionally recognized basic stem types of Latin verbs. I have tried to show that these stems, whether or not they are listed in the permanent lexicon, have two important properties. First, they are not meaningful. Second, the abstract categories of present, perfect, and 3 stem enjoy a special status in Latin grammar as independent parts of the morphological system of the language. Realization rules of the language refer to these abstract categories and not to specific forms when selecting forms on which to operate.

Many stems are of this abstract type, but some are much more concretely specified. Consider the following fact. In Latin verbs of the *aa* and *ee* conjugations, the future and imperfect tenses are formed by adding certain person and number suffixes to a form of the verb that is built on the present stem by means of the suffix *VVb*.[60] For the other conjugations, however, while the imperfect is formed on this same stem, the future is formed with the vowel *ee* attached to the present stem.[61] The relevant forms are given in table 14.

The imperfect of all verbs is formed on what I will call the *b* stem, while the future of only *aa* and *ee* verbs is formed on the *b* stem.[62] The *b* stem thus has a status of sorts outside the rules that refer to it, since it is referred to by more than one realization rule. But the *b* stem is not abstract in the way the basic stems are, since it is always formed with the suffix *VVb* on the present stem. It thus contrasts with the basic stems, which are quite varied in their forms, sometimes arbitrarily so.

We see then that Latin has two kinds of stem types, those characterized by a single relatively concrete form and those that are not.[63] The two sorts of stem types seem to be quite widely distributed among the world's languages (a

Table 14
Future and Imperfect Forms

Conjugation	*Future 2 sg.*	*Imperfect 2 sg.*	*Gloss*
aa	laudaabiis	laudaabaas	'praise'
ee	mordeebiis	mordeebaas	'bite'
e	acuees	acueebaas	'sharpen'
i	capiees	capieebaas	'take'
ii	muugiees	muugieebaas	'bellow'

conjecture I will not try to prove here), and Latin does not seem to be exceptional in having recourse to both sorts. As far as I know, the literature does not explicitly distinguish these two different kinds of stems terminologically or otherwise. In my investigations, I have not found any cases where the morphology distinguishes the two kinds, in the sense that rules that build on abstract stems have different properties from rules that build on phonologically characterized stems. I will therefore not burden the reader with any terminology to separate the two sorts. Nevertheless, the distinction should be kept in mind, since it may have consequences that I am unaware of.

One interesting difference between the two kinds in Latin is whether individual instances of a particular stem type must be listed in the permanent lexicon. We saw above that many, though not all, basic verb stems must be listed, as Lieber and others have shown. I argued, contra Lieber, that this listedness was unconnected to their being stems, since many basic stems are not and can not be listed. The existence of *b* stems further strengthens my original claim, since, though stems, they are never listed.[64] It is possible that the historical or psychological reason for the contrast with respect to listedness is the difference in abstractness or, put differently, the availability of a number of mechanisms for realizing phonologically the same morphosyntactic category.

9. CONCLUSIONS

We can now define a stem as the form of a lexeme on which a realization rule operates. If this definition holds, we must recognize the existence of sometimes abstract, purely morphological entities within human languages. These entities can be easily accomodated within a lexeme-based theory of morphology in which the relation between form and meaning is indirect.

BRACKETING PARADOXES IN MANIPURI

Shobhana L. Chelliah

INTRODUCTION

In the theory of Lexical Phonology (LP) (Kiparsky 1982; 1983; Mohanan 1986), morphological processes and phonological rules that apply exclusively within the word are interspersed and organized in a series of hierarchically ordered levels. Research has shown that such an organization of word formation often leads to a mismatch between phonological structure and morphological-semantic bracketing (Kiparsky 1983; Pesetsky 1985; Sproat 1985; Marantz 1988; and Cohn 1989, among others).

Cohn (1989), presents a discussion of the cyclic application of stress in Indonesian which argues that bracketing paradoxes can be resolved if the morphological-semantic structure of words—derived on the basis of subcategorization requirements and semantic compositionality—is taken as basic. Building on work done by Booij and Rubach (1984) and Nespor and Vogel (1986) in the theory of Prosodic Hierarchy (PH), Cohn develops an effective mechanism for deriving phonological structure from morphological-semantic bracketing. According to the theory of PH, (morpho)syntactic strings are composed of hierarchically organized prosodic units, building up from the syllable to the foot, the phonological word, the clitic group, the phonological phrase, and the intonational phrase. Cohn shows how the parsing of the morphological-semantic structure into prosodic units can adequately define the domain of application of phonological rules.

In this paper, I will present an account of bracketing paradoxes in Manipuri[1] that supports the analysis of Indonesian presented by Cohn. In particular, I will show that although a level-ordered LP analysis of the interaction of morphology and phonology in Manipuri does correctly define the domain of application of phonological rules, the structure imposed on words to derive these domains is at variance with the morphological-semantic structure of the word. However, when the morphological-semantic structure is taken to be basic and parsed in terms of prosodic units, these units prove adequate in delimiting the domain of application of phonological rules. In this way, the bracketing paradox in Manipuri is resolved. Finally, the prosodic analysis will be used to give an account of some bracketing paradoxes observed in English.

1. LEVEL ORDERING IN THE LEXICAL PHONOLOGY OF MANIPURI

I will now present the data from Manipuri, giving first the phonological evidence present for the existence of level ordering in the lexical phonology of the language. Consider the Voicing Assimilation Rule (VAR), where syllable-initial voiceless unaspirated stops are voiced between voiced segments. As illustrated in [1a], VAR applies with the suffixation of the infinitive marker *-pə*, when it is suffixed to a stem that ends in a voiced segment. When the stem ends with a voiceless segment, the initial stop of the suffix does not voice. Similar examples are given in [1b] through [1d] with the affixation of the genitive, dative, and associative markers, respectively.[2]

[1]	**a.** stem +– pə 'inf'	čabə	'to eat'	pikpə	'to be small'
	b. stem +– ki 'gen'	tʰagi	'of the moon'	pʰuritki	'of the shirt'
	c. stem +– tə 'dat'	čində	'on the hill'	ləmpaktə	'on the ground'
	d. stem +– kə 'ass'	migə	'with man'	kʰutkə	'with the hand'

VAR also applies in compounds where the second stem of the compound has a falling tone.[3] Thus in [2a] the initial voiceless stop of *pòy* 'wander' voices when compounded with a stem that ends in a voiced stop. Similarly VAR applies on the stem *-čín* 'border' in [2b], and on the stem *-čaw* 'big' in [2c]. Examples [2d] through [2f] show compounds where the second has a high-level tone: VAR does not apply in these cases.

[2]	**a.** ləmbòybə ləm-pòy-pə path-wander-agen 'wanderer'	**b.** kumjìn kum-čın year-border 'early part of the year'	**c.** sàjàwbə sà-čàw-bə body-big-agen 'one who is corpulent'
	d. tə̀mpak tə̀m-pak water-broad 'ocean'	**e.** ika i-ka water-rise 'flood'	**f.** tinkaŋ tin-kaŋ insect-mosquito 'small insects; mosquitoes and the like'

VAR, however, fails to apply with prefixation. For example, in [3a], with the affixation of *i-* 'first person pronominal', the stem *pa* 'father' does not voice. Other examples of VAR's failure to apply with prefixation are given in [3b] with the prefixation of *mə-* 'third person pronominal' in [3c], with the attributive marker *ə-*, in [3d], with the prefixation of *mə-* 'method of Ving', and in [3e] with the nominalizing prefix *khu-:*

[3]		*root*	*pronominal prefix* i-, mə- + *root*	
	a.	pa 'father'	ipa	'my father'
	b.	pu 'grandfather'	məpu	'his/her grandfather'

	c.		**d.**		**e.**	
		ətənbə		məpa		khuthi
		ə-tən-pə		mə-pa		khu-thi
		att-short-inf		mode-read		nom-ugly
		'that which is short'		'way of reading'		'ugliness'

As is illustrated in the minimal pairs in [4], although tone is relevant for voicing in compounds, it is not relevant for either suffixation or prefixation.

[4]	**a.**	əpàybə uček	versus	əpaybə kolom
		ə-pày-bə uček		ə-pay-bə kolom
		att-fly-rel bird		att-hold-rel pen
		'the bird that is flying'		'the pen that is held'

b. čàbə 'for fishes to swim in the water' versus cabə 'to eat'
c. mìgi 'of a spider versus migi 'of a man'

The fact that VAR applies only in a particular morphological environment can be neatly represented in the theory of LP, where word formation processes and phonological processes are organized in a series of hierarchically ordered levels. In the LP model, the correct characterization of VAR can be made by placing the morphological environments where VAR applies on a level earlier than the environments where the rule fails to apply and by pairing VAR with this earlier level. This level ordering is shown in [5]:

[5]	*level*	*morphology*	*phonology*
	level 2	suffixation	VAR, other level 2 phonology
	level 3	prefixation	level 3 phonology

This level ordering assures that the application of the VAR is restricted to level 2 (L2), where suffixation takes place. VAR will not apply at level 3 (L3), where prefixation takes place, since it is turned off at the end of its own level of application. In this way, the application of the rule to morphological environments created at the later level is blocked.

Voicing in compounding and suffixation as formalized in [6a] and [6b], respectively, can be collapsed into the single rule in [6c]:

[6] **a.** Voicing in Compounds (VAR):
C→[+ voice] / [(C)V] [__ V̀(C)]

b. Voicing with suffixation (VARC):
C→[+ voice]/ [[(C)V]__V(C)]
σ σ

c. Voicing in compounds and suffixation (VAR):
C→[+ voice] / (C)V__V(C)
σ σ

Besides simplifying the statement of voicing, [6c] is more desirable than the two distinct rules given in [6a] and [6b], as it ensures that morphological boundaries need not be written into the phonological rule. This is important since it is claimed that a major advantage of LP over a traditional SPE treatment of the interaction of morphology and phonology is that level ordering eliminates the necessity for boundary symbols (Pesetsky 1985, among others). I will return to this issue in sections 2 and 4.

Compounding of stems with a falling tone in the final stem can occur at L2 along with suffixation. Compounds on which VAR does apply will be created at L2 and thus paired with the application of VAR as formulated in [6c]. Compounds on which VAR does not apply will be created at L3, just as in the case of prefixation, to escape VAR.

The interleaving of morphology and phonology, as shown in [7], gives further evidence for LP in Manipuri. Examples [7a] and [7b] illustrate the application of the Lateral Deletion Rule (LDR), where *l* deletes after *k* (the *l* of the durative aspect marker *-lə* in [7a] and the perfective aspect marker *-ləm* in [7b] delete). A rule applies subsequently whereby intervocalic *k* changes to glottal stop.[4] In examples [7c] and [7d] LDR fails to apply; here the *l* in *-lək,* a suffix that indicates that the action originates at a distance from the speech event, does not delete but surfaces as *r*.

[7] **a.** yoˀəbə
yok-lə-pə
rear-dur-inf
'rear up'

b. laˀəmmi
lak-ləm-li
come-perf-prog
'carried here'

c. putʰorəˀi
pu-tʰok-lək-i
carry-out-dsource-pres
'carries out'

d. čoŋtʰorəˀəgə
čoŋ-tʰok-lək-lə-kə
jump-out-dsource-dur-ass
'jumping out'

Characterizing LDR is complicated by the presence of the Velar Stop Deletion Rule (VDR), by which *k* is deleted before *l*. Examples [6c] and [6d] illustrate the application of VDR: the *k* of *-tʰok* is deleted with the suffixation of the directional suffix *-lək*. However, VDR is seen not to apply in cases like [6a] and [6b], where LDR applies instead.

Consider the necessary ordering between the rules of LDR and VDR. In the derivation of a form like *čoŋtʰorəˀəgə* 'jumped out': if LDR is assumed to apply before VDR, the incorrect form given in [8a] is derived; if VDR is assumed to apply before LDR, the incorrect form given in [8b] is derived.

[8]	**a.**	/čoŋ-tʰok-lək-lə/	LDR applies
		*[čoŋ-tʰok-ək-ə]	environment for VDR no longer available
	b.	/čoŋ-tʰok-lək-lə/	VDR applies
		*[čoŋ-tʰo-lə-lə]	environment for LDR no longer available

Thus, mere ordering of LDR before VDR or ordering of VDR before LDR will not derive the correct result. However, both rules do apply to the form. The formalism used to characterize the application of these rules must be able to ensure that VDR applies with the affixation of *-lək* but is turned off with the affixation of *-lə*. Furthermore, LDR must be turned on only with the affixation of *-lə*. The correct characterization of these facts, reviewed in [9], is possible in LP.

[9]	*rule*	*does apply with the affixation of:*	*does not apply with the affixation of:*
	LDR	-lə, -ləm	-lək
	VDR	-lək	-lə, -ləm

In order to make certain that LDR does not apply with the suffixation of *-lək,* the rule can be paired with the suffixation of *-lə*, and *-ləm* at a level different from that of *lək* affixation. Similarly, in order to avoid the application of VDR with *-lə* and *ləm,* VDR can be paired with the affixation of *-lək* at a different level from the application of LDR.

Since the level-ordered lexicon reflects the order in which morphemes are concatenated, an additional way to determine the level ordering of *-lək, -lə* and *-lə*m affixation, is to consider the linear order of these morphemes. From a form like *cŏŋtʰorəˀəgə*, it is clear that *-lək* affixation occurs before the affixation of *-lə*. Thus, *-lək* affixation is assumed to occur, along with the application of the VDR, at a level before the affixation of *-lə*. A level-ordered derivation illustrating the application of the LDR and VDR following these observations is given in [10].

[**10**]	*level of* -lək	čoŋ-tʰok-lək	VDR applies
	affixation	čoŋtʰolək	
	level of -lə	čoŋtʰolək-lə	LDR applies
	affixation	čoŋtʰoləkə	
	surface form	[čoŋtʰorəˀəgə]	after further morphology and phonology apply

The level ordering of the rules of VAR, LDR, and VDR can now be determined. First, in the linear order of morphemes given in [11], *-lə* is affixed before the infinitive marker *-pə* [11a] and before the associative marker *-kə* [11b]; thus *-lə* affixation must occur before affixation of these markers.

[**11**] **a.** čarəbədi
ča-lə-pə-ti
eat-dur-inf-ex
'if (I) am eating'

b. čarəgə
ča-lə-kə
eat-dur-ass
'after eating'

Also, as shown in the form *čoŋtʰorəˀəgə*, *-lək* is affixed after the derivational marker *-tʰok* in the linear order. Since *-lək* must be affixed before the affixation of *-lə*, I will assume that *-tʰok* and *-lək* are affixed at a level before the affixation of *-lə*. Based on these facts about the interaction of morphological and phonological processes and the linear order of morphemes, the level ordering of the lexical phonology of Manipuri is represented in [12].[5]

[**12**]	*level*	*morphology*	*phonology*
	L1	-lək, -tʰok[6]	VDR
	L2	infinitive-pə	VAR
		case markers	LDR
		aspect-lə	
		directional -ləm	
		compounds:	
		(final stem has a falling tone)	
	L3	prefixation	L3 phonology
		all other compounds	

2. BRACKETING PARADOXES IN MANIPURI

This level ordering, while correctly pairing morphological and phonological processes, leads to bracketing paradoxes: the phonological structure (PS) and the morphosyntactic structure (MS) do not always match. Bracketing paradoxes will occur when noun stems modified by one of the L3 pronominal prefixes or verb stems derived from nouns by use of the attributive suffix must additionally take an L2 case marker. An example of such a paradox is given in [13a], where VAR applies with the suffixation of the dative marker *-tə*, requiring the PS as indicated in [13b]. As shown in [13c], the MS bracketing is at variance with this PS.

[13] **a.** məyumdə
mə-yum-tə
3PP-house-dat
'to his house'

b. L2 yum-tə VAR
yumdə
mə-yumdə
[məyumdə]

c. PS: [mə+[yum+tə]]
MS: [mə+yum]+tə]]

It has previously been noted (Hoeksema 1985; Aronoff 1988; Booij and Rubach, among others), that when compounds are inflected, the inflection attaches phonologically to only one stem of the compound and that this sometimes results in bracketing paradoxes. In Manipuri, bracketing paradoxes of this sort will result for any compound noun that is derived at L3 in order to escape VAR, when this compound is followed by a case marker. Recall that case markers have voiced allophones and are affixed at L2. Consider for example the compound given in [14a] with a corresponding phonological derivation given in [14b]:

[14] **a.** ikagi
i-ka-ki
noun-verb-case
water-rise-gen
'of flood water'

b. L2 ka-ki VAR
ka-gi
L3 ikagi
[ikagi]

c. phonological bracketing: [i+[ka+ki]]
MS: [[i+ka]+ki]

In [14a] compounding does not occur at L2 since the L2 rule VAR does not apply between the stems *i* and *ka;* however, the case marker must be affixed to *ka* at L2 to allow for the application of VAR. Thus, as shown in [14c], the PS for *ikagi* is [i+[ka+ki]], but the MS is [[i+ka]+ki], where the genitive marker is affixed to the whole compound. This type of bracketing paradox could be avoided by opting for two distinct rules of voicing (i.e., [6a] and [6b]). Since the domain of application of voicing in compounds is written into the phonological rule, [6a] would not apply in cases of compounding where the second stem has a high and not a falling tone. In that case there would be no need to carry out compounding at two levels; if all compounding could take place at L2, the observed paradox would not be obtained. However, as discussed in section 2, [6c] is also problematic for LP. For the moment, in order to avoid the problem of the bracketing paradox, I will assume that voicing in Manipuri should be characterized by the two rules [6a] and [6b]. A solution to this problem along with a solution to the bracketing paradox observed in [13a] will be given in section 4.

3. POSSIBLE SOLUTIONS TO BRACKETING PARADOXES

3.1. Deriving MS from PS

One class of solutions proposed to bracketing paradoxes claims that the phonological structure of words—in LP, this would be the structure imposed by the phonological cycle and level ordering—is basic and that it should be manipulated to arrive at the morphological-semantic structure. Kiparsky (1982b) and Pesetsky (1985) are representative of this view.

Consider the Manipuri data in the light of Kiparsky's (1982b) solution for a bracketing paradox in English that is similar to the one illustrated for Manipuri. Take examples like *ungrammaticality*. As an L1 suffix, *-ity* attaches to *grammatical* first. *Un-*, an L2 prefix, must only attach to adjectives and therefore should not be able to attach to the noun *grammaticality*. How is *-un* able to peek through the noun and see the adjective stem? In Kiparsky's view these violations must be seen as exceptions to the Bracket Erasure Convention, which stipulates that internal brackets are erased at the end of every level. Kiparsky's analysis is that, as the Projection Principle is relevant in morphology, subcategorization requirements of affixes must be met at every level. Thus, since *-un* subcategorizes for an adjective, the requirements of the Projection Principle override all other conditions and allow for *un-* to see the adjective stem in *grammaticality*. Such a solution is not effective in solving the violations given in [13] and [14] as there is no subcategorizational restriction against a prefix being affixed to a fully inflected form, or any subcategorizational requirement for a stem to be compounded with a fully inflected word. Thus, there is no motivation for reanalysis due to the subcategorization requirements of an affix, and Kiparsky's solution to English bracketing paradoxes is inapplicable in Manipuri.

3.2. Deriving PS from MS

A second class of solutions to bracketing paradoxes claims that PS should be deduced from MS. Proponents of this claim include Booij and Rubach (1984), Sproat (1985), Marantz (1988), and Cohn (1989). Cohn comes to this conclusion based on the notion that cyclic phonological rules that necessitate the interspersing of morphological and phonological processes can reveal the order in which words are constructed. She points out that in Indonesian, cyclic stress rules must be applied in the same order necessary for compositional semantics. From this she concludes that the only possible account of bracketing paradoxes in Indonesian must take MS to be primal. In section 4 I will present evidence to support this claim. Analysis of the Manipuri data will show that the primacy of MS can be proved not only on the basis of cyclicity (a phenomena expressed in LP by the interspersing of phonology and morphology) but also by the interaction of morphological processes and noncyclic rules (as characterized by the level ordering of VAR, suffixation, and prefixation in Manipuri).

4. A PROSODIC ANALYSIS OF BRACKETING PARADOXES IN MANIPURI

4.1. Theoretical Background

In the theory of the Prosodic Hierarchy (PH), dealing primarily with postlexical phenomena, Nespor and Vogel (1986) show that for a variety of languages the domain of certain phonological rules cannot be stated in terms of syntactic constituents. The authors motivate the existence of prosodic constituents, derived from a parsing of syntactic strings, which do correctly delimit the domain of phonological rules. A syntactic string is considered a prosodic constituent if a rule of the grammar refers to it in its formulation or if the string is the domain of application of a phonological rule (Nespor and Vogel 1986, 59).

Booij and Rubach (1984) and Cohn (1989) extend the theory of PH to interaction of phonology and morphology with lexical phonological rules. It is argued that where PS and MS are not isomorphic, prosodically defined phonological constituents can be used to appropriately delimit the application of phonological rules in the lexicon. A good example of how this works is given in Booij and Rubach's prosodic solution to a bracketing paradox in Polish, where all phonological rules are blocked by prefix junctures. For instance, the Polish rule of Vowel Deletion in verbs (V → Ø / _ V) applies regularly across all morpheme junctures except prefix junctures:

[15] **a.** wy + obrazić — imagine

b. prze + analizować — reanalyze

Since prefixes do not form the domain of application for the rule of Vowel Deletion, in a prosodic analysis prefixes and stems can be said to form two separate prosodic constituents and the Vowel Deletion Rule, along with all other rules that never apply across prefix junctures, can be said to apply within, and never across, prosodic constituents.

The smallest prosodic constituent relevant to such an analysis is the phonological word (PWord). A PWord maybe a stem, prefix or a stem plus all its suffixes. In the case of compounds, if no phonological rules apply across the stem junctures, then the prosodic structure of the compound will be:

```
[16]  PWord          PWord
        |             /  \
      stem        stem    affix
```

If on the other hand, there are specific rules that do apply exactly between these junctures, then the stems of the compounds will be part of the same phonological constituent. The prosodic constituent above the level of the PWord is the clitic group (Cohn 1989; Nespor and Vogel 1986). A clitic group (CGroup) bounds the domain of application of a phonological rule that applies within the boundaries of a prosodic unit larger than a PWord (for example, refer to Cohn's discussion of the Main Stress rule in Indonesian (1989; 201).

Cohn (1989), based in part on work done by Chen (1985) and Selkirk (1986), provides a formal implementation of PH within the lexicon to deal with bracketing paradoxes in Indonesian. As in LP, her treatment reflects the interleaving of morphological and phonological processes; however, whereas LP delimits the domain of application of phonological rules through level ordering, she shows that the prosodically defined PWord can be used for such delimitation. The morphological structure of a word, determined through subcategorization and compositionality, is seen as basic and the phonological structure is derived from it.

4.2. The Solution to the Bracketing Paradox in Manipuri

4.2.1. VAR(C) in Suffixation, Prefixation, and Compounding

Adapting the formalism used by Cohn, I will now show how the Manipuri facts can adequately be described in terms of PH:

[17] **a.** The prosodic domains for the application of phonological rules:

(i) VAR: the PWord
(ii) VARC: the CGroup

b. Well-formedness of affixation and stem adjunction:

(i) When a suffix is added to a stem, the stem and the suffix form a single PWord, and the entire string forms a CGroup.
(ii) When two strings are compounded, the entire string forms a CGroup.
(iii) Reparsing occurs after each morphological process.

Utilizing the framework presented in [17], consider the derivation of the form *čiŋdə*, where VAR does apply:

[18]		
	Derivation of	[čiŋdə]
	Input and Initial parsing	$[_c]_w$ čiŋ]]
	Suffixation	$[_c[_w$ čiŋ]]tə
	Reparsing	$[_c[_w$ čiŋtə]]
	Phonology with the PWord (VAR)	$[_c[_w$ čiŋdə]]

In [18] the input is parsed into a PWord and a CGroup. After suffixation, reparsing is triggered and the relevant phonological rules apply. Since the phonological rules are noncyclic, following Booij and Rubach (1987), I assume that they apply in one block after all morphology has taken place. Consider next the derivation of *ipagi* 'of my father', where VAR does not apply:

[19]	Derivation of	[ipagi]
	Input and Initial parsing	[$_c$[$_w$ pa]]
	Prefixation	[$_c$[$_w$ i]][$_c$[$_w$ pa]
	Reparsing	———
	Suffixation	[$_c$[$_w$ i]][$_c$[$_w$ pa]ki
	Reparsing	[$_c$[$_w$ i]][$_c$[$_w$ paki]
	Phonology with the PWord (VAR)	[$_c$[$_w$ i]][$_c$[$_w$ pagi]
	Phonology within the CGroup (VARC)	———

In [19] the form is constructed compositionally, with prefixation preceding suffixation. Since no lexical phonological rules apply across the prefix juncture, I assume, as do Booij and Rubach (1984) in the case of Polish (as mentioned in section 4.1.), that the prefix is an independent prosodic unit (i.e., a PWord). As VAR applies only within PWords, voicing does not occur at the prefix juncture. Furthermore, as VARC applies only within the CGroup, the environment for its application is not present here and it does not apply.

Now consider the derivation of the compound *mijàwdə* 'to the big man', where VARC does apply:

[20]	Derivation of	[mijawdə]
	Input and Initial parsing	[$_c$[$_w$ mi]]
	Compounding	[$_c$[$_w$ mi] [$_c$[$_w$ čàw]
	Reparsing	[$_c$[$_w$ mi] [$_w$ čàw]]
	Suffixation	[$_c$[$_w$ mi] [$_w$ čàw]]tə
	Reparsing	[$_c$[$_w$ mi] [$_w$ čàwtə]]
	Phonology within the PWord (VAR)	[$_c$[$_w$ mi] [$_w$ čàwdə]]
	Phonology within the CGroup (VARC)	[$_c$[$_w$ mi] [$_w$ jàwdə]]

In [20], after compounding, the string is parsed so that both stems form a single CGroup. As the domain of application of VARC is the CGroup and as the falling tone of the second stem provides the right environment for its application, VARC applies.

Finally, consider the derivation of a compound where VARC does not apply:

[21] Derivation of [ikagi]

Input and Initial parsing	$[_c[_w\ \mathrm{i}]]$
Compounding	$[_c[_w\ \mathrm{i}]\ [_c[_w\ \mathrm{ka}]$
Reparsing	$[_c[_w\ \mathrm{i}]\ [_w\ \mathrm{ka}]]$
Suffixation	$[_c\mathrm{i}[_w\ \mathrm{ka}]]\mathrm{ki}$
Reparsing	$[_c\mathrm{i}[_w\ \mathrm{kaki}]]$
Phonology within the PWord (VAR)	$[_c\mathrm{i}[_w\ \mathrm{kagi}]]$
Phonology within the CGroup (VARC)	——

In [21] the string, after compounding, is reparsed so that the two stems are part of the same CGroup. Although its domain of application is the CGroup, VARC fails to apply since *ka*, the second of the stems in the compound, does not have a falling tone. Suffixation follows compounding in keeping with the semantic composition of the word.

We can now return to solve the problem about the formulation of the voicing rule in compounds. Since the domain on which the rule can apply is constrained by a prosodic domain, the CGroup, it is no longer necessary to specify the stem boundary in the formulation of the rule.

4.2.2. LDR and VDR

As we have seen, a significant outcome of the analysis presented in section 4.2.1. is that it eliminates the need for level ordering set up in section 1, where I also showed how the correct characterization of the phonological rules LDR and VDR can be derived through a level-ordering analysis. Let us now consider if words like *cǒŋtʰorəˀəgə* 'jumped out' can be analyzed into constituents in such a way as to pair the application of VDR with the suffixation of *-lək,* and the application of LDR with the affixation of *-lə*

By the principles set up to determine prosodic constituency, *tʰok* and *-lək* must be part of the same prosodic constituent since VDR refers to that string in its formulation. I assume that the domain of application of VDR is the PWord. The remainder of the analysis hinges on the morphosyntax of the sequence *ləgə*, for which I must present some background information on the verb morphology of Manipuri. In Manipuri, independently existing suffixes are often combined to form complex suffixes. Most often the meanings signified by these complex suffixes is idiosyncratic. The suffix *-ləgə* is an example of such a complex suffix, where the suffix *-lə* 'durative aspect' is combined with *-kə* 'associative case' to signal meanings like 'having Ved, after Ving'. Morphosyntactically then, *-ləgə* is a single unit. This fact can be used to motivate the status of *-ləgə* as a prosodic word. Further motivation comes from the fact that a real phonological juncture exists between *čoŋ-tʰok-lək* and *-ləgə*: LDR does not apply across this boundary. Given the PWord status of *coŋ-tʰok-lək* and *-ləgə*, consider the derivation in [23] ((-) indicates where a segment has been deleted):

[23]

Derivation of	[čoŋtʰorəˀəgə]
Input and Initial parsing	[$_c$[$_w$ čoŋ]]
Suffixation	[$_c$[$_w$ čoŋ]] tʰok
Reparsing	[$_c$[$_w$ čoŋtʰok]]
Suffixation	[$_c$[$_w$ čoŋtʰok]]lək
Reparsing	[$_c$[$_w$ čoŋtʰoklək]]
Suffixation	[$_c$[$_w$ čoŋtʰoklək]]ləgə
Reparsing	[$_c$[$_w$ čoŋtʰoklək][$_w$ ləgə]]
Phonology within the PWord (VAR, VDR)	[$_c$[$_w$ čoŋtʰo-lək][$_w$ ləgə]]
Phonology within the CGroup (VARC, LDR)	[$_c$[$_w$ čoŋtʰo-lək][$_w$ -əgə]]
Further phonology (postlexical) (k→)ˀ/V_V;l→r/V_V)	[$_c$[$_w$ čoŋtʰorəˀəgə]

Since *-ləgə* is a PWord, it is not reparsed to form part of the PWord *coŋtʰoklək*. Since VDR takes only the PWord as its domain of application, it cannot apply across the PWord boundary and so is prevented from bleeding LDR. However, since the domain of application of LDR is the CGroup, it can bleed the application of VDR. For this reason, the restriction on phonological rule application given in [24] is necessary.

[24] Where *x* is higher than *y* on the Prosodic Hierarchy, a phonological rule that takes *y* as its bounding domain must apply before a phonological rule that takes *x* as its bounding domain.

The rule in [24] ensures that VDR will apply before LDR thus allowing for the derivation of the attested form. In effect, [24] allows us to obtain the results of level ordering without imposing a phonologically based structure on the word.

5. BRACKETING PARADOXES IN ENGLISH

Two types of examples have been presented in the literature that counter the prediction made by the theory of level ordering in LP that L1 affixes will always precede L2 affixes. First, Kiparsky (1983) and Pesetsky (1985) discuss examples like *ungrammaticality,* where (as described in section 3.1.) because of the subcategorization requirements of the prefix *un-*, the MS of the word is [*un* [*grammatical*]]*ity*]. This means that the L1 suffix *-ity* occurs outside the L2 affix *un-* in the linear order of the string. Second, Aronoff

(1976) presents examples like *readability* and *computerization,* where suffixes that affect stress placement (the L1 suffixes *-ity* and *-tion*) occur outside suffixes that are neutral with regard to stress (the L2 suffixes *-able* and *-ize*).

Recall that a syntactic string can be considered a prosodic unit if exactly that string is the domain of application of a phonological rule. The rule of Stress Placement helps to establish the prosodic constituency of words like *ungrammaticality*. Since there are no phonological processes that take place between the prefix and the stem, the two form independent PWords. On the other hand, the Stress Placement Rule does apply across the boundary of the suffix *-ity,* thereby arguing for a prosodic constituent that includes the stem and suffix. As illustrated in [25] (taken directly from Cohn 1989, 212), the analysis of the word into these prosodic constituents allows for the correct placement of stress in the word:

[25]	Cycle 1:	Input:	[grammatical]
		Parsing:	$[_W$ grammatical]
		Stress:	$[_W$ grammátical]
	Cycle 2:	Affixation:	ùn$[_W$ grammátical]
		Parsing:	$[_W$ ùn] $[_W$ grammátical]
		Stress:	applies vacuosly
	Cycle 3:	Affixation:	$[_W$ ùn] $[_W$ grammátical] ity
		Parsing:	$[_W$ ùn] $[_W$ grammáticality]
		Stress:	$[_W$ ùn] $[_W$ grammáticálity]

Note that the prefix is added to the stem at an early stage of the derivation, so that the word is constructed compositionally. Since *un-* is in a separate constituent from the stem, assuming that the Stress Placement Rule has the PWord as its domain of application, the prefix is outside the scope of the structural description of the Stress Placement Rule and is not counted in the assignment of stress. After *-ity* is added to the stem, parsing makes a PWord that contains both the stem and the suffix; as the domain of the Stress Placement Rule is the PWord, the stem-suffix sequence does undergo the rule.

Syllabification reinforces this constituent analysis of the string. Booij and Rubach (1984, 14), note that the syllabification of *ungrammaticality* is *un=gram=ma=ti=ca=li=ty* (= signifies a syllable boundary), where the *i* of the suffix *-ity* is the nucleus of the syllable that has as its onset a segment from the stem (i.e., *ca*). The prefix *un-*, on the other hand, forms a syllable of its own. Thus, syllabification treats the stem and the suffix as a single a constituent; on the other hand, the prefix is treated as if it were an independent unit.

I will now show how this analysis can be used to account for the type of bracketing paradoxes exemplified in *readability* and *computerization.* Since level ordering is not built into PH, no claims are made about the order in which affixes will appear. However, as has been pointed out in Aronoff and Sridhar (1987), the stem *read* and the and suffix sequence *-ability* are stressed as individual words: this fact needs to be accounted for. Applying the principles for determining prosodic constituency stated above, it is possible to analyze *read* and *-ability* as individual PWords. First, note that in the syllabification of the word, the stem and the suffix sequence are part of different syllables: *read=a=bi=li=ity*. However, just as in the case of *ungrammaticality,* the *i* of the suffix *-ity* forms the nucelus of a syllable that is part of the suffix *-able*. Since Syllabification does not take place between the stem and suffix juncture, *read* forms a different PWord from the rest of the word. Since Syllabification treats *-ability* as a single unit, the suffix sequence forms an independent PWord. The peculiar stress pattern of *readability* can now be accounted for: as *read* and *-ability* are independent PWords, they are stressed individually and each PWord receives word stress.

5. CONCLUSION

In this paper, I have given an account of the rules of VAR, VARC, LDR, and VDR in Manipuri. The analysis presented supports the claim that morphological-semantic structure should be taken as basic and that phonological structure should be deduced from it. Since the domain of application of the phonological rules of Manipuri could be delimited using prosodic units like the PWord and the CGroup, the validity of such constituents as well as the inclusion of prosodic information in the lexicon is also supported. I have also suggested how the PH framework developed in Cohn (1989) for the interaction of morphology and cyclic phonology can be used to account for the interaction of noncyclic lexical rules and morphology. Finally, I have shown how the PH framework can be used to solve a type of bracketing paradox in English that is problematic for LP.

DERIVATION IN SYNTAX

Frank Drijkoningen

INTRODUCTION

In this paper I wish to defend the claim that processes of derivational morphology occur in syntax proper, and that the properties of the constructions illustrating them are to be explained by a theory allowing adjunction of category-changing affixes to the independently motivated X-bar levels of the verbal projection.

In order to set the scene, consider a well-studied English construction, the gerundive nominals discussed in Chomsky (1970). The classical analysis of this construction—an analysis that has never been challenged fundamentally—explains its properties by stating that a verb phrase (VP) has been nominalized. Since a syntactic structure (the VP) is input to the process of nominalization, the construction cannot be treated in the lexical component. On the other hand, the construction clearly uses a category-changing affix, such that morphological properties are involved too. In terms of this paper, gerundive nominals illustrate a derivational process (nominalization) occurring in syntax proper (the input being a syntactic structure). My main goals in this paper are to motivate the existence of this type of construction by enlarging the number of constructions with similar properties and to elaborate and refine the theory covering them.

In the first section I will take up the deverbalization rule of Jackendoff (1977) and criticize some claims connected to his specific implementation. In the second section I will analyze participles of various kinds and argue that they all are adjectivalizing syntactic affixes. In the third section I will take up the nominalizing syntactic affixes, and in the fourth section I will briefly discuss the interaction between nominalization and adjectivalization in syntax. The class of affixes thus isolated has a number of interesting properties in common, which are discussed more extensively in section 5. In the conclusion I will summarize my proposals and results.

1. DEVERBALIZATION

Jackendoff (1977, 221) proposes a Deverbalizing Rule Schema:

[1] $X^i \rightarrow Af\ V^i$

The rule is meant to describe a class of systematic exceptions to the otherwise general X-bar schemata. Although the deverbalizing rule schema conflicts with some standard assumptions concerning syntactic structure, it does not have a devastating effect on the overall definition of X-bar projections, as some clear restrictions are made. First, the X-bar level may not change, thus the general tenet of controlled level-assignment is retained. Second, the rule only mentions verbs on the right-hand side; the schema does not apply to all potential Xs. Finally, the rule has to be triggered by a specific limited class of elements, indicated by Af.

Although the idea formalized by [1] seems attractive to me, I have some general criticisms before entering into the details of specific constructions.

To make things more concrete, Jackendoff (1977) ultimately proposes the following instantiations of the schema:

[2] **a.** Gerundive Nominals
$N'' \rightarrow ing\ V''$

b. Tensed Complements
$V''' \rightarrow \{that,\ as,\ than,\ wh\}\ V'''$

c. Free Relatives
$N''' \rightarrow wh\ V'''$

d. Gerundive PPs
$P'' \rightarrow ing\ V''$

e. Passive VPs
$A'' \rightarrow en\ V''$

This set of rules, however, can be divided in two subsets: group A includes [a], [d], and [e]; group B consists of [b] and [c]. Group A contains true affixes as the realization of Af: *-ing* and *-en* are affixes in a morphological sense and hence are to be attached to the verb at some more superficial level. Group B does not contain affixes in a morphological sense; if the relevant elements are anything for morphology, they rather would be unanalyzable independent words, and as such not very interesting. This bifurcation is accepted by Jackendoff, who claims that Af may be either a grammatical formative or an affix (p. 221). For a theory of affixation in syntax, however, I think it is advisable to concentrate only on group A. In other words, I propose the following constraint on rule [1]:

[3] Af in [1] may only be instantiated by an affix.

This restriction strikes me as very plausible, not in the least because it seems odd to have to explicitly state [3] in the first place.

A second point concerns Jackendoff's remark that gerundive nominals are dominated by a node with nominal properties, but that they do not contain a noun head (p. 52), or, rather, contain a verb head (p. 221). This makes the deverbalization schema quite exceptional with respect to the general idea behind any X-bar theory: a projection of X, but no X, or, rather, a Y. This problem can be mended by postulating that affixes may themselves bear a categorial indication (cf. Selkirk 1982): *-ing* as used in gerundive nominals then is a nominal affix. This makes the X-bar aspect of the deverbalization rule more in line with the general tenet of X-bar theory: a projection of X with an X present. Of course, it remains stipulated that this X-head is an affix, just as it remains stipulated that this affix adjoins to a verbal projection of a certain level.

Once we adopt the combination of Selkirk's proposal that affixes bear categorial indications and Jackendoff's deverbalization schema, there are some nontrivial consequences, consequences beyond just updating Jackendoff's proposal. It entails in general that the categorial head of the construction is the category of the class of elements called Af. First, this again casts severe doubts on the examples of group B, and in two different ways. On the one hand, the categorial status of the WH-element in COMP is predicted to be relevant for the categorial status of the tensed complements, clearly an undesired state of affairs. On the other hand, it is predicted that an element such as *than* or *as* is verbal if the projection is to be verbal, not evidently the correct result either. So, if categorial matches between the Af-head and the projection are desirable, group B falls out. When we return to group A again, there is also a member of group A that becomes improbable in view of categorial indications—that is, rule [2d].

In general, in morphology no instances of preposition-making affixes have been found: though it is fairly common to build adjectives, nouns, or verbs, prepositions are not productively constructed by means of affixes because they form a closed class. If one considers then rule [2d], describing gerundive PPs, one is now forced to claim that *-ing* is an affix bearing the category P. This seems undesirable to me in that *-ing* does not look at all like a preposition. Note that it is not in principle impossible to have affixes that look like prepositions and that may be analyzed as syntactic prepositional affixes (e.g., infinitival *to*). The type of criticism presented here does not only bear on Jackendoff's account of this specific "gerundive PP" construction (for which an alternative will be suggested in section 3), but can also be formulated against other concrete analyses, like, for instance, the rule N″ → P V″ proposed for Spanish by Wilkins (1986).

A last remark concerns the levels. All instances that have been found (group A) are cases in which the affix adjoins to the VP. This entails at least that the full potential of the proposal has not been used. Full use of the possibilities is very well possible, as I will show below. In this respect it is relevant to note that Jackendoff implicitly seems to bar adjunction of an affix to the lowest syntactic projection, in the sense that the value of *i* in [1] may not be 0. I see no particular reason for this restriction barring adjunction of an affix to a syntactic head, which is quite standard in current syntactic theory (cf. Chomsky 1986).

To conclude, in what follows the full potential of [1] will be used, with three added qualifications, that the Af must be a morphological affix, that the Af must bear a categorial indication, and that this categorial indication must correspond to the category of the projection.

With respect to the syntactically defined verbal projection, I will assume [4] as standard in what follows.[1] A concrete argument for this situation is given in the section on nominalizations.

[4]

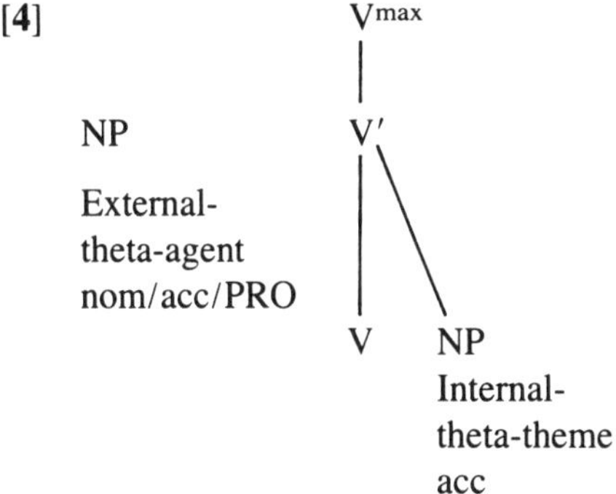

The situation depicted in [4] is subject to a number of qualifications, the most important of which I will give here. The order of the NPs with respect to their verbal sister depends on the language and is therefore irrelevant at the abstract theoretical level. The direct object is an internal argument with a theta-role that I will assume to be theme. The higher NP is the external argument with a theta-role that I will assume to be agent.[2] Hence, at D-structure the maximal verbal projection[3] dominates all arguments, all theta role–bearing elements. With respect to case theory, the verbal projection is part of a higher clausal projection, IP, and one NP will normally move to the specifier position of this projection,[4] the external argument in the case of transitive and intransitive verbs, and internal argument in the case of ergative verbs. In this [Spec, IP]

position the argument will receive nominative case, accusative case (Exceptional Case Marking) or be an ungoverned PRO. If the internal argument remains in position, it will receive accusative case.

A last note concerns the languages under consideration. In principle the argumentation will be based on French and English. However, in some circumstances one or the other may not be illustrative due to some language-specific property. In cases where neither is illustrative, Dutch and/or German will be used. (Some comments may be found in the notes in cases where hesitation could be possible.)

2. ADJECTIVALIZATIONS IN SYNTAX

In the literature it has often been noted that verbs with participial endings tend to have a number of adjectival properties when compared to verbs bearing other endings (Chomsky 1981; Van Riemsdijk 1983; Reuland 1983; rule [2e] above), so the most plausible candidates for syntactic adjectivalizations are various kinds of participles.

I will assume that there are essentially three types of participles, as given in [5].

[5] **a.** Present Participle (PRES-PART)
un homme PRO *parlant* quatre langues
a man PRO *speaking* four languages

b. Perfective Participle (PERF)
il a *parlé*
he has *spoken*

c. Passive Participle (PASS)[5]
il a été *tué*
he has been *killed*

If [4] is the basic syntactic structure, defining three syntactic verbal levels, and [1] the affixation rule to be used, allowing adjectivalization of every syntactic verbal level, the prediction is that there should exist three types of adjectivalizations of syntactic verbal projections. As there exist three different types of participles, I will argue that each participle selects a different verbal level, and that all three participles are adjectival. The overall picture for which evidence will be presented shortly is given below, where [6a] only differs from [6b] in perspective.

[6] **a.** PRES—PART [+V + N] adjoins to V^{max}

PERF [+V + N] adjoins to V′ NP

PASS [+V + N] adjoins to V NP

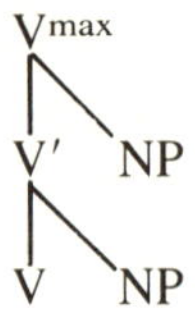

b. (i) $A^{max} \rightarrow$ PRES-PART V^{max}
(ii) $A' \rightarrow$ PERF V'
(iii) $A \rightarrow$ PASS V

The arguments to be presented are of three types. First, the categorial status of the affix must be motivated. Second, the categorial status of the projection must be evidenced. Third, the level of adjunction must be argued for.

Let me start with the present participle and the arguments concerning its level of adjunction. When one adjoins an affix to the maximal verbal projection, it is predicted that the maximal verbal projection itself has undergone no changes: in [6b] the V^{max} on the right-hand side is a V^{max} with all its standard properties illustrated in [4]. Thinking in terms of arguments and theta roles, this entails that all arguments and theta roles may be present. This prediction is borne out in [7] illustrating respectively transitive, ergative, and intransitive verbs.

[7] a. l'homme PRO mangeant des pommes
the man PRO eating apples

b. l'homme PRO arrivant en retard
the man PRO arriving too late

c. l'homme PRO dormant dans la rue
the man PRO sleeping on the street

In other terms, the complete theta grid is licensed by adjoining PRES-PART. Licensing in this sense is close to the licensing defined in Fabb (1984), who argues that all elements must be licensed in order to be able to assign the Theta roles contained in their theta grid. In his theory affixes like INFL license verbs: this can be retained with respect to the standard structure in [4] in the sense that INFL licenses the complete verbal projection, such that all theta roles can be associated to their syntactic positions.

The present participle thus falls in exactly the same class of affixes as INFL: adjoining INFL or adjoining PRES-PART to the maximal verbal projection has the same effect in terms of arguments and theta roles. Thus, by proposing that the present participle adjoins to the maximal verbal projection, it is parallel to the more standard ±TENSE affixes and makes one distributional class with them. And indeed it is impossible to find both ±TENSE and PRES-PART in one clause, a distributional fact which has been the reason for Rizzi (1982) and Reuland (1983), for example, to rewrite INFL as PRES-PART. In combining this with the evidence for the adjectival nature of PRES-PART constructions, PRES-PART would be an adjectival inflectional affix.

To these two arguments concerning licensing in terms of theta roles and distributional facts, I add one specific argument here, based on French present participles. In the normal case, negation in French consists of two parts, *ne* and *pas;* in tensed clauses *ne* precedes the finite verb and *pas* follows it. In infinitival clauses on the contrary, both *ne* and *pas* precede the infinitive, as illustrated in [8].

[8] a. l'homme ne vient pas
the man not comes not

b. l'homme a décidé de PRO ne pas venir
the man has decided "for" PRO not not to-come

Now, the present participle patterns with the finite verb and not like the infinitive, as illustrated in [9].

[9] a. l'homme PRO ne venant pas
the man PRO not coming not

b. *l'homme PRO ne pas venant
the man PRO not not coming

In other words, present participles are finite verbs in their behavior with respect to the elements indicating negation in French, as also noted in Emonds (1978). Similar arguments can be based on floating quantifiers in French (Drijkoningen 1989). This concludes my evidence for the level of adjunction postulated for PRES-PART in [6].

The most prominent evidence for the adjectival nature of the projection headed by PRES-PART comes from Dutch and German. As illustrated for Dutch in [10], all constituents follow the head noun except for adjectival constituents and except for present participles.

[10] a. de man die vier talen spreekt
the man that speaks four languages
b. de man op straat
the man on the street
c. de aardige man
the nice man
d. de [PRO vier talen sprekende] man
the [PRO four languages speaking] man

The external distribution of the construction headed by the present participle thus corresponds to the distribution of adjectival constituents.[6]

The most prominent evidence for the adjectival nature of the present participle marker can be found in German, in which all adnominal adjectives agree with the head noun in features for number, gender, and case, but not in person. Verbs, on the other hand, agree with the subject in features for number and person, but not in gender. If the present participle were verbal, it would take endings for number and person but not for gender, and if on the other hand the present participle is adjectival, it would take endings for all cases, number, and gender, but not for person. As evidenced by [11] and [12], the present participle behaves like any other adjective: gender is expressed but person cannot be expressed.

[11] **a.** ein kleiner Mann
a little (masc,sg,nom) man

b. einen kleinen Mann
a little (masc,sg,acc) man

[12] **a.** ein [PRO mehrere Sprachen sprechender] Mann
a [PRO several languages speaking (masc,sg,nom)] man

b. einen [PRO mehrere Sprachen sprechenden] Mann
a [PRO several languages speaking (masc,sg,acc)] man

My conclusion for the present participle is that all its properties are explained by [6b(i)]: The complete constituent is a maximal adjectival projection, headed by an adjectival affix that subcategorizes for a maximal verbal projection, such that all standard verbal properties with respect to theta role and case are also retained.

Let me then continue with the passive participle. Passivization has a clear effect on the situation in terms of theta roles and case, in particular absorption of the external theta role and of the internal case, as illustrated in [13].

[13] **a.** le président a été tué
the president has been killed

b. le président PRO tué hier
the president PRO killed yesterday

If my proposal in [6b(iii)] is correct, the verb has been adjectivalized from the start. The question, What do adjectives have in their theta grids? becomes relevant now. If one compares adjectives and verbs, adjectives lack one non-prepositional NP. It might be the internal argument or the external one; in the absence of an external argument, the internal argument moves to the more superficial subject position, so there is no answer to be based on the fact that the adjective has a sort of subject. However, if the D-structure external argument is generally agent, adjectives never assign this role, unless perhaps to a more internal PP (e.g., *readable for John*). It seems, therefore, that the internal theta role argument also exists for adjectival constituents, but not the external argument. In other words, I assume [14] to be the adjectival parallel (to be compared to [4]) stating that adjectival projections have only one NP position, of the internal type.

[14]

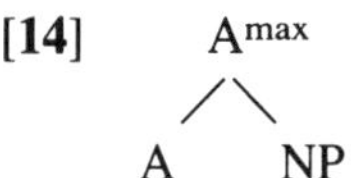

Internal-theta-theme

Returning then to passive participles, making the verb adjectival at the lowest level entails that the internal argument position is still present and can be assigned theme, but that there is no further position for the external argument, such that agent cannot be assigned. In other words, adjectivalizing a verb at a low level has an effect on the external argument agent in that it cannot be assigned to a position present in the structure. As the process occurs in syntax, and as in syntax the Projection Principle must be obeyed, I follow Jaeggli (1986), who argues that the external theta role is assigned to the passive morpheme itself and hence visible for other syntactic processes.[7] Just as with adjectives, the internal argument will move to the superficial subject position in the case of passive, where the argument will receive a case (or be PRO). Note that this entails that A^{max}, just as V^{max}, is dominated by a higher projection (IP/small clause) with a nonthematic subject position.

With respect to the distribution of the passive participle, arguments parallel to those of the present participle can be given. In Dutch, the passive participle is prenominal too, as in [15].

[15] de [PRO gisteren vermoorde] president
the [PRO yesterday killed] president

With respect to the other endings selected by the passive participle, it again selects endings normally associated to adjectives, as illustrated in [16] for French.

[16] **a.** les filles ont été heureuses
the girls have been happy (fem,pl)

b. les filles ont été vues
the girls have been seen (fem,pl)

c. les filles PRO vues hier
the girls PRO seen (fem,pl) yesterday

My conclusion is that the behavior of constructions with passive participles is correctly explained by [6b(iii)]. The construction occurs in adjectival positions, is headed by an adjectival affix and the situation with respect to theta role and case has been changed: from the lowest level on, the construction has become adjectival in nature, which entails the absence of one NP position, the external position for agent, a role that hence has to be assigned to another element—the passive morpheme itself, according to Jaeggli (1986).

Turning next to the perfective participle, consider first its influence on the theta grids and case. With respect to accusative case nothing changes, which makes the perfective participle crucially different from the passive one. If the verb assigns accusative case in a standard clause, it still assigns accusative if the verb is the perfective participle, as illustrated in [17].

[17] l'homme a tué le président
the man has killed the president

This entails that V′ is completely intact. The part dominated by V′ in [4] has not been changed by adding the perfective morpheme. Hence, the level of adjunction should at least be the intermediate projection. Consider the prediction if the perfective participle adjectivalizes V′: if adjectives do not license positions for external arguments as argued above, then the adjectival projection headed by PERF still does not provide a position for the external argument. So, while adjectivalizing at the lowest level has effect on internal case, adjectivalizing at the intermediate level has no effect on internal case. However, as adjectives do not license positions for external arguments, it does not matter at which lower level the adjectivalization has occurred: in both the case of the passive participle and of the perfective participle, the external argument position is not licensed. Consider now the following examples relating to the generalization in Burzio (1986):

[18] **a.** *une personne PRO compris cette théorie
a person PRO understood this theory

b. une théorie PRO comprise par cette personne
a theory PRO understood by this person

c. une personne PRO arrivée en retard
a person PRO arrived too late

d. *une personne PRO dormie toujours
a person PRO slept always

Ergative verbs pattern with passivized verbs [18b] and [18c], and intransitives and transitives pattern differently. The crucial difference between the two cases is that passivized and ergative verbs have only the internal argument and theme, whereas both intransitives and transitives select an external argument agent. Examples [18a] and [18d] then provide direct evidence for the fact that the perfective participle in itself is not capable of licensing a position for the external argument. Without additional licensing, perfective participles do not license the position for the agent. As the theta grid itself has not been altered either, [18a] and [18d] are simply filtered out as violations of the projection principle: agent cannot be associated to a position in the structure, as adjectival projections do not license this position.

Why then is [17] grammatical, if the perfective participle does not license the position for agent? The answer is that, if the projection has been altered at the level of V′, there still is the possibility of adjoining an affix at the highest syntactic level, the level of V^{max}. As the external position is not licensed from "below" (i.e., by the perfective participle in [18]), adjoining an affix that licenses external positions revives the external position, such that agent can be assigned in the normal way. As INFL has the function of licensing the external position, adding INFL to the projection makes assignment of agent possible again. In other words, PERF does not license the position for θ-agent, hence there are no small clauses with agent; on the other hand, INFL licenses the position for agent, hence adding INFL to the construction headed by PERF renders the theta situation correct. The fact that simply adding INFL renders the relevant constructions grammatical again is also evidenced by [19].

[19] **a.** l'homme PRO ayant compris cette théorie
the man PRO having understood this theory

b. l'homme PRO ayant dormi toujours
the man PRO having slept always

With respect to the adjectival distribution of the projection headed by the perfective participle, Dutch can be cited again [20]. For the sort of other endings associated to the affixed verb, French is illustrative [21].

[20] de [PRO gisteren aangekomen] man
the [PRO yesterday arrived] man

[21] les femmes PRO arrivées hier
the women PRO arrived (fem,pl) yesterday

My conclusion is that the behavior of constructions containing perfective participles is explained by [6b(ii)]. The construction distributes like adjectival projections, the affix takes inflectional endings normally associated to adjectives, and the adjunction to the intermediate level explains on the one hand why the situation in terms of V′ has not changed, but on the other hand why the situation is changed in small clauses. In the case of the perfective participle the situation can be mended by licensing the position for the external argument agent through another affix of a higher level.[8]

In this section the following type of arguments were presented for the proposal in [6]:

[22] **a.** If a language associates inflectional markers to adjectives, the same set of markers is associated to the participles.

b. If a language distributes adjectives in a way distinguishing them from other categories, participles distribute like the adjectives.

c. Adjectivalization at different levels has different effects on the properties of the verbal base in terms of the theories of theta role and case.

The arguments in [22c] are again schematized in [23], indicating changes with respect to [4].

[23]		*External NP*	*Internal NP*
	a. PRES-PART	no changes	no changes
	b. PERF	changes (not licensed)	no changes
	c. PASS	changes (absorbed)	changes (no case)

In other words, adjectivalization at the lowest level changes everything; adjectivalization at the intermediate level changes the situation for the upper part of the projection, while the lower part undergoes no changes; adjectivalization at the highest level leaves the standard verbal projection unharmed.

To this a certain number of additional remarks have to be made. First, though it is certainly true that participles distribute like adjectives in a number of cases, the reverse is not always true. There are some positions for adjectival constituents that are not positions for participles as illustrated here for Dutch and French in [24], and there are cases of absence of expected agreement in French [25].

[24] **a.** *il est parlant quatre langues

b. *hij is vier talen sprekend
he is speaking four languages[9]

[25] *Une femme parlante quatre langues.
A women speaking (fem) four languages.

My main argument is that there is a bifurcation between syntactic and lexical affixes. Participles are headed by an adjectival syntactic affix. This distinction can be translated into a feature on the affixal head: [±lex] or alternatively [±synt]. As this is a feature on the head, it can be percolated up to the maximal projection, and then be used to describe the difference between plain adjectival phrases and adjectivalized verbal constituents in a number of cases, among which are the distributional differences in [24].[10] As a feature on the head, it can be used to describe the impossibility to associate adjectival inflections to present participles in French in [25].

I should add, however, that this device is somewhat descriptive or mechanical. Its main function is to account for differences between the participles and the ordinary adjectives, which have always been a major obstacle for analyses in which participles are adjectival. In this sense not even a descriptive device for this problem has ever been proposed. Note, however, that the feature is predictable from the subcategorization frame of the affixes involved and hence need not be stipulated in their lexical entry, a redundancy rule would suffice. More generally, it just is the descriptive reflex of the general bifurcation I argue for.

This feature may also be used in stating morphological generalizations about the shape of the affix. As the perfective and the passive participle both generally have the same form, and as this form also generalizes with the adjectival participle created in the lexicon, there is one affix with the following subcategorization frame:

[26] *ed* (PASS, PERF, ADJ-PASS): [— V [-max] [αlex]].

All three participles subcategorize for a verbal element, lexical or syntactic, head or projection, except for the maximal projection.[11] Note that the rare discrepancies (cf. Aronoff 1989) between the three cases can still be accounted for in the lexical entry—for example, by splitting [αlex] into [+lex] versus [−lex] and by referring to the rare verb that has the split.

Now that I mentioned the adjectival passive created in the lexical component, my last remark concerns the question, What are the differences between these adjectivalizations in syntax and adjectivalizations in the lexical component? So far there seems to be no difference, as I restricted the discussion of the theta roles to the two most prominent ones. One of the differences is that the formation of passive participles in the lexical component is restricted to the verbs bearing theme (Anderson 1977; Williams 1981) or to sole complements (Levin and Rappaport 1986). The formation of passive participles in syntax is not restricted in this way. The same difference holds for the the formation of present participles in the lexical component; that process seems to be restricted to nonsubject experiencers (Brekke 1988). In other terms, syntactic adjectivalizations are (thematically) unrestricted, while lexical adjectivalizations are—or at least may be—restricted to a specific thematic situation. My view on this matter is as follows. There is one clear difference between affixation in syntax and affixation in the lexical component. If affixation applies in the syntax the verb has projected its properties onto the syntactic structure in accordance with the Projection Principle. If affixation applies in the lexical component the verb has not yet projected its properties onto the structure. Affixation in syntax then observes the Projection Principle, so it cannot undo the mapped properties, because that would result in a violation of the principle. This process can hence only be unrestricted with respect to the properties mapped. In the lexical component this does not hold. The unrestrictedness of syntactic participles thus follows from this "one bridge too far" idea. One is in syntax, the Projection Principle holds, so the verb must project its properties. The verb can be turned into an adjective, but its properties cannot be undone because of the Projection Principle. So, either one does not adjectivalize or one adjectivalizes the verb with the properties it has mapped. If one adjectivalizes the verb before it has mapped its properties onto the syntactic structure—that is, before syntax, in the lexical component—then the projection principle does not hold, so restrictions on the type of verbs input to the adjectivalizations are possible. Put in other terms, syntax observes the projection principle and syntactic adjectivalization cannot ignore this, while in the lexicon the Projection Principle does not hold, so lexical adjectivalization may be restricted to a certain class of verbs.

To conclude this section, I have shown that there exist processes of adjectivalization in syntax, defined as the adjunction of affixes to the three independently defined syntactic verbal levels. The syntactic process of adjectivalization necessarily observes the Projection Principle, with (thematic) unrestrictedness as a consequence, while the lexical process of adjectivalization need not obey the Projection Principle, so that (thematic) restrictions may occur. From the Projection Principle it also follows that it is the Verb that has mapped its theta grid onto the structure. This explains the "mainly verbal" character of participles. On the other hand, this does not exclude category changes, which accounts for the "adjectivelike" character of participles.

3. NOMINALIZATIONS IN SYNTAX

In this section I will consider the English nominalizations in [27] in a way comparable to the one for adjectivalizations.

[27] **a.** Clausal nominalization (NOM-INFL)
(i) John destroying the city
(ii) PRO destroying the city

b. Gerundive Nominal (GER)
John's destroying the city

c. Lower gerundive nominal (LOW-GER)
John's destroying of the city

d. Lexical Nominalization (LEX-NOM)
(i) John's destruction of the city
(ii) the destruction of the city

The full theory of affixation explained above allows for four levels of nominalization: three syntactic levels and a lexical one. LEX-NOM being the undoubted lexical level, I will argue that examples [27a] through [27c] corresponds to a descending level of nominalization in syntax.

In this section I do not present arguments for the nominal properties of the constructions, which are well studied (e.g., Reuland 1983) and quite straightforward. As for existing differences between nominal phrases and nominalized verbal constituents, the feature [±lex] explained above is useful again for the description of them.

My main purpose is to motivate the levels of adjunction. As with the participles, the main line concerns the effects in terms of case and theta role.

In considering the different nominalizations in [27], the effects in terms of case with respect to a standard verbal structure are schematized in [28].

[28]

	External NP	*Internal NP*
NOM-INFL	acc/PRO	acc
GER	gen	acc
LOW-GER	gen	no acc/*of*
LEX-NOM	gen/*the*	no acc/*of*

This pattern corresponds to the pattern observed with the participles. At the lowest level both the internal and the external argument position have undergone a change; at the intermediate level there is no change with respect to the internal arguments, but a change for the external argument; at the highest level there is no change at all. The theory predicts that although almost everything seems to be possible in English nominalizations, it is impossible to change the situation for the internal arguments but to leave unharmed the situation for the external argument. Nominalization at the lower levels automatically entails a change at the higher levels too. This prediction is borne out by [29].

[29] * John destroying of the city

The highest level of nominalization is the level of adjunction normally postulated for INFL (cf. the discussion of the present participle above). As inflectionhood can be tested in French on the basis of the elements indicating negation, consider [30]:

[30] a. imaginez-vous les ordinateurs de l'OTAN ne fonctionnant pas
imagine the NATO computers not functioning not

b. *imaginez-vous les ordinateurs de l'OTAN ne pas fonctionnant
imagine the NATO computers not not functioning

I postulate a nominally specified inflection here, which entails that the construction is an IP, with S-bar deletion for case and the possibility of PRO. Hence, [27a(ii)] also falls into this class.

I analyze Jackendoff's "gerundive PPs" (*I kept* [*Bill running*]) inside this class of constructions.[12]

As for the intermediate variant, it has always been assumed that it involves nominalizing the VP, thus giving the specifier of the construction nominal properties, and leaving the complements of the ordinary verbal nature. On the basis of the differences between the gerundive nominal and the clausal nominalization, I will motivate the structure given in [4]. The "older" VP analysis leads to the structures in [31]:

[31] **a.** **b.**

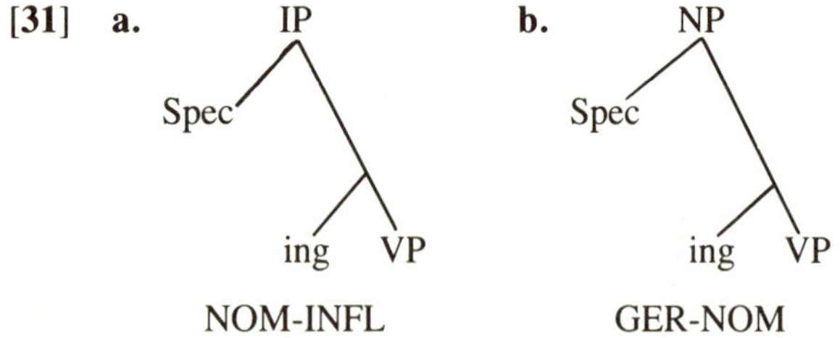

NOM-INFL would subcategorize for a VP, as well as GER. If now both affixes are nominal, a clear conflict arises with respect to the nature of the case to be assigned to the element in specifier position. For [a] a variant of S-bar deletion would allow for accusative case, but this must be prohibited in [b]. In [b] on the other hand genitive case must be assigned, and accusative case prohibited. Intuitively, the situation in [b] is more NP-like than the situation in [a]. At the lower level no changes obtain for both, the verb assigns case and theta role in its standard way inside V′. As for the external argument, GER assigns case in the nominal way, and is hence more nominal than NOM-INFL. It is therefore impossible that both subcategorize for the same node VP in its "older" definition. The conflict is dissolved immediately by adopting the underlying structure in [4] and the following affixations:

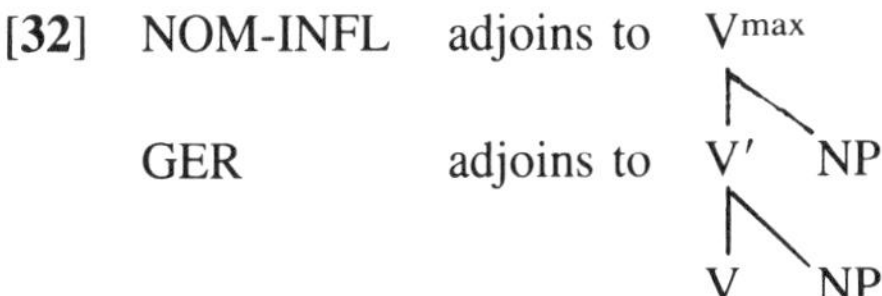

With the highest nominalizer, the theta grid is licensed in the exact way verbs do. As this highest nominalizer is INFL, in the specifier position of this projection the subject may bear accusative in the case of some external case assigner or be PRO. With the intermediate nominalizer however, the verb is left intact for its internal arguments and hence there is no change at this level. On the higher level of this nominalized V′, the licensing is done in the way nouns license arguments. As in principle nouns allow the external theta role/argument to be assigned, there is no specific problem for theta theory (as there was one for PERF). In terms of case theory however this external argument will bear genitive case.[13]

There is no specific problem for theta theory, but on the other hand, as the nominalization takes place in syntax, the projection principle must be obeyed. This entails that in gerundive nominals the external argument must be present, and cannot be omitted, which explains the ungrammaticality of the constructions in [33].

[33] **a.** * the destroying the city

b. * the city's destroying

c. * the city's destroying by John

Note also that this entails that *ing* in this lower variant cannot be assigned the external theta role, as opposed to the PASS-morpheme.[14]

As for the lowest level of nominalization in syntax, I think of the "mixed" variant in Chomsky (1970), of which [27c] is the example. As the discussion bears on the lowest level, argumentation comparable to the one concerning lexical (adjectival) participles and syntactic (verbal) participles should be made. In the spirit of the arguments above, my suggestion for the mixed variant LOW-GER is that it is derived on the lowest level in syntax, such that the projection principle holds, as opposed to LEX-NOM. This prediction can be borne out in two ways. On the one hand, it is well known that LEX-NOM has effects on the theta grid (optionality of the external theta role) such that both the external argument with a genitive case and determiners like *the* may occur. In syntax however, the external role has been projected, such that it must be realized if LOW-GER is derived in syntax. In other words, the determiner *the* would lead to a violation of the projection principle parallel to [33]. This prediction seems to be borne out in [34].

[34] ?? the refusing of the offer[15]

It is also predicted that the Affectedness Constraint of Jaeggli (1986) does not hold, but unfortunately this cannot be checked, because the constraint states that the external theta role cannot be eliminated. The constraint thus stipulates something similar to the Projection Principle in that it forces certain theta roles to be present in the structure.

In this section I have shown that there are three different types of syntactic nominalizations in English, each differing from the others just by a difference in level of adjunction to the verbal projection. The Projection Principle holds for them, there are no particular changes in terms of theta roles, so the main difference turns around the situation in terms of case theory. Crucial evidence for the postulation of the underlying structure in [4] has been presented on the basis of the difference between the gerundive nominal and the higher variant of nominalization, the inflectional.

4. MIXING ADJECTIVAL AND NOMINAL SYNTACTIC AFFIXES

If adjectivalization and nominalization are both possible in syntax, it must be asked whether there are limits: Can every nominalized or adjectivalized verb be input recursively to a new process of adjectivalization or nominalization?

The first case is repetitive adjectivalization. Adjectivalizing and even readjectivalizing an already adjectivalized verb is possible: the use of the three different participles in one clause is allowed, as illustrated in [35].

[35] the president, PRO having been shot at yesterday, will appear

So, the present participle may adjoin to an adjectivalized projection, just as the perfective participle may. For the passive participle, however, there is no evidence, as it is the lowest.[16] This entails the following subcategorization frames for the affixes:

[36] **a.** PRES-PART [— $[+V]^{max}$]

b. PERF [— $[+V]'$]

c. PASS [— $[+V-N]$]

The second case is repetitive nominalization. Contrary to the expectation, this is impossible, as illustrated below, where [37] is an instance of nominalizing at the maximal level a projection already nominalized at the intermediate level, and [37] an instance of nominalizing at the intermediate level a projection already nominalized at the lowest level.

[37] **a.** * John having destroying the city

b. * John's having destroying of the city

So it seems that nominalizers select verbs in their subcategorization frames, as in [38]:

[38] **a.** NOM-INFL [— $[+V-N]^{max}$]

b. GER [— $[+V-N]'$]

c. LOW-GER [— [+V−N]]

The third case is a first mixture, adjectivalizing a nominalized projection. The prediction of the frames in [36] is that this is impossible. This prediction is borne out below where [39a] should be an instance of adjoining PRES-PART to GER-NOM, and [39b] an instance of adjoining PERF to LOW-GER.

[39] **a.** * the man [PRO having destroying the city]

b. * the man [PRO had refusing of the offer]

The fourth and last case is the second type of mixture: nominalizing an already adjectivalized projection. The prediction of the frames in [38] is that this is impossible. This prediction is not borne out, as witnessed by [40]:

[40] **a.** John's having destroyed the city

b. John's being incited to react

This entails a revision of [38]:

[41] **a.** NOM-INFL [— $[+V]^{max}$]

b. GER [— $[+V]'$]

c. LOW-GER [— [+V−N]]

The above subcategorization frames indicate an obvious generalization. Although both adjectivalizing and nominalizing a verbal projection is possible, when nominalization has occurred, the category switch is complete, so it can no longer be the input for a new change. On the other hand, when adjectivalization has occurred, the category switch is less complete, so further affixation still is possible. In other words, the basis for the derivational processes in syntax is not only verbal, as in [1], but rather [+V].

From this state of affairs, one important prediction emerges: the existence of verbal syntactic affixes. The problem for the moment is that there are no clear criteria. Adjoining a verbal affix to a verbal projection would not directly change its distribution, which remains verbal. The other inflectional endings adjoinable to this verbal affix would not differ from the inflections normally associable to verbs. The licensing in terms of theta roles would not be affected, nor the assigned cases. There is only one type of argument left. As shown, the present participle falls in the class of INFL (adjectival INFL), and the clausal nominalization uses the nominalizer *ing* (nominal INFL). In order to make the system complete, in the class of INFL the verbalizer must still be attested. The other affix standardly falling in the class of INFL is ±TENSE. This suggests that ±TENSE is verbal INFL, although one could argue that infinitival *to* is prepositional INFL, which leaves me with +TENSE as verbal INFL. As for the lower levels, I suggest English progressive *ing* could well be a verbal syntactic affix.

5. CONSEQUENCES

A major effect of the proposed theory is that a specific class of affixes has been isolated from other affixes. That class has the following properties:

[42] **a.** They bear a categorial indication.

b. They are the categorial heads of the construction.

c. They subcategorize for the syntactically defined projections.

d. The syntactically defined projections of [c] are [+V].

What kind of affixes are these, derivational or inflectional? On the one hand, the fact that they are object of syntactic study would make them inflectional, if one follows the definition of Anderson (1982). On the other hand, properties [42a] and [42b] are standard properties of derivational processes, if one follows Selkirk (1982).

Or, from another point of view: On the one hand, if inflection is meant to cover features of the type number, gender, person, case, and the like, the affixes under consideration would not be inflectional. On the other hand, if derivation is meant to cover the creation of new words, the affixes under consideration would not be derivational.

Suppose one discriminating property is whether the affix is part of syntactic study or not, a distinction between so-called lexical affixes and so-called syntactic affixes. Suppose the other discriminating property is whether they are the categorial head of the construction (and hence have a categorial indication themselves) or not (and thus indicate a number of properties)—a distinction between so-called derivational affixes and so-called inflectional affixes—then four possibilities exist:

[43] **a.** derivational affixes treated in the lexical component

b. inflectional affixes treated in syntax

c. derivational affixes treated in syntax

d. inflectional affixes treated in the lexical component

This entails a somewhat inherent definition of *derivational* versus *inflectional* combined with a more operational approach based on the locus of analysis. Cases [43a] and [43b] are standard. Case [43c] is the one considered above. The claim defended here is that an affix changes the category and is derivational in this sense does not necessarily mean that it is treated by the lexical component.

Several other points of view are possible, and I wish to give some arguments against at least two of them. First, one might not believe in a distinction between derivational and inflectional affixes. Second, one might not believe in a distinction between affixation in syntax and affixation in the lexicon.

My arguments involve clear-cut distinctions between the affixes. The class of derivational syntactic affixes has one very salient and, in fact, very ordinary property with respect to all other affixes, a property that can also be used to define their uniqueness. While the number of lexical affixes that can be adjoined to some base is in principle not determined, verbs allow only one element of the class of syntactic derivational affixes, as illustrated in [44]:

[44] **a.** standard+iz+abil+ity

b. * kill+ed+s ("meaning" kill + PASS + INFL)

c. * kill+ed+ing ("meaning" kill+ PERF + GER)

It is exactly the class of derivational syntactic affixes that has this property. A verbal element allows for only one element of the class of affixes considered in this paper. Since standard clauses have one verb and one INFL, in the presence of two syntactic affixes one auxiliary will be necessary; in the presence of three syntactic affixes two auxiliaries will be needed. Every verbal base only allows for one derivational syntactic affix, and if there are more derivational syntactic affixes present, more verbal bases are needed (auxiliary verbal bases, auxiliaries).

In order to explain (44) it is at least necessary to make two sets of affixes. With no additional criteria, the division of the elements between the sets is arbitrary. My claim is that this division is not arbitrary but reflects a principled difference between syntax and the lexical component.

The facts noted in [44] have two other consequences. On the one hand, it entails that at some abstract level of representation, auxiliaries are not present. This favors an analysis in which auxiliaries are inserted at some later point of the derivation parallel to *do*-support.[17] On the other hand, [44] is a pattern obtaining in English, Dutch, French, German, and similar languages, but not universally true. Ancient Greek, for example, allows for all syntactic affixes to be added to one and only one verbal base without any need for auxiliaries. In this sense [44] is a pattern that forms the basis for a parametrizable difference in agglutination across languages.

A distinction between the syntactic affixes considered in this paper and affixes treated in the lexical component is therefore well motivated and has some interesting corollaries in the fields of auxiliary theory and the field of parametrization of agglutination.

The bifurcation based on [44] does not have to do with inflection, as inflectional affixes can be adjoined without specific limit to a verb, as in [45]:

[45] **a.** les filles ont été tuées (V+PASS+fem+pl)

b. ein mehrere Sprache sprechender (V+PRES−PART+masc+sg+nom) Mann

This entails that the affixes considered in this paper are again crucially different from other affixes—inflectional affixes this time. Whereas inflectional affixes (on an inherent definition) can be added in an undetermined number to verbs, derivational syntactic affixes cannot.

So the patterns in [44] and [45] set the derivational syntactic affixes apart from all other ones, and thus motivate their uniqueness with respect to lexical derivational affixes as well as with respect to syntactic inflectional affixes.

Returning then to [43], my proposal seems to entail that it is not inconceivable that inflectional affixes (on an inherent definition) are treated in the lexical component, case [43d]. I suggest that these are the cases in which inflectional affixes are parts of words, but have no syntactic influence—for instance, cases in which the left-hand member of a right-headed compound bears some inflectional indication.

6. CONCLUSION

I have shown in this paper that there is a specific class of affixes in English and similar languages, a class of affixes that adjoins in syntax to the independently defined levels of verbal structure and that changes the category of the structures while retaining originally projected verbal properties. The class thus isolated cannot be lexical because of the pattern in [44], and cannot be inflectional because of the pattern in [45]. As the process occurs in syntax and as the result is a category change, the class should best be considered to consist of derivational syntactic affixes.

GRAMMATICIZATION THEORY AND HEADS IN MORPHOLOGY

Martin Haspelmath

INTRODUCTION

It has been recognized for some time that the notion of 'head', which plays an important role in syntax, can also usefully be applied to the internal structure of words. This insight dates back at least to Bally (1932),[1] but most recent work on heads in morphology is directly or indirectly inspired by Williams (1981). Williams proposes that derivational and even inflectional affixes in English should be treated as heads—just like second members of compounds, except that they do not occur independently. At least as far as derivational morphology is concerned, this proposal has been accepted by many generative morphologists (Toman 1983, Selkirk 1982, Höhle 1982, Scalise 1984, Wunderlich 1986), and heads also play an important role in Categorical Morphology (Hoeksema 1988).[2]

However, in some other approaches to morphology that focus on functional, cognitive, and diachronic explanations for word structure, no use is made of this notion (cf. Plank 1981; Bybee 1985; and Natural Morphology (Dressler et al. 1987)). Since heads are widely used in very different syntactic theories (Zwicky 1985, Hudson 1987, including functionally oriented approaches (e.g. Dik 1978), one might ask why this notion is so far restricted to formally oriented approaches to morphology and whether functionalist morphologists would not be well advised to adopt it, too.

In this paper I will try to do two things: On the one hand, I will point out possible advantages of the notion of 'morphological head' for one substantive approach to morphology, Grammaticization Theory (cf. Lehmann 1982, Heine and Traugott forthcoming). On the other hand, I will suggest that grammaticization theory can explain some morphological phenomena that have been observed and discussed by generative morphologists. I hope this paper will serve as a modest contribution to the task of exchanging ideas between rival and sometimes radically different theories.[3]

Section 1 deals with derivational morphology and its origin in compounding, and in section 2, I argue that inflectional morphology that originates in periphrastic constructions behaves in a quite analogous manner. In section 3, I show how feature percolation can be understood from the point of view of grammaticization; section 4 presents some data from highly synthetic languages showing that word-syntactic approaches are even more useful for such languages.

1. COMPOUNDING AND DERIVATIONAL MORPHOLOGY

The use of the notion of 'morphological head' is fairly straightforward in English compounds as in [1] (the headhood of the second noun is indicated here by an arbitrary double-branch line notation).

[1] **a.** ozone hole
b.

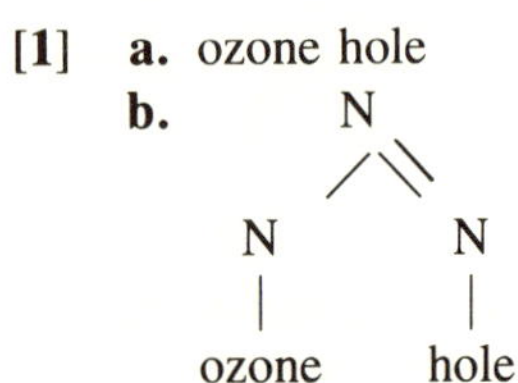

In compounds such as [1], the right-hand constituent clearly has a privileged status within the compound: it determines the syntactic category of the compound as well as other inherent features like gender and declension class, and it takes additional affixes like plural and case affixes (in Zwicky's (1985) terms, the right-hand constituent is the morphosyntactic determinant and the morphosyntactic locus of the compound). Since the privileged status of the second compound member is closely parallel to the privileged status of the head in a syntactic phase, no controversy has arisen about the practice of calling the righthand compound constituent the head of its word (cf. even Dressler et al. (1987, 101ff.) within Natural Morphology).

Now Williams observes that words derived by affixes share a number of characteristics with compounds. Derivational affixes can be treated just like the second members of compounds—that is, as the heads of their words, as in [2]:

[2] **a.** jobless
b.

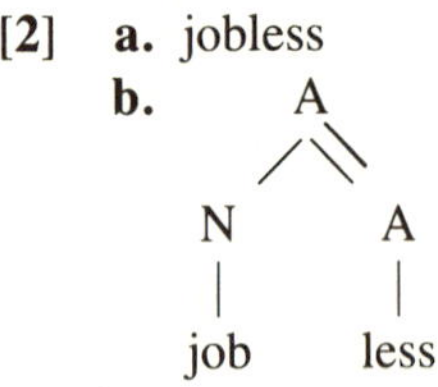

Like second members of compounds, derivational affixes determine the syntactic category of the derived word as well as other features, and inflections appear on the affix, not on the stem. The only difference, according to Williams, is that that they are bound, which is formally expressed by a subcategorization frame. For *-less,* this will read [N_____], which says simply that for *-less* to appear in a well-formed word structure, its sister must be a noun on the left side. Thus, derivational affixes are nothing but special lexical items of their particular category (i.e., *-less* is a bound adjective).

For functionally oriented approaches, this claim is at first sight not very attractive. As Hudson (1987, 113ff.) emphasizes, the intuitive appeal of the notion of 'head' in syntax is that it expresses the 'kind of' relation. According to Zwicky, "In a combination X + Y, X is the 'semantic head' if, speaking very crudely, X + Y describes a kind of the thing described by X" (1985, 4). In compounds this works just as well as in syntactic phrases: an *ozone hole* is a 'kind of' *hole,* if someone goes *window-shopping* they go 'kind of' *shopping,* a *color-blind* person is 'kind of' *blind,* and so on. But it does not seem to work with derivational affixes: a *king-dom* is not a 'kind of' *-dom,* a *friend-ly* person is not 'kind of' *-ly,* and if someone *exempli-fies* something, they do not 'kind of' *-fy* it.

However, if we recall some of the insights of Grammaticization Theory, a somewhat different picture emerges. According to this theory, affixes go back to earlier free lexical items that are reduced semantically and phonologically and become bound to the stem. For many English affixes the diachronic origin in a full lexical item has long been known to historical linguists—for example, *-hood* (cf. Gothic *haidus* 'kind, manner'), *-dom* (cf. Old English (OE) *dōm* 'judgment, doom', Old High German *tuom* 'position, condition'), *-less* (cf. OE *lēas* 'devoid (of), free (from)'), *-ly* (OE *-līc,* second member of exocentric compounds based on Germanic **līk-* 'appearance, form, body'; thus *friend-ly* is originally 'having the appearance of a friend'). For some English affixes, the origin in free lexical items is to some degree even synchronically transparent—for example, *-ful* (cf. *full*), *-man* (cf. *man*).

Although the increasing use of a word as the second member of a compound with accompanying semantic generalization and phonological erosion is not exactly the paradigm case of grammaticization (in which a lexical item in a syntactic periphrastic construction gradually evolves into an inflectional affix), it is clearly a completely analogous diachronic process.

Now it is clear that all grammaticization changes share the general characteristic of gradualness. This is as true for more central cases as it is for the evolution of derivational affixes. There is no evidence for a radical reanalysis at any particular point in the development of such items. Diachronic gradualness is necessarily reflected in synchronic variation in descriptive ambiguities, and this is indeed what we find here. For instance, descriptive works on German and English derivational morphology use a category 'suffixoid' (Fleischer 1975, 70) or 'semi-suffix' (Marchand 1969, 356), intermediate between suffix and second compound member, to describe items such as German *-gut, -zeug, -werk,* and English *-like, -worthy, -way(s), -wise, -monger*.

Once we are aware of the diachronic origin of derivational affixes in lexical items, we can also reconsider the semantic 'kind of' relation. Since *-hood* is not a free form anymore, we cannot literally say, for example, that *parenthood* is a kind of *-hood,* but there is no problem with saying that *-hood* refers to a state or condition (and in pre-Old English there was a free lexical item **haiduz* with a very similar meaning), and that *parenthood* is a kind of state or condition. The situation here is analogous to the head status of auxiliaries discussed in Hudson (1987, 115). He argues that an Aux + VP phrase like *may control those penguins* can also be understood as a kind of possibility, not necessarily as a kind of controlling (though of course not literally as a kind of 'maying'), so that there is no obstacle to taking the auxiliary as the head of the whole phrase. Like derivational affixes, auxiliaries are more grammaticized than lexical items.

Thus, the two different points of view, distribution and grammaticization, converge here. Both tell us that there is no principled difference between lexical items and derivational affixes. The main difference is that affixes cannot occur alone, and this is merely a consequence of their greater degree of grammaticization. I cannot show in detail here how Grammaticization Theory predicts this property and other properties of grammaticized elements. For a full discussion of the kind of theory that I am assuming, see Lehmann (1982). Briefly, the theory is concerned with the covariation of a whole range of properties that are characteristic of grammaticized items and with the explanation of this covariation in terms of the systematic diachronic changes that result in increased grammaticization. The properties whose covariation is predicted are called parameters of grammaticization by Lehmann (1982; 1985a). One of these parameters is increasing bondedness, the increasingly tight syntagmatic cohesion of the grammaticized item with another word. As a lexical item gradually turns into a grammatical item, it first becomes a clitic and is finally fully attached to its host, in other words, it becomes obligatorily associated with a subcategorization frame. So the major distributional difference between derivational affixes and compound heads is predicted by grammaticization theory. But Grammaticization Theory predicts more properties of derivational affixes than purely formal principles can express. Some of them are:

(i) Compared to roots, affixes are generally shorter and phonologically reduced in other ways. Compare English *-dom* versus *doom, -ful* [fl] versus *full,* and *-ly* versus *like*. It is predicted by Lehmann's parameter of reduced phonological integrity.

(ii) Compared to roots, affixes typically have a rather general meaning. For instance, English *-less* 'not having' is more general than OE *leas* 'deprived (of)' (earlier: 'unattached, loose'), and English *-ful* 'having' is more general than *full*. This property is predicted by the parameter of reduced semantic integrity.

(iii) Affixes are much less numerous than roots in any language. This is predicted by the parameter of increasing *paradigmaticity*, the tendency for grammaticized items to cluster in increasingly small, homogeneous paradigms.

So it appears that in order to achieve maximal explanatory power, formal principles need to be complemented by substantive principles of grammaticization: the covariation of the above parameters (and others) can be shown to follow from the way in which speakers change their language unconsciously (cf. Lehmann 1985a, 314–17; Lüdtke 1980). On the other hand, Grammaticization Theory could gain by accepting the idea of affixal heads. Indeed, this is a natural consequence of the gradualness of grammaticization changes that set them off from changes involving a radical reanalysis. For instance, the change whereby the English root *pease* was reanalyzed as consisting of a root *pea* plus a plural suffix *-s* (*pease* > *pea- s*) cannot have been gradual.[4] Such changes of reanalysis probably occur when children acquire the language and interpret the output that they are exposed to differently from the way adult speakers do. It is not surprising that the discontinuity in the transmission of the language leads to discontinuities in the rules of the grammars. However, grammaticization changes occur because of the nature of language use or language activity, and since there is no discontinuity in language activity, we do not expect discontinuities in grammaticization changes. Nevertheless, a number of studies in grammaticization have made use of the concept of reanalysis (see Heine and Reh 1984, 95ff.). If the relations between affixes and roots are seen as quite different from the relations between syntactic constituents, then the assumption of radical reanalysis accompanying grammaticization is inevitable. This undesirable assumption can be avoided if primarily syntactic notions like 'head' are accepted in morphology. As Lehmann puts it: "So we . . unwittingly [slide] from syntax into morphology, and there is no way to tell the point where the type of relation applicable in syntactic analysis ceases to be applicable. Grammaticization causes syntactic relations to continue as morphological relations" (1985b, 90).

Before moving on to inflectional morphology, let me briefly mention two problems for the Affixal Head Theory that have been discussed in the literature. The first concerns evaluative (diminutive and augmentative) affixes, as in Portuguese *filh-inh-a* 'little daughter', derived from *filh-a* 'daughter'. Words with such affixes have exactly the same properties as the words from which they are derived, so it has been concluded (for instance, by Bally 1932[5], Scalise (1988, 233–37) that evaluative affixes are not heads. This conclusion accords well with Grammaticization Theory because as far as we know evaluative affixes do not arise diachronically from free lexical items that undergo grammaticization.[6] They are typically sound-symbolic extensions of the stem (involving high-frequency sounds for diminutives and low-frequency sounds for augmentatives) with a primarily pragmatic meaning, and we may speculate that they arise by spontaneous creation.

Another problem was already noticed by Williams (1981, 250): whereas most affixal heads in English are suffixes, there appears to be one exception—the prefix *en-*, as in *enrich* or *enrage,* which seems to turn adjectives and nouns into verbs. This would be an oddity not only from the distributional point of view, but also from the point of view of grammaticization. Whereas other verbalizing affixes derive historically from verbs, as expected (English *-fy* in *codify, exemplify, frenchify,* for example, is ultimately from Latin *facere* 'do, make'), *en-* is (ultimately) derived from an adverb (Latin *in* 'in'). More recently, convincing distributional arguments have been put forward for the view that the verbalizing morpheme here is zero and that *en-* is prefixed for different reasons (Walinska de Hackbeil 1985, Scalise 1988, 238–41), so again the diachronic evidence from grammaticization and the purely synchronic evidence point toward the same conclusion.

2. PERIPHRASTIC CONSTRUCTIONS AND INFLECTIONAL MORPHOLOGY

In applying the notion of 'head' to morphology, Williams (1981) does not stop at derivational morphology because he rejects the distinction between derivational and inflectional morphology. He therefore proposes the same treatment for inflectional affixes such as tense affixes and case affixes: they, too, are the heads of their respective words, (example [3] is Williams's (1981, 250); example [4] is mine).

[3] **a.** cited
b.

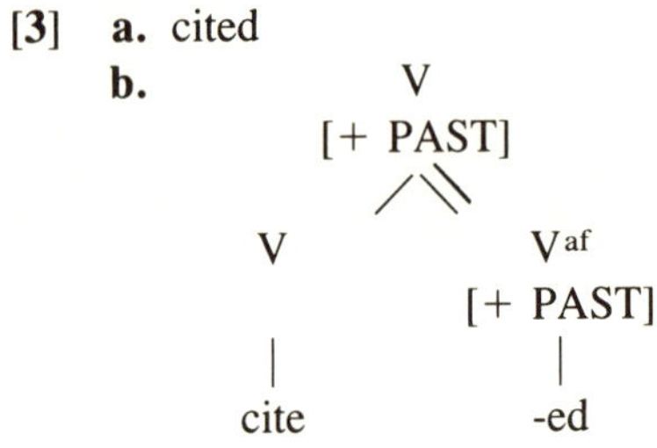

[4] **a.** Russian: karandaš-om 'with a pencil'
b.

N
[+ INSTR]

N — N af [+ INSTR]

karandaš — -om

At first sight such an analysis might seem even more unusual and radical than the analysis of derivational affixes as heads. But the arguments against a strict separation of inflection and derivation are quite strong. Bybee (1985), working within a rather different theoretical perspective from Williams's, also concludes that there is no sharp boundary between inflection and derivation.

Now what does an affixal head analysis look like from the point of view of Grammaticization Theory? Again, I think, it makes sense. We know that tense and aspect affixes typically arise from auxiliaries (Bybee, Pagliuca, and Perkins, in preparation), and that case affixes typically arise from adpositions (Kahr 1976). (In fact, one of the proposed etymologies of the English past tense marker *-ed* is a periphrastic construction involving the auxiliary *do*.) According to this hypothesis, the erstwhile structures for [3] and [4] are as in [5] and [6].

[5] VP → VP V_{aux} (tree: VP dominating VP and V_{aux}, head marked on V_{aux})

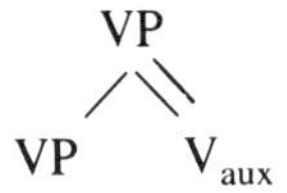

[6] PP → NP P (tree: PP dominating NP and P, head marked on P)

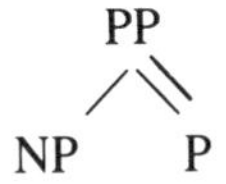

We also know where adpositions usually come from: spatial nouns of some sort (cf. Svorou 1988).

[7] NP → NP $N_{spatial}$ (tree: NP dominating NP and $N_{spatial}$, head marked on $N_{spatial}$)

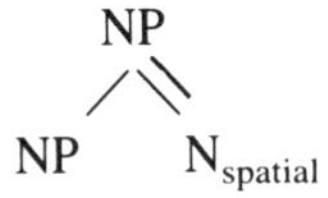

Here, V_{aux} and $N_{spatial}$ (or P) clearly are the heads of their phrases. The case is exactly analogous to the one we saw above for derivational morphology: what starts out as the head of a syntactic phrase and becomes grammaticized to a grammatical affix is described as the head of a word on purely distributional evidence. Generative morphology and Grammaticization Theory arrive at similar conclusions, and again it becomes unnecessary to assume a radical reanalysis at any single point.

4. PERCOLATION PROBLEMS

While Williams's proposal has been widely accepted for derivational affixes, the extension to inflectional morphology has not been so successful. Selkirk (1982, 74–77) and others (e.g., Scalise 1988) reject the idea of the headhood of inflectional affixes because of problems with the percolation of features in cases of multiple affixation. But this is not a necessary conclusion, as will become clear in the discussion below.

The problem is the following: If percolation is allowed to transmit only head features (as implied in a well-known formulation of percolation, the Head Feature Convention), then only the features of the outermost affix can be percolated. Selkirk discusses a hypothetical example, which I for concreteness replace with a real one. Consider the Turkish imperfective evidential *yazı-yor-muş-un:*

[**8**] **a.** yazı-yor-muş-un
write-impf-evid-2sg
'(it is said that) you are writing'

b.

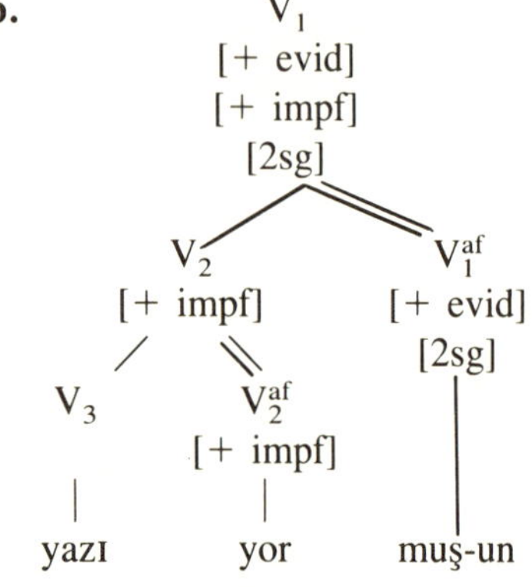

If only heads can pass up features, then the feature [impf] can not be transmitted to the top V node. Selkirk therefore proposes to modify the definition of the percolation convention with the effect of allowing the feature of a nonhead to percolate if the head is not specified for that feature.[7] Thus, in [8] [+impf] is transmitted from V_2 to its mother V_1 because the head $V_1{}^{af}$ is not specified for [±impf]. But with this reformulation of percolation, Selkirk notes, we need no longer consider inflectional affixes to be heads at all.

Selkirk's proposal solves the percolation problem, but it forces her to strictly separate inflectional and derivational morphology,[8] contradicting the finding of Bybee (1985) and others that the difference is gradient rather than absolute. In addition, the view that inflectional affixes cannot be heads contradicts the picture that emerges from the grammaticization perspective, as we saw in the preceding section.

However, the main empirical problem with any kind of percolation solution is that percolation cannot handle structures from morphologically more complex languages in which one affix occurs twice in the same word and contributes twice to the word's feature specification (or meaning). For instance, in Udmurt the causative suffix can be repeated, giving a double causative; in Turkish, the passive suffix can be repeated, giving an impersonal passive of a passive ('there is being killed in the war'); in Korean, the past tense suffix can be repeated, giving a remote past. Percolation would allow the meaning of an affix (its feature value) to enter only once into a complex word.

Such cases suggest that affixes can contribute to the feature specification of the whole word in much the same way that syntactic constituents contribute to the meaning of the sentence: by compositionality. This is not surprising if we consider that affixes often do the same jobs that words or even phrases do in other cases. For instance, example [9] shows a possible German translation of the Turkish word in [8] (to avoid word order complications example [9] is shown in the form it takes in subordinate *that*-clauses).

[9]

a. (das du) am Schreiben sein sollst
that you on: the writing be ought
'(that) you are said to be writing'

b.

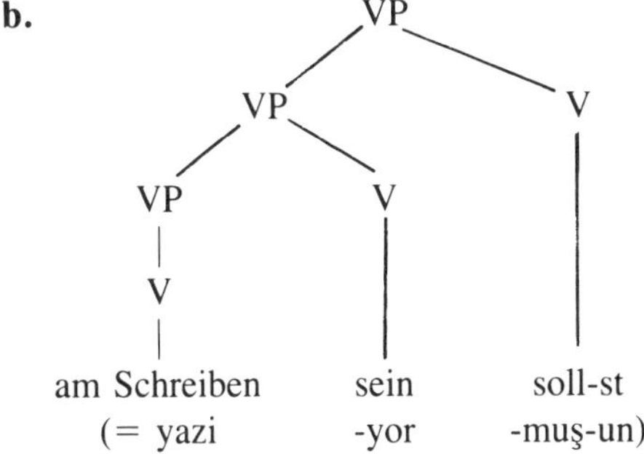

The structure of the German analytic construction of [9] is very similar to the Turkish synthetic construction in [8] and completely isomorphic, the only difference being that a phrase-level category in [9] corresponds to a lexical category in [8]. Thus it is very plausible that an analogous principle of interpretation is at work in both cases, namely compositionality.[9] Note also that the feature bundle in [8] is the wrong result. The features should not be organized in a simple unordered list, but rather hierarchically, corresponding to the hierarchy of constituents: [[+impf] +evid, 2sg]. That such hierarchical organization of features or grammatical meanings is necessary is shown by cases where either order is possible, but with different meanings, as in the Quechua cases discussed in Muysken (1981).

The parallelism between [8] and [9] cannot be fortuitous (cf. also Wunderlich 1986 on such cases), and from the point of view of grammaticization it is expected rather than surprising. Complex synthetic words as in [8] are simply more grammaticized versions of complex phrases as in [9]. Again, as in sections 2 and 3, we see that it is useful to look at word-internal structures from the point of view of the syntactic structures that typically give rise to them via changes of grammaticization.

5. BEYOND THE INDO-EUROPEAN MORPHOLOGICAL TYPE

Much of recent morphological theory was formulated on the basis of Indo-European languages of Europe, such as English (Selkirk 1982), Romance (Mayerthaler 1981, Scalise 1984), or Latin (Matthews 1972). This formulation resulted in an unfortunate bias,[10] because these languages not only represent a rather peculiar morphological type (inflecting/fusional), they also have a rather impoverished morphological structure, compared to languages with a higher degree of synthesis. But it seems clear that morphological theory should be developed on the basis of the most intricate morphological systems rather than the simplest ones.

Languages with a higher degree of synthesis use morphologically complex words to express the same content that other languages express in syntactic constructions. It is therefore not surprising that morphological constituents show more syntaxlike behavior in highly synthetic languages than in highly analytic languages. We already saw an example of synthetic morphology in the preceding section, and we will see two more examples in this section.

The first example is word-internal government in nominal case suffixation in Georgian (Kartvelian). Bauer (1990), in an examination of a number of head properties in morphology, does not find a good example of government by a morphological head in English. But Georgian offers just such an example (my data are from Vogt 1971).

Georgian has about eighteen cases, which can be divided into primary cases and secondary cases. The primary cases already existed in Old Georgian, whereas the secondary cases only arose in the modern period by way of further grammaticization of postpositions and their eventual attachment to the noun. Thus, the partial case paradigm of *kalak-* 'town' in [10] goes back to the Old Georgian forms in [11].

[10] *Modern Georgian*

Primary cases:	nominative	kalak-i	
	genitive	kalak-is	
	dative	kalak-s	
Secondary cases:	prodessive	kalak-is-tvis	
	ablative	kalak-is-gan	
	inessive	kalak-ši	(⟨kalak-s-ši)

[11] *Old Georgian*

Cases:	nominative	kalak-i	
	genitive	kalak-isa	
	dative	kalak-sa	
Postpositional phrase:		kalak-isa tvis	'for the town'
		kalak-isa gan	'from the town'
		kalak-sa šina	'in the town'

We see that the Old Georgian postpositions govern different cases: *šina* governs the dative case, *tvis* and *gan* govern the genitive case, and so forth. But after the morphologization of the postpositions into case suffixes, this difference persists. In Modern Georgian, the prodessive suffix *-tvis* and the ablative suffix *-gan* govern the genitive case, and the inessive suffix *-ši* governs the dative case (the dative suffix *-s* is deleted by a phonological rule: *kalak-s-ši* > *kalak-ši*). Given the data presented so far, one might ask why an analysis is not possible in which the former primary case suffix is part of the secondary case suffix: prodessive *-istvis,* ablative *-isgan,* and so on. The reason is that case inflection is not completely uniform. For instance, the genitive of the first person singular pronoun *me* 'I' is *čem,* and the prodessive is *čem-tvis,* not **me-istvis* or the like. Furthermore, the secondary case suffixes are still independent enough to undergo coordination reduction. Thus, besides *ded-is-tvis da mam-is-tvis* 'for mother and for father', one can also say *ded-isa da mam-is-tvis* 'for mother and father'. Here both coordinate constituents are in the genitive case (the first coordinate has the long ending *-isa,* which occurs when *da* 'and' and certain other particles follow), but only the second coordinate has the additional prodessive suffix. It is difficult to see how such phenomena could be expressed in a theory that does not allow syntactic notions like 'head' or 'government' in morphology.[11]

Our next example are word-internal arguments in Abkhaz (Abkhazo-Adyghean; data from Hewitt 1979). Abkhaz is a typical pronominal argument language (cf. Jelinek 1984)—that is, a language in which pronominal affixes on the verb are not mere agreement markers but arguments governed by the verb (or verb stem).

[12] (sarà barà) bə-z-bòvt'
I you.f.sg 2sg.f.abs-1sg.erg-see:dyn:fin[12]
'I see you'

In [12] the free pronouns are completely optional, and the real arguments of the verb are the pronominal affixes. This is thus another example of word-internal government: the relationship between the verb stem and the affixal pronominal arguments is quite analogous to the relationship between the verb and its NP arguments in the English sentence *I see you.* Since no older stages of Abkhaz are attested, we do not have diachronic evidence to show that the pronominal prefixes result from the grammaticization of earlier free pronouns, but evidence abounds that this is a common path of grammaticization (for instance, in colloquial French the corresponding expression *je te vois* seems to behave much like the Abkhaz word in [12], although it is not treated as a single word in normative French spelling). Compared to our first example of morphological government, the head-dependent relationship is reversed here: it is not the affix that is the head of its word and governs its stem, rather the stem is the head of the word and governs its affixes.

Abkhaz, which is very highly synthetic, also allows several layers of affixal head-dependent relationships. A striking example are pronominal arguments governed by affixal "postpositions," which occupy the prefix position between the absolutive pronoun and the ergative pronoun in transitive sentences:

[13] (∅−) à-le-y-šəyt′
3sg.abs-3sg.obl-with-3sg.m.erg-kill:fin
'He killed it with it'

[14] yn-š°ə-z-àħ-c°′oyt′
3sg.abs-2pl.obl-for-1pl.erg-break.off:dyn:fin
'we'll break it off for you'

Such "prefixal postpositions" have the standard properties of postpositions: they never occur without their argument, they govern a special Oblique form of the pronominal prefix, they always immediately follow their argument. They must therefore be heads, but at the same time the prefixal "postpositional phase" is governed by the verb stem in much the same way as the verb's pronominal arguments. We therefore have to assume the following structure for [14].

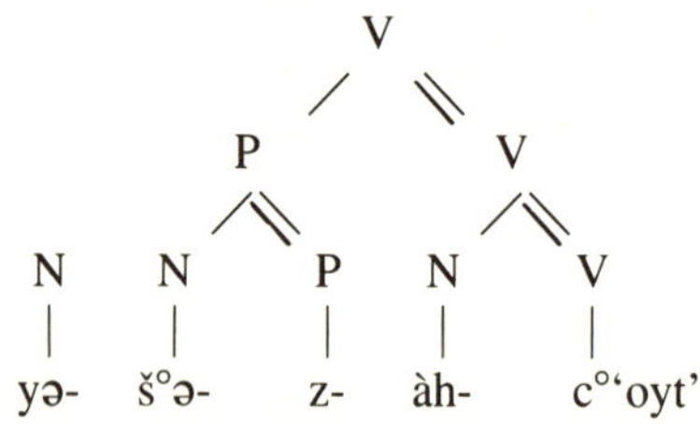

Such examples make it quite clear that it is not enough to ask whether the affix (as in Williams 1981 or the base (as in Anderson 1980) is the head in a morphologically complex word. Just as in syntax, any morphological element may be a head or a dependent, regardless of its status or position in the word, depending only on its inherent valence (or "subcategorization") properties and the valence properties of other elements in the vicinity.

This situation can again be understood from the history of affixes: not only syntactic heads may undergo grammaticization and finally affixation (e.g., adpositions, main verbs and auxiliaries, complementizers, second compound members), but also syntactic dependents—both arguments (e.g., pronominal verbal arguments, pronominal possessors, pronominal adpositional arguments) and adjuncts (e.g., negative elements, locative adverbs). The preference for the grammaticization of either heads or dependents is a major typological parameter. The world's languages can be divided into predominantly dependent-marking and predominantly head-marking languages (Nichols 1986). The grammaticization of heads leads to dependent-marking patterns and affixes that are heads, whereas the grammaticization of dependent arguments leads to head-marking patterns and affixes that are dependents. Since Indo-European languages are of the predominantly head-marking type, affixal heads have played a much more prominent role in discussions of morphological theory than affixal dependents.

I am aware that the data and the discussion in this section raises many issues and problems of which I was able to address only a few. My main goal was to emphasize that morphological theory has to consider a broader range of language types, in particular highly synthetic languages and head-marking languages, and that the syntactic similarities between words and affixes (due to the diachronic origin of affixes in words) are brought out more clearly in highly synthetic languages.

6. CONCLUDING REMARKS

In this paper I have discussed one morphological area where it appears that different morphological frameworks might profit by learning from each other: on the one hand, Grammaticization Theory need not posit radical reanalysis of syntactic relations in addition to gradual attachment of a grammatical item to its host if the notion of 'head' in morphology is adopted. On the other hand, some purely formal principles seem to be amenable to deeper explanation by the substantive principles of grammaticization theory.[13] Indeed, Grammaticization Theory also suggests how the current debate on the relation between morphology and syntax (see, in particular, Di Sciullo and Williams 1987, Baker 1988) might be resolved. According to Di Sciullo and Williams, morphology and syntax are separate subcomponents of grammar with only minimal interaction, whereas Baker assumes a much larger extent of overlap, allowing even syntactic movement in morpholgy.

Now, if morphological structures arise through the grammaticization of syntactic structures, as embodied in the well-known slogan Today's Morphology is Yesterday's Syntax, then the similarities between the two grammatical domains might be ascribed to this historical relationship. Their differences, on the other hand, could be ascribed to the much greater degree of grammaticization that words exhibit in comparison to sentences.

I do not want to convey the impression here that all problems have been solved. One notorious problem for word-syntactic approaches to morphology is the existence of process morphology. Some morphophonemic alternations can be understood as representing an extreme degree of formal grammaticization (phonological erosion)—for example, English *goose*/*geese* from Proto-Germanic **gans*/**gans-iz*, where only the feature [+front] is left of the original plural suffix *-*iz*. But when such morphophonemic alternations become morphologically productive, as in the German umlaut, independent principles of morphology are at work and word-syntactic approaches are of limited value (cf. also the disclaimer in Selkirk 1982, 2–3).

A potential problem for the continuity hypothesis of Grammaticization Theory are evolutionary paths that involve a change in word class (syntactic category), like the change from structures as in [7] to structures as in [6], where a spatial noun turns into an adposition. Don't we have to assume a radical reanalysis from N to P at some point anyway? Probably not, if we accept the notion of gradience of word class membership. Given many well-known cases of synchronic descriptive ambiguities (e.g., is English *(on) behalf (of)* an N or a (complex) P?), there is independent motivation for this notion.[14]

Although many problems remain, I hope to have shown that an exchange of ideas can be useful for rival approaches to morphology, even if not all ideological differences can be resolved.

CATEGORIAL MORPHOLOGY AND THE VALENCY OF NOUNS

Jack Hoeksema

1. VALENCY AND CATEGORIAL MORPHOLOGY

Categorial Grammar differs from many other current systems of syntactic description, such as Lexical Functional Grammar and Government and Binding Grammar, in that it does not recognize thematic relations as a crucial component of the description of argument structure. Argument selection is defined in strictly categorial terms—that is, a transitive verb is described as anything that combines with an NP to form a VP, and no mention is made of the grammatical function of the NP (direct object) or its thematic role (patient, say). There is a certain Spartan quality about a system this simple, and this is one of the reasons why I like it. It is also the reason why categorial grammar fails to provide an insightful account of argument selection, others would say. Of course, we could all be right. Truth and simplicity are not always bedfellows. Is Categorial Grammar too simple to be true? This paper takes some aspects of the valency problem under the microscope[1] and concludes that, in spite of claims to the contrary, nominalizations in the modern languages Dutch, English, and German do not require the rich vocabulary that current competitors of Categorial Grammar have at their disposal. In particular, thematic grids à la Williams (1981), Di Sciullo and Williams (1988), or Stowell (1981) are not needed (grammatical functions can be defined away in Categorial Grammar, cf. Dowty 1982). This conclusion is compatible with Levin and Rappaport's (1986) finding that a set of restrictions on the subjects of adjectival passives is not to be explained in terms of a thematic requirement ("only themes can be subjects of adjectival passives"), but rather in terms of subcategorization properties (only the sole NP complement to a verb can be the subject of the corresponding adjectival passive). Levin and Rappaport's analysis can be recast in categorial terms without much ado; the analyses it replaces, such as the ones in Wasow (1980) and Bresnan (1982), cannot.

Before embarking on my mission, I briefly sketch the outlines of the categorial system I am assuming. For more detail, I refer the reader to Hoeksema (1985). I should also add here that categorial grammars are usually employed in tandem with a semantic interpretation. To the extent that thematic relations can be reduced to (i.e., defined in terms of) lexical semantics, an interpreted categorial grammar can also make use of them—however, most current work assumes that no such definition is possible and that thematic relations must be treated as primitives of the theory of grammar. (But see Jackendoff 1983; 1987 and Dowty 1988, among others, for attempts at embedding thematic relations into a more comprehensive theory of lexical semantics, in which they are more than unanalyzed labels of argument types.) The argument of this paper, then, is primarily directed against theories that postulate an unanalyzed set of entities that figure in some thematic grid which can be manipulated by rules of word formation. I do not doubt that such notions as 'agent' and 'goal' have content and that they play a role in lexical semantics. Indeed, some of the very arguments I use below rely on intuitions about those notions, presupposing therefore that they are real. But first of all, thematic relations are gradient in a way that is not expressed by the usual thematic-grid notation (i.e., there are prototypical agents and less prototypical agents), and second, their relation to syntactic selection is indirect and not part of the syntax of word and phrase formation. As a case in point, consider agent nominals of the form Verb-er. As the name itself indicates, words of this type are first and foremost used to indicate agents of actions: *drinker, killer, boxer*. However, the term *agent nominalization* is somewhat misleading. It is too specific on the one hand (nonagents formed by the same process may also be found, especially instrument names (*potato peeler, paper cutter*), but also experiencer names (the word *experiencer* itself may serve as an example), goals (*receiver*), and so on) and not specific enough on the other hand (as it does not express the fact that besides the preference for agents there is a preference for humans—*runner* and *smoker* are words that apply to humans, even though the underlying verbs can also be predicated of inanimate objects: *running water* and *smoking gun*).

What I would say about this kind of nominalization is this: It is used to form subject names[2] from verbs (cf. also Booij 1986 for further motivation of this claim, especially for Dutch) and it is not fully productive within the entire class of verbs. Sometimes a class of verbs systematically lacks agent nominalizations, such as the class of raising verbs (cf. the ill-formed **seemer, *appearer, *tender*). In other cases, agent nominalizations are blocked by other lexical items (a standard example is the blocking of *stealer* by *thief*).

More important for the purposes of this paper, agent nominalization shows preferences for certain semantic classes—but these preferences are not categorical[3]—and does not revolve entirely around the notion 'agent'. In particular, I argue below that there is no motivation for claiming that *-er* serves to bind the agent role in the thematic grid of the underlying verb.

1.1. Categories

Within the framework of Categorial Grammar, categories are either simple (such as NP or S) or complex. Complex categories take the form of a fraction:

[1] $$\frac{\mathrm{X}}{\mathrm{Y}}$$

The fractional notation states that the expression may combine with an expression of category Y to form an expression of category X. This is usually called the rule of application:

[2] $$\frac{\mathrm{X}}{\mathrm{Y}} + \mathrm{Y} \rightarrow \mathrm{X}$$

The fractional category is called the main functor of this combination, Y its argument and X the result of application. The denominator of the fractional thus concerns horizontal or subcategorization relations; the numerator concerns vertical or percolation relations. The formation of complex categories is recursive, and so X and Y need not be simple categories themselves. For example, the category of ditransitive verbs such as *give* has a complex numerator:

[3] $$\frac{\;\frac{\mathrm{VP}}{\mathrm{NP}}\;}{\mathrm{NP}}$$

This category signifies that the operator in question combines with a noun phrase in order to form an expression with the category of a transitive verb. This expression in turn may combine with a noun phrase to form a verb phrase. Observe that the length of the lines is used here to indicate the structure of the functor category. Compare the above category with the one below:

[4] $$\frac{\mathrm{VP}}{\;\frac{\mathrm{NP}}{\mathrm{NP}}\;}$$

In [4] the length of the lines betrays a rather different animal, a functor that calls for another functor of the type that combines with NPs to form NPs. In each case the main numerator is the category above the longest line and the main denominator is the category beneath it.

1.2. Order

Word order, when predictable, can be stated in the form of word order conventions (Flynn 1983). Following the notation of Lambek (1958), we write NP\VP (NP under VP) to indicate a transitive verb that takes its NP argument to the left (as is usual in SOV languages, such as Japanese and German) and VP/NP (VP over NP) to indicate a transitive verb that takes its NP argument to the right (as is usual in SVO languages such as English and French). For more complex categories, we can use parentheses to indicate the structure expressed by the length of lines in the earlier vertical notation. So the category of ditransitive verbs could in principle correspond to any of the following four directional categories: (VP/NP)/NP, NP\(VP/NP), (NP\VP)/NP, and NP\(NP\VP). In general, since a horizontal line in the nondirectional notation may correspond to any of two directional slashes, the number of directional categories correspond to a nondirectional category with n lines is 2^n. Word order conventions can now be stated as rules that interpret undirectional (vertical) complex categories as directional complex categories (with forward and backward slashes):

[5] **a.** $\frac{\mathrm{VP}}{\mathrm{NP}} \rightarrow$ VP/NP (English, French, Swedish, etc.)

b. $\frac{\mathrm{VP}}{\mathrm{NP}} \rightarrow$ NP\VP (Japanese, Korean, Turkish, Tamil, etc.)

For combining categories, we now need two mirror-image rules, called forward and backward application:

[6] a. Forward application: A/B + B → A

b. Backward application: B + B\A → A

When word order is not predictable by rule, it is simplest to put directional categories in the lexicon. For instance, in a language with both postpositions and prepositions, such as German, some items are listed as members of the category PP/NP (the prepositions) while others are listed as NP\PP (the postpositions). In the area of morphology, this is a common state of affairs. For instance, both *en-* and *-en* map adjectives into verbs (cf. *enlarge* and *darken*), but one is a prefix (with V/A as one of its categories) and the other is a suffix (with category A\V). Prefix or suffix status is not predictable in English, and hence best treated as a lexical fact, a fact about these particular formatives. Word order conventions, then, have the status of default rules within the categorial system.

1.3. Schematic Categories

It is often useful to have available underspecified or schematic categories. A schematic category corresponds to a set of regular, fully specified, categories. For example, it might be necessary to generalize over the set of categories

[**7**] $S, \quad \frac{S}{NP} \quad \frac{\frac{S}{NP}}{NP}$, etc.

For this purpose, Ades and Steedman (1982) introduced the dollar sign notation:

[**8**] $\frac{S}{\$}$

The symbol $ abbreviates any sequence of arguments, including the empty sequence. So the above category stands for all functors mapping zero or more arguments into the category S. The usefulness of schematic categories is obvious in areas such as nominalization. A nominalization suffix such as *-ing* combines with verbs of many valencies. Without the use of a schematic category, it becomes necessary to introduce a different category for *-ing* for every verb category: an *-ing* for intransitive verbs, one for transitive verbs, one for ditransitive verbs, one for verbs taking a single PP argument, and so on. Even in morphology, that would be an intolerable lack of generality.

Considering that nominalizations turn sentences into nominals, we see that the basic category of nominalization affixes is

[**9**] $\frac{N}{S}$

However, due to their status as affixes, they are not actually in construction with sentences but with the heads of sentences, verbs. Verbs are functions into S, that is, they are characterized by the schema

[**10**] $\frac{S}{\$}$

This paves the way for a proper categorization of -ing: we can give it the schematic category

[**11**] $\frac{S}{\$} \backslash \frac{N}{\$}$

from which its combinatorial properties follow. For example, the derivation of *erupting* is as follows: first $ is instantiated as NP, to get a category that then combines with the intransitive verb *erupt* to yield a noun with a single NP argument:

[12] erupt: $\frac{S}{NP}$ (lexical category assignment)

-ing: $\frac{S}{NP}\backslash\frac{N}{NP}$ (instantiation of schema: \$ = NP)

erupting: $\frac{N}{NP}$ (from the above by backward application)

Compare this derivation with the derivation of *waiting* as in *the men's waiting for Godot*. Here, we derive a nominalization that can take a subject argument and a PP object marked by *for*. In line with my suggestions for case marking in the following section, I will designate such an object *NP[for]:*

[13] wait: $\frac{\frac{S}{NP}}{NP[for]}$ (lexical category assignment)

-ing: $\frac{\frac{S}{NP}}{NP[for]}\backslash\frac{\frac{N}{NP}}{NP[for]}$ (instantiation of schema)

waiting: $\frac{\frac{N}{NP}}{NP[for]}$ (from the above categories by backward application)

From the examples above we see that the arguments of the verb are inherited by the nominalization as a consequence of adopting the schematic category. Similar effects can be achieved by using function composition (Moortgat 1985; 1988; Kang 1988). For more detailed discussion of schematic categories and their relation to function composition, see Hoeksema (1985; 1989). The NP argument of a nominalization must take a particular form—for example, that of a PP headed by *of* or a genitive NP. This is the domain of case assignment rules. Much more could be said here, in particular regarding the interaction of these assignment rules, but this discussion will have to be set aside for some other occasion.

1.4. Case

Case assignment rules are similar to the word order conventions in that they spell out details left open in the category specifications. For example, it is not appropriate to specify in the lexicon for every English transitive verb that it combines with accusative NPs, since that is predictable by rule:

[14] $\frac{VP}{NP} \rightarrow \frac{VP}{NP[acc]}$

The use of case assignment rules of this kind is not too common in the literature on categorial grammar. Often, a very different approach to case assignment is taken, following a suggestion by Lambek (1958), in which case is expressed by type raising. In such an approach, a nominative NP is an element that combines with a (finite) verb phrase to give a sentence, an accusative NP is an element that combines with a transitive verb to give a verb phrase, and so on. This approach, which eliminates the need for case features, is attractive mainly from a semantic point of view (see Hoeksema 1989, chap. 6, for discussion) but fails as a theory of case marking. In a language such as Icelandic, which has accusative and dative subjects as well as dative, accusative, and genitive objects, it is impossible to describe case in purely combinatorial terms, without the use of features. Moreover, it is hard to see how a genitive object of a transitive verb (which would have the category (VP/NP)\VP in Lambek's scheme) and a genitive modifier of a noun (with category N\N) could be treated in a uniform fashion by the morphology, given their quite diverse combinatory properties, unless case features are added.

Marking by genitive case or the preposition *of* can also be dealt with by means of case assignment rules. For example:

[15] $\frac{\text{N}}{\text{NP}} \rightarrow \frac{\text{N}}{\text{NP[Gen]}}$

$\frac{\text{N}}{\text{NP}} \rightarrow \frac{\text{N}}{\text{NP[of]}}$

These rules interact with word order conventions:

[16] $\frac{\text{N}}{\text{NP[Gen]}} \rightarrow \text{NP[Gen]}\backslash\text{N}$

$\frac{\text{N}}{\text{NP[of]}} \rightarrow \text{N/NP[of]}$

(for German, the ordering N/NP[Gen] is also permitted). The marker *'s* and *of* have the following entries:

[17] **a.** 's: NP\NP[Gen]

b. of: NP[of]/NP

Case features may be assigned by rule, as above, or be lexical. For example, the German verb *helfen* has the peculiar property of assigning dative case to its object. This does not follow from any rule of German, and hence must be noted in the lexicon with the entry *helfen:* NP[Dat]\VP.

This means that case assignment rules have the property of being default rules. They only apply to categories unspecified for case features. As we saw above, this is also a property of word order conventions.

The preceding remarks entail that the case marking of verbal arguments is only inherited by the arguments of deverbal nominalizations when the case is lexical. Regular or default case is not inherited. There is a parallel here with passive, where the same applies (cf. especially the discussion of "quirky" case in Icelandic in Zaenen et al. 1985).[4] In English nominalizations, accusative case is never inherited, but prepositional marking is:

[18]	think of John	his thinking of John
	talk about us	her talking about us
	look for Pete	our looking for Pete

This is also evident from the impossibility of genitive case for prepositional objects:

[19]	**a.**	John's talking		the talking about John
		Martha's waiting		the waiting for Martha
		Compare:		
	b.	the donkey's spanking	=	the spanking of the donkey
		the city's destruction	=	the destruction of the city

Inheritance of preposition selection by nominalizations was noted as early as Grimm (1837) for German, but its theoretical significance is still debated, as we will see.[5] This concludes the discussion of the categorial system to be applied below.

2. AGENT NOMINALIZATIONS

2.1. Inheritance

Agent nominalizations are especially interesting from the perspective of this paper, because they differ from event nominalizations in a number of ways. As noted by Randall (1982) and others, only transitive and intransitive verbs appear to be truly happy with the suffix *-er:*

[20]	run	runner
	eat	eater
	sing	singer
	raiders of the lost ark	
	lover of Baroque fountains	
	explorer of Antartica	
	Rome's founders	

Compare this with

[21] *counter on the U.S. cavalry
*claimer that Armageddon is near

*attempters to escape
*keeper (of) blacks down
*starter making money

In the case of PP complements, only such PPs as are naturally interpreted as adnominal modifiers are readily permitted; PPs that require an argument interpretation are (almost always) ruled out. Hence the difference between the two forms in [22]:

[22] **a.** painter without hands

b. *painter with his hands

The qualification *almost always* is necessary for a careful account of the data. For instance, the phrase *fighters against apartheid* does not force the interpretation 'fighters who are against apartheid' analogous to, say, *women against apartheid* or *fire fighters against apartheid,* but also permits and in fact prefers the PP to be interpreted as an argument of the verb *to fight:* 'someone who fights against apartheid'. This is clear in a sentence such as *Botha and Viljoen were involuntary fighters against apartheid.* Here a paraphrase such as 'involuntary fighters who were against apartheid' is not available. Another example, observed at a linguistics conference:

[23] as a believer in Gesamtbedeutung, I . . .

Similar examples can be found in Dutch (Sassen 1980) and German (Droop 1977), where the restrictions on PP inheritance are about the same as in English (see Booij 1988; Booij and Van Haaften 1988; and Hoekstra and Van der Putten 1988 for a discussion of Dutch). The following Dutch examples are partly from Sassen, partly my own:

[24]	reizigers naar Groningen	'travelers to Groningen'
	strijders tegen apartheid	'fighters against apartheid'
	zoekers naar waarheid	'seekers to (=for) truth'
	heerser over heel Azië	'ruler over (=of) all of Asia'
	luisteraars naar ons programma	'listeners to our program'[6]
	jager op oorlogsmisdadigers	'hunter on (=of) war criminals'
	medewerker aan onze uitzending	'collaborator to (=on) our program'
	handelaar in onroerend goed	'trader in real estate'
	leidinggevers aan internationale bedrijven	'leadershipgivers to international businesses = managers of multinationals'
	lijders aan tuberculose	'sufferers from tuberculosis'
	deelnemers aan de conferentie	'participants to (=in) the conference'

Note also the existence of verbal compounds with verbs taking a PP complement. In such compounds, the left member of the compound corresponds to the PP argument: Dutch *Engelandvaarder* (cf. *varen naar Engeland* 'sail to England'), *AIDS-lijders* (cf. *lijden aan AIDS* 'suffer from AIDS, to have AIDS'), English *city dweller, science reporter* and so on.

Some German examples of PP inheritance with agent nominalizations, taken from Droop (1977: 83), are:

[25]	Kämpfer für den Freiheit	'fighter for freedom'
	Teilnehmer an der Veranstaltung	'participant in the activity'
	Befreier von der Fremdherrschaft	'liberator from foreign rule'

Some examples from Booij (1988, 60) may serve to show that inheritance of PP arguments is not always possible:

[26]	houden van kaas	'hold of cheese = like cheese'
	*houder van kaas	'lover of cheese'
	vertrouwen op de mens	'trust on the man = rely on man'
	*vertrouwer op de mens	'relier on man'
	wonen in Amsterdam	'live in Amsterdam'
	*woner in Amsterdam	'liver in Amsterdam'

Similar examples could be cited for German:

[27]	warten auf Regen	'wait for rain'
	*Wärter auf Regen	'waiters for rain'
	wohnen in Berlin	'live in Berlin'
	*Wohner in Berlin	'liver in Berlin'

Since I agree with Booij and Hoekstra that it is easier to find examples of verbs taking PP arguments whose agent nominalizations do not allow them than it is to find convincing cases of inheritance, I take it that inheritance is not the rule but the exception. I also agree with Booij that this is best interpreted as showing that agent nominalization is not productive with verbs that take PP complements, since the formations are also ruled out without the presence of a PP (cf. **woner, *vertrouwer,* etc. in Dutch and **relier, *liver,* etc. in English).[7] However, it is a common phenomenon that rules apply productively in one domain and only occasionally elsewhere. Agent nominalization is not productive for verbs that take PP arguments, but when it does create new items, it shows inheritance of the PP argument. To be sure, it has been denied that these cases involve the inheritance of PP arguments (Hoekstra 1986; Booij and Van Haaften 1988), a matter to which I return below. First, however, let us consider whether agent nominalizations show argument inheritance in the area in which they are clearly productive, that of transitive and intransitive verbs. The question of why agent nominals are productive in precisely the area of transitive and intransitive verbs will be sidestepped here. I refer the reader to the discussion in Randall (1982) of various proposals concerning this matter.

2.2. Inheritance of Direct Objects

In the productive domain, the evidence is quite clear: agent nominalizations from intransitive verbs take no arguments (the subject argument is bound by the suffix), and agent nominalizations of transitive verbs take an NP argument corresponding to the object of the verb. Accordingly, *sleeper* takes no objects (**sleeper of sofas*) but *watcher* does (*Kremlin watcher, avid watcher of late-night horror movies*). The behavior of *-er* points to the following category, where the angled brackets indicate conditional optionality in the manner of phonological notation.[8] That is, either the bracketed symbols are all present or they are all absent:

[28] -er: $$\frac{\frac{N}{\langle NP \rangle}}{\frac{VP}{\langle NP \rangle}}$$

It might seem that the uppermost bracketed NP argument need not be present, even if the lowermost one is. However, that is probably due to a more general phenomenon. Arguments of nouns are generally optional, whereas verbs may have obligatory complements. This difference between nouns and verbs has been noted from time to time (Hoeksema 1985; Dowty 1988). Dowty (1988, 90) gives the following paradigm to illustrate the phenomenon:

[29] the gift of a book from John to Mary
the gift of a book from John
the gift of a book to Mary
the gift from John to Mary
the gift from John
the gift to Mary
the gift of a book
the gift

In the next section, I discuss Dowty's theoretical assessment of this striking phenomenon. First however, let us examine how the categorial model copes with it. In Hoeksema (1985), a rule of argument drop is proposed that allows nominals to omit their complements:

[30] $$\frac{\frac{N}{\$}}{X} \rightarrow \frac{N}{\$} \qquad \text{where } X = NP, S', PP \text{ etc.}$$

Consider how this rule applies in Dutch to an agentive nominal from a transitive verb:

[**31**] bereid 'prepare' bereider 'preparer'

$$\frac{VP}{NP} \rightarrow \qquad \frac{N}{NP} \rightarrow N/NP[van]$$

$$\downarrow$$

N (by argument reduction)

So a transitive verb is transformed by *-er* suffixation into a transitive (or relational) noun, which then is optionally turned into an intransitive noun. Inheritance, in this view, is obligatory, but its effects are not categorical, due to the operation of the Valency Reduction Rule. I disagree here with Booij and Van Haaften (1988) and Booij (1988), who maintain that nouns derived from genuine transitive verbs must have an overt argument. They motivate their claim with triples such as the following:

[32] *bereider 'preparer'
ijsbereider 'ice-preparer [for skating, JH]'
bereider van ijs 'preparer of ice'

However, it must be added that nouns such as *bereider* have an intransitive use, albeit this use is restricted to contexts where the object of preparation is given (Booij calls these elliptic contexts). For instance, the following piece of discourse is possible:

[33] De soep is vergiftigd; we moeten de bereider vattan
the soup is poisoned we must the preparer seize

This kind of intransitive use is not possible for the verb *bereiden,* except in the notorious recipe context, in which all transitivity strictures are lifted, as they are in English (cf. *Shake well before baking*). Another example that Booij and Van Haaften give is *maker*. The Dutch verb *maken,* like its English cognate *to make,* is transitive, and the Dutch noun *maker* is characterized by the following triple:

[34] *maker
lijstenmaker 'frame maker'
maker van lijsten 'maker of frames'

Again, we note that the star is not appropriate in general:

[35] Op deze foto ziet U een guillotine voor muizen. De trotse maker staat er naast.
on this photo see you a guillotine for mice the proud maker stands there next-to
'In this photo, you see a guillotine for mice. The proud maker is standing next to it

To sum up the findings so far: agent nominalizations of transitive verbs inherit the direct object argument. This argument, however, does not have to be overt, but may be given by the context. There is a parallel here with relational nouns that are not morphologically complex, such as *father*. Normally, such relational nouns require an argument, but when this argument is obvious from the context, overt expression is not necessary:

[36] "Who is the father?" (speaker pointing at a baby)

There is a striking lack of agreement between our findings for Dutch and Randall's (1982) findings for English on the one hand, and Fanselow's (1988) discussion of the pertinent German data. According to Fanselow, German transitive verbs never permit inheritance of the object argument by the agent nominal. The claim appears to be immediately falsified by such examples as:

[37]	der Fahrer des Lastwagens	'the driver of the truck'
	der Käufer des Mantels	'the buyer of the coat'
	der Leser des Buches	'the reader of the book'

which Fanselow notes. He claims, however, that real transitive verbs, the kind that do not let go of their arguments under any circumstances, do not permit inheritance:

[38]	*der Hemmer des Appetits	'the inhibitor of appetite'
	*der Löser des Problems	'the solver of the problem'
	*der Verletzer der Grenze	'the violator of the border'

The apparent inheritance in the earlier cases is then viewed as an artifact of another possibility, namely that "within certain limits that will yet have to be determined, non-derived agentive nouns allow for an NP-complementation interpreted with the relation implicit in the noun's meaning" (Fanselow 1988, 106). Examples illustrating this point are:

[39]	der Autor des Buches	'the author of the book'
	der Arzt von Maria	'the doctor of Maria'
	der Pilot der 747	'the pilot of the 747'

The relation implicit in the meaning of *pilot,* for instance, can be lexicalized by the verb *to fly,* since x is the pilot of y if and only if x flies y (modulo some slight subtleties that need not concern us here). So the phrase *der Pilot der 747* can be viewed in the same light as a phrase with a deverbal nominalization such as *the* "flier of the 747". If Fanselow is right, then German agent nominalization differs from its Dutch and English counterparts in a surprising way, since the latter clearly show inheritance of subcategorized arguments. However, a quick look at some relevant facts tells us that things are not so different in German. First, there are some genuinely transitive verbs that have agent nominalizations with entirely acceptable objects:[9]

[40] der Verursacher des Unglücks — 'the causer of the accident'
ein Bewunderer von Goethe — 'an admirer of Goethe'
der Verfasser dieses Buches — 'the writer of this book'

Compare:

*er verursacht — 'he causes'
*sie bewundert — 'she admires'
*er verfasst — 'he writes'

Second, even with some of Fanselow's own examples, argument inheritance is not quite as bad as he claims it is. For example, the Cambridge-Eichborn German dictionary (vol. 2) gives an example with the noun *Verletzer:*

[41] Verletzer eines Patents — 'infringer of a patent'

Finally, agent nominalizations that appear to disfavor syntactic arguments permit these arguments in verbal compounds. Fanselow notes this himself and gives the following examples:

[42] ein Appetithemmer — 'an appetite inhibitor'
ein Problemlöser — 'a problem solver'
ein Grenzverletzer — 'a border violator'

To avoid having to say that here a noun such as *hemmer* takes its argument to the left in the form of a compound specifier, Fanselow proposes the analysis *[[N V]er],* following Lieber (1983). In this structure, the argument of the verb is directly satisfied, and there is no need for inheritance by the agent nominalization. However, this proposal fails to satisfy, as N + V compounding is not productive in English, Dutch, or German, languages in which verbal compounding of the type N + V + er is extremely productive. (This point was made in Hoeksema 1981 and Booij 1988.) Another problem with the proposal is that it cannot be extended to other kinds of verbal compounding in which the affix is a prefix (see Hoeksema 1985 for more discussion). Such cases show the prefix on the verb, rather on the noun or noun-verb combination. In short, there does not seem to be an alternative to the structure N + [V + er]. But then the issue of inheritance returns with full force. Conclusion: Contrary to Fanselow's claims, German agent nominalization does not differ crucially from Dutch or English agent nominalization in the way direct object arguments are inherited.

3. INHERITANCE: SEMANTIC OR SYNTACTIC?

3.1. Nominal versus Verbal Argument Structure

We saw above that arguments of nominalizations are optional, even when the underlying verb subcategorizes for obligatory complements. A rule was suggested to cope with this situation, but no particularly deep explanation was offered.

Dowty (1988) suggests that the nominal domain differs crucially from the verbal domain in the way predicates are associated with their arguments. In the verbal domain, subcategorization principles apply, of the kind formalized in categorial grammar. In the nominal domain, association proceeds by what Dowty calls the Neo-Davidsonian method, along semantic lines: an event nominalization does not require NPs, PPs, or the like, but allows various expressions to indicate agents, goals, themes, and so on, insofar as these are appropriate to the kind of event. For this reason, arguments to nouns are optional. Dowty admits that his "hypothesis is not unequivocally supported by available evidence." It is also not compatible with the categorial theory of argument inheritance. The main flaw of the proposal is that it does not deal with the selection of semantically arbitrary or vacuous prepositions.[10] In the above example, the prepositions *from* and *to* have a clear semantic motivation. However, in *a look at this year's spring fashion* the choice of the preposition *at* does not appear to be guided by semantic intuitions, but rather by the fact that the corresponding verb *to look* has the idiosyncratic property of selecting *at*. Similarly for the following cases

[43]	they approve of violence	their approval of violence
	acquaint her with Joe	her acquaintance with Joe
	go about your business	my going about my business

It is necessary to dwell on these matters, because it is not just Dowty who advocates the thematic approach to the argument structure of nominalizations. Hoekstra, for instance, proclaims that "in nominal constructions the formal realization of arguments is determined by their thematic role with respect to the head" (1986, 568). Similar claims about the primary status of thematic relations can be found in Booij and Van Haaften (1988) and Rappaport (1983). It should be noted though that neither Dowty nor Hoekstra subscribes to the notion that thematic relations come in a small number of primitive types, such as agent and theme, but talk about thematic relations as a convenient abbreviation for those aspects of lexical meaning that involve the arguments of predicates. As I mentioned in the beginning of this paper, I have no quarrel with this aspect of their theories.

To the extent that the selection of prepositions by verbs is not predictable from the meaning of those verbs, the selection of the same prepositions by corresponding nominalizations is not a semantic matter, but a lexical matter. Event nominalizations, therefore, are problematic for the point of view advocated by Dowty and Hoekstra. Now, it may be that a semantic theory can be worked out that will correctly predict the choice of *about* by *go* and the selection of *of* by *approve*. So far, however, no such theory exists, and in the absence of such a theory, it is better to rely on the duller mechanism of lexical subcategorization to do the work.

This is not to deny that lexical semantics plays an important role in nominalizations and many other areas of word formation. To the contrary, it is clear that the choice of complements is largely determined by meaning. The choice of prepositions is often not arbitrary, the choice of sentential rather than nominal complements is not random for, say, propositional attitude verbs, and so on. However, it is important to keep in mind that there is a set of cases that cannot be reduced to semantics. For instance, the English verb *to think* takes *that*-complements and accusative infinitive (AcI) complements, among other things, but not subjectless infinitival complements.[11] Its Dutch counterpart, *denken,* on the other hand, does not accept AcI complements (these are restricted to verbs of perception and causative verbs in Dutch) but can be used as a control verb. These differences reflect certain generalizations that can be made over the lexicons of Dutch and English, but they do not follow from a difference in meaning.

Returning now to the case of agent nominalizations, there are two inheritance phenomena to be considered in some more detail: the unproductive inheritance of prepositional complements and the productive inheritance of direct object argument. With regard to the first, Booij (1988) remarks that the occurrence of PP complements with deverbal nouns is not very telling, since semantically related underived words can also select prepositional complements. For example, next to *reizigers naar Groningen* 'travelers to Groningen', there is *treinen naar Groningen* 'trains to Groningen', and next to *heerser over Europa* 'ruler over Europe' there is *koning over de Nederlanden* 'king over the Netherlands'. Hence whatever mechanism allows the cases with underived words (and it is clear that this is a semantic mechanism that has nothing to do with inheritance) could also be responsible for the acceptability of the cases with deverbal nouns.

I have three objections to Booij's argumentation. First, it is simply not very plausible for some of the data. For instance, another example that Booij cites is *lijders aan pleinvrees* 'sufferers from agoraphobia' (literally 'sufferers to agoraphobia'). The choice of the preposition *aan* (just as the choice of the English preposition *from* in the translation of this example) is not predictable if we only consider the meaning of the word *lijder,* but it is predictable if the selection properties of the base verb *lijden* are also considered, (cf. *lijden aan pleinvrees* 'to suffer from agoraphobia'). Second, some of Booij's examples are not convincing. Take again the case of *heerser/koning over Europa* 'ruler/king over Europa'. As it happens, with the noun *koning,* the preposition *van* is preferred over the preposition *over:*

[44] de koning van/?over Denemarken wordt onthoofd
'the king of/over Denmark is beheaded'

However, with the noun *heerser,* the preferences are reversed:

[45] de heerser over/?van Europa was Karel de Grote
'the ruler over/of Europe was Charlemagne'

If the same forces were at work in both cases, we would expect converging, not diverging, preferences. Third, it seems from the acquisition data reported in Randall (1982) that children distinguish between agent nominals such as *writer with a candy bar* (which is often given the interpretation 'someone who writes with a candy bar', in spite of the fact that this is not a possible interpretation for adult speakers of English) and underived noun + PP combinations such as *chef with a fork.* Randall takes her findings to be evidence that children overextend morphological inheritance for a while, before they learn that only objects can be inherited productively.

As for inheritance of direct objects, it is even less clear what a theory based on thematic roles has to offer. The choice of the marker *of* (Dutch *van,* German *von,* or genitive case) can be predicted without any recourse to thematic relations by a default case marking rule. These markers are not restricted to particular thematic relations, in much the same way that the nominative and accusative cases are not restricted to particular roles such as agent or patient. This is perhaps most evident from the fact that in event nominalizations the *of* phrase can represent either the subject (agent) or the object (theme), as in such classic examples as *the shooting of the hunters.*

Zucchi (1989) notes some additional problems with the thematic role account. As Dowty (1986) points out, the triple *dine, eat,* and *devour* clearly shows that subcategorization is not determined fully by lexical semantics. All three verbs relate to the consumption of food, but the first is strictly intransitive, the second can occur either with or without a direct object, and the third is strictly transitive. Now, if nominalizations do not involve the mechanism of subcategorization, then these differences ought to be neutralized. Zucchi observes that they are not. For example, the nominalization *the dining of the missionaries* does not have a reading according to which the missionaries are the ones being eaten, in spite of the fact that very event of dining presupposes the existence of material to be eaten. Another way of stating Zucchi's observation is that Dowty's (and Hoekstra's) thematic account predicts not only the argument drop phenomenon described earlier, but also the possibility of argument addition for nominalizations—to wit, the expression by means of prepositional phrases of arguments that are only implicit with the corresponding verbs. Such argument additions, however, are not found, suggesting that the categorial account, which stipulates argument drop but not argument addition, is a better approximation of the truth.

By phrases offer more compelling evidence for thematic relations. Unlike passive constructions, action nominalizations do not readily permit *by* phrases unless these denote an agent (Dowty 1988 attributes this observation to the early days of case grammar and cites Fillmore 1977). Some relevant examples to illustrate this point are:

[46] the death of Caesar/*by Caesar
the love of sex (*by primates)

the knowledge of chess (*by Capablanca)
the well-being of the public (*by the public)

Contrast this with the acceptability of nonagentive *by* phrases in passives:

[47] this was known by most chess masters
it is nice to be loved by those one loves
the shooting was heard by all gamblers

The situation in Dutch and German is the same, which suggests that the above observations are onto something. However, a simple theory of thematic relations is still going to have to deal with such problematic cases as:

[48] the reception of the diplomats by the queen
the perception of final devoicing by infants
the possession by the Church of certain funds[12]

Here the *by* phrases express the roles of goal or recipient and experiencer, respectively. Again, the data are the same in Dutch, as the following translations of the phrases in [48] attest:

[49] de ontvangst van de diplomaten door de koningin
de waarneming van final devoicing door kinderen
het bezit door de Kerk van zekere fondsen

While it might be thought that being a goal or an experiencer does not exclude agenthood (cf. especially Jackendoff 1983 for such a point of view), I can think of a few cases where there does not seem to be any kind of agentivity, for example, in Dutch:

[50] **a.** het bereiken van de middelbare leeftijd door onze ambtenaren
the reaching of middle age by our civil servants
'our civil servants' reaching middle age'

b. het niet begrijpen van Nederlandse zinnen door buitenlanders
the not understanding of Dutch sentences by foreigners
'the failure of foreigners to understand Dutch sentences'

c. het kwijt raken van kredietkaarten door onze klanten
the lost getting of credit cards by our customers
'the loss of credit cards by our customers'

The worst problem for the thematic relation account is the fact that agents of intransitive verbs do not occur as *by* phrases in the corresponding nominalization:

[51] *the fight by Sam
*the departure by Amy
*the defection by the sailors

Using the categorial system and its rules of case assignment, it is easy to distinguish transitive from intransitive cases.[13] In a thematic account, where prepositions simply mark thematic relations, the difference between transitive and intransitive verb nominalizations makes no clear sense. I conclude that *by* phrases are used to express the subject arguments of transitive nominalizations and that there are some ill-understood conditions on this way of expressing these arguments. These conditions appear to be of a semantic nature, but cannot be described straightforwardly in terms of thematic roles.

3.2. Thematic Hiercharchy and Inheritance

Departing from her earlier work, Randall (1988) proposes that inheritance is constrained by a thematic hierarchy. Morphological rules that suppress arguments also must suppress all arguments lower on the thematic hierarchy:

[52] theme
agent
source/goal/location, etc.

So if a rule suppresses the agent argument (e.g., agent nominalization), then also any lower arguments expressing goal or source or location (etc.) must be suppressed. (An argument is "suppressed" by a morphological rule when the application of that rule bars an overt realization of that argument. Thus the subject or agent argument of an agentive nominal cannot be expressed, as is clear from the observation that *killer of John* could not possibly be interpreted in such a way that John is the subject, rather than the object, of the verbal relation *kill.*) Theme arguments may remain intact, and so we derive the finding that *-er* derivations inherit the object (=theme) arguments of their bases but not anything else. Of course, the exceptions noted above still apply. And this time they may cause some more concern. Under the categorial account, a phrase like *fighther against apartheid* results from a transgression on the part of the rule of *-er* affixation. Instead of staying within its domain of transitive and intransitive verbs, it has gone astray and applied itself to a verb that takes PP complements. The inheritance of the PP argument itself is *not* exceptional: it follows automatically from the rule application. The phenomenon of rules applying outside the domain within which they are productive is common. It would be more ominous if we have to lift pervasive conditions on the projection of argument structure, such as the one invoked by Randall, to permit cases of PP inheritance. Apart from this qualm, and the general problem that it assumes that some morphological rules directly refer to thematic roles, an assumption I have been challenging throughout this paper, I have the following critical comment to make on Randall's proposal. Unlike the categorial account, it does not predict that alongside **putter of men on the moon* and **hander of scalpels to surgeons,* the phrases **putters of men* and **handers of scalpels,* as well as the lexical items **putters* and **handers,* are also bad. By removing some arguments (which ought to be possible, given the optionality of arguments of nominals), we should be able to restore acceptability. In **putters of men,* say, there is no inherited argument that has a lower status than agent.

For the affix *-able,* which suppresses the theme or object argument of transitive verbs, Randall predicts that no inheritance is possible, since the theme role is the highest on the thematic hierarchy. As evidence for this claim, she cites (1988, p. 135):

[53] *Men are puttable on the moon.
*African elephants are comparable with Indian elephants.
*Those stamps are not pastable onto envelopes.
*These nuts are not removable from their bolts.

However, as evidence this is less than convincing. The second and fourth of the preceding examples are acceptable to my ear, and so are the following examples:

[54] These items are deductible from income tax.
That property is definable in first-order logic.
Is this enforceable by legal proceedings?[14]
What is its applicability to sociolinguistics?

As for **puttable on the moon,* it seems that the nonexistence of the word *puttable,* rather than a constraint on inheritance, is responsible for the oddness of this phrase. There is no reason, I conclude, to prefer a theory of inheritance that appeals to some ranking of thematic roles.

3.3. Thematic Constraints on the Genitive

The various constraints on what may appear as a prenominal genitive NP in English noun phrases have frequently been treated as reflecting sensitivity to thematic relations. A recent proposal (Rozwadowska 1988) states the constraints as follows (p.152):

[55] N-rule: Neutral cannot appear in specifier position of a nominal.

By *neutral,* a special thematic relation is intended, defined as follows (p.151):

[56] Neutral: An entity X holds a thematic relation NEUTRAL (N-role) with respect to a predicate Y if:
(i) X is in no way affected by the action, process, or state described by Y;
(ii) X does not have any control over the action, process, or state described by Y.

Condition (i) rules out affected objects, condition (ii) rules out agents.

This correctly predicts that a predicate such as *destroy,* with an agent and an affected theme arguments, allows either argument to show up in the specifier position of the corresponding nominalization, whereas a predicate such as *enjoy,* with an experiencer and an experienced argument, allows only the experiencer argument to show up there:

[57] **a.** the enemy's destruction of the city
the city's destruction by the enemy

b. John's enjoyment of the film
*the film's enjoyment by/of John

The experiencer can be assumed to be affected, and hence does not count as neutral; the experienced, on the other hand, being neither affected by, nor in control of, the event, is neutral and hence barred from the specifier position.

A problem with Rozwadowska's account is that according to her own definitions, temporal arguments are neutral and therefore ruled out as specifiers of nominals. Yet examples such as the following are fine:

[58] yesterday's execution of the first twenty-five prisoners
tomorrow's attempts at promoting world peace

Moreover, since the N-rule does not refer specifically to nominalizations from verbs (a point emphasized by Rozwadowska), it also rules out cases such as *John's sister* or *Prizzi's honor,* given that the roles of John and Prizzi here have to be neutral. Finally, there are cases of "objective" genitives whose interpretation can only be viewed as neutral in Rozwadowska's sense, such as the following from Quirk et al. (1972, p.188):

[59] the tenants' scrutiny by the landlord
the man's examination by the doctor

While the existence of these counterexamples does not rule out the possibility of a satisfactory account in terms of thematic relations at some point in the future, it is clear that neither Rozwadowska's theory, nor related ones on which she builds (cf. Anderson 1979, Amritavalli 1980, and Rappaport 1983) are descriptively adequate (for a critical discussion of the latter, I refer to Rozwadowska's paper). The case for thematic relations still has to be made in this area of research.

3.4. The Role of Semantic Analogy

Finally, a word should be said about the cases of prepositional selection that cannot be explained by argument inheritance. For example, it is a fact about the noun *attack* that it selects the preposition *on*. The verb *to attack,* on the other hand, does not mark its argument with a preposition—it is a regular transitive verb. There is a certain amount of randomness in the choice of prepositions, as Droop (1977, 77) illustrates with the following German examples:

[60] Verlust an Zeit 'loss on (=of) time'
Hass auf den Tyrannen 'hatred on (=of) the tyrants'
Forderung nach mehr Freiheit 'demand to (=for) more freedom'
Achtung vor dem Gegner 'esteem before (=for) the opponent'
Liebe zu einer Frau 'love toward a woman'

Note that some of these examples involve derived nouns. Since the selection of the preposition cannot be explained as the result of the morphological rule that derived them from their verbal base, this means that these nouns have acquired an idiosyncratic feature through lexicalization.

The above examples notwithstanding, a number of people, including Droop (1977) and Hoekstra and van der Putten (1977), have pointed out that the choice of prepositions by nouns is not entirely random. Rather, it often reflects the influence of lexical semantics, as evidenced by the fact that semantically similar nouns frequently require the same preposition:

[61] attack on Pearl Harbor
assault on the garrison
raid on Entebbe
run on the liquor store
attempt on his life[15]

The suspicion that the choice of preposition is not arbitrary is reinforced by the observation that similar nouns in Dutch select the preposition *op* 'on':

[62]

aanslag op de Paus	'attempt on the Pope'
aanval op drugsmisbruik	'attack on drug abuse'
overval op een goudtransport	'assault on a gold transport'
bombardement op Rotterdam	'bombing raid on Rotterdam'
moord op Allende	'murder of Allende'

As the last example shows, the parallelism between Dutch and English is not perfect, since *murder* does not take *on*. Conversely, the counterpart of English *war on poverty* is *oorlog tegen de armoede*, with the preposition *tegen* 'against', rather than *op*. Other English words that might be expected to take *on*, such as *offensive* or *crusade*, prefer *against* instead. The picture that arises from these and many other such cases is that the choice of the preposition is guided by analogical mechanisms: words with similar meanings tend to select the same ranges of prepositions, but no surefire rules can be set up. It seems arbitrary that the preposition *on* can be used with the meaning 'about' in combinations such as *book on chess*, *paper on organometallics*, and so on (in German or Dutch, the corresponding prepositions do not have this additional use), but given that it can, it comes as no particular surprise that *on* can also be used in this way with semantically related nouns such as *e-mail* (as in 'send me some e-mail on your dissertation proposal'). It is also interesting to note that sometimes semantic selection principles apply across word classes, as in the case of *on* meaning 'about': *book on* and *write on* show that both nouns and verbs can select this marker. The earlier cases with *attack on,* on the other hand, do not seem to have a class of corresponding examples with verbs.

For the above examples, it is not very useful to appeal to thematic relations in order to explain the choice of prepositions. The lexical-semantic classes involved do not lend themselves easily to a classification in terms of agents, sources, goals, and the like, but rather cluster around some core meaning, such as 'attack'. In other cases, we find that the choice of preposition may serve to express aspects of meaning that are entirely orthogonal to the ones focussed on by thematic relation theory à la Gruber (1965) or Jackendoff (1983), such as temporal distinctions. An interesting set of examples from German to illustrate this point is given in Sommerfeldt and Schreiber (1980, p.21):[16]

[63] **a.** die Freude des Jungen auf den Geburtstag
the joy of-the boy on the birth-day
'the boy's joyful anticipation of his birthday'

b. die Freude des Jungen über das Geschenk
the joy of-the boy about the present
'the boy's joy about the present'

c. die Freude des Jungen an dem Geschenk
the joy of-the boy to the present
'the boy's enjoyment of the present'

Here, the preposition *auf* signals that the joy is directed at a future event, the preposition *über* indicates enjoyment of an earlier or present object or event, and the preposition *an* expresses simultaneity of joy and the object of joy.

4. CONCLUSIONS

This paper identifies two main forces that determine the valency of derived nouns: (1) inheritance of arguments from their base and (2) selection of arguments under analogy with semantically similar words. For argument inheritance, categorial grammar offers a simple and economic mechanism to describe the relevant facts. One categorial system is described here in some detail; it has, besides the usual combinatory rules of left- and right-application, rules of case marking and word order, which function here as default rules and can be overridden by lexical information. The system is applied to nominalization data from English, Dutch, and German, in particular agent nominalizations and event nominalizations. Contrary to much current work in morphology, no role is envisaged for thematic relations in the account of how nominalizations inherit the argument structure of their underlying verbs. A number of claims that morphological rules must make reference to a thematic grid, a thematic hierarchy, or constraints expressed in terms of thematic relations, are shown to be based on erroneous or problematic assumptions. The paper also argues against the hypothesis in Dowty (1988) that verbs and nouns select their arguments in different ways, the former by syntactic subcategorization, the latter by a semantic mechanism (making reference to such notions as 'agent' and 'goal'). There is solid evidence that nominalizations, just as verbs, may select for semantically irrelevant morphosyntactic properties. This supports the view that the mechanisms for selection are the same across the major lexical categories.

SOME CONCEPTS IN AHTNA ATHABASKAN WORD FORMATION

James Kari

INTRODUCTION

The Athabaskan languages of western North America are a homogeneous family of about thirty-five languages. A verb in an Athabaskan language consists of a stem, at least one suffix, and a series of rigidly sequenced prefixes. Athabaskan languages seem to be among the world's most elaborate prefixing languages. Some of the languages, such as Ahtna of Alaska's Copper River area, have twenty-seven distinct prefix positions in the verb complex, with an inventory of about 150 prefixes and suffixes, as well as a slot for incorporates (Kari 1989; 1990).

Athabaskan languages are now attracting increasing attention because of the challenges they provide to theories of word formation and to mechanisms for the linearization of morphemes. To begin a study of Athabaskan morphology and word formation, one should review standard sources in the field, including works by Morice, Jetté, Sapir, Hoijer, and Young and Morgan. Krauss (1973) provides an excellent overview of this literature. In the 1970s Leer's work on the historical phonology of the Athabaskan root (Leer 1979) gave a firm basis for distinguishing canonical root structure and verb stem alternations in the modern languages. Coordinate with Leer's work was my 1979 study on the nature of verb themes and verb theme categories, and the structure of the suffixation system for aspect. In the 1980s documentation and research in the language family has expanded with the massive Navajo dictionary by Young and Morgan (1980; 1987), several analyses of Navajo phonology and word formation (Speas 1984; 1986; 1987; Wright 1984; 1987; Hargus 1986), grammars of Sarcee (Cook 1984) and Slave (Rice 1989), a lexical phonological analysis of Sekani (Hargus 1988), an analysis of Halfway River Beaver morphology and phonology (Randoja 1989), a computerized dictionary of Ahtna (Kari 1990), and a recent functional grammar analysis of the Koyukon verb (Fortescue 1990).

In this paper I will summarize the conceptual framework I have applied to the Ahtna verb. Since 1973 I have been involved with a number of concurrent lexicographic projects in Alaska on Ahtna (Kari 1990), Dena'ina, Lower Tanana, and Koyukon (Jones, Axelrod, and Jetté forthcoming) and have done parallel field work in several other Athabaskan languages. My approach has developed in stages, and is a descendent of the approach to the Athabaskan verb launched by Sapir in the 1920s and advanced by Hoijer in the subsequent generation (e.g., Hoijer 1974). My approach is lexicographic in the sense that the theory and terminology have been shaped by the many interesting practical problems of representing the Athabaskan verb in dictionary formats.

Athabaskan linguistic history is interesting in itself (see Krauss 1986, for example). While there may be no consensus on certain points (such as what constitutes derivation vs. inflection), and serious flaws with some inherited terminology (e.g., *classifier prefixes,* or *deictic prefixes*), there is a general approach to the Athabaskan verb that has endured from earlier work. Table 1 presents some basic concepts that pertain to the Athabaskan verb.

Due to the pervasive positional rigidity of the affixes in the Athabaskan verb complex, the recent literature shows an intensification of interest in the templatic nature of Athabaskan languages. The abstract verb theme is the minimal specification of the verb as template (cf. Randoja 1989). On the other hand, the verb complex, once it is thoroughly explored, can be viewed as the maximally specified templatic expression of surface morphemes (cf. Kari

Table 1
Basic Terms Pertaining to the Athabaskan Verb

verb complex: a complete inventory of verbal affixes, with an explication of the linear order of morphemes (see table 2)

verb theme: the abstract lexical specification of a verb, including thematic prefixes, abstract root, transitivity, and theme category

verb base: a derivation of a verb theme, in abstract form, without full specification of inflectional affixes

verb composite: the fully specified abstract structures that underlies the phonetic verb form

derivative: a derived form of a verb theme

phonetic verb form

NOTE: This table follows, for example, Hoijer 1945, Sapir and Hoijer 1967, Hoijer 1974, Kari 1974, and Young and Morgan 1980.

1989). Furthermore, the verb phonology can be broken into several contrasting domains: For example, prefixes versus roots versus suffixes, or conjunct (inner) prefixes versus disjunct (outer) prefixes. Aspects of verb phonology can be treated coherently in terms of constraints on syllable structure within domains of the verb, (cf. Hargus 1988, Rice 1989, Randoja 1989). Leer (1989a) has recently extended the templatic analogy further by pointing out templatic properties of nouns that are partly congruent with verb structure. Also the abstract structure of the small set of directionals is a pared-down version of the verb complex, with a prefix slot, a root, and a set of suffixes (Leer 1989b).

In the course of integrating verbal affixes with roots in the *Ahtna Athabaskan Dictionary,* I tried to account for the relative position of the verbal affixes and the surface structure of fully inflected verbs (Kari 1989; 1990). The position class model for Ahtna in Kari 1989 and 1990 distinguishes twenty-seven distinct prefix positions before the root and four suffix positions after the root. (See table 2 in section 3 below.) I divide the prefixes into five zones. These zones allow for flexibility in characterizing the precise order of prefixes, which can vary in interesting ways in the daughter languages, as well as some new rubrics that are either more accurate as to function (e.g., a pronominal zone rather than a chimerical and misleading deictic position that has been ensconced in the Athabaskan literature, Kari 1989, 443, 447–48), or that are neutral to function (e.g., a qualifier zone).

Kari (1979, 58–62) presented a preliminary model of Ahtna word formation that sets forth some ideas about dynamic properties and derivational levels in the verb, from abstract verb theme to phonetic verb form. This model of Ahtna word formation is refined in Kari (1990:38–60) and is discussed here in sections 1 through 6. In the final section I summarize this approach and how it can be compared to and integrated with Young and Morgan's 1987 treatment of derivation and aspect in Navajo.

1. A MODEL OF AHTNA WORD FORMATION

The model of Ahtna word formation tries to address several general facts about the Ahtna (and Athabaskan) verb. We routinely see enormous derivational and inflectional productivity in sets of verbs. With practice, the linguist can assign derivatives to abstract verb themes. The underlying structure of the verb theme with thematic prefixes before a root and an abstract meaning is a recognizable template. Word composition is of the type called the interrupted synthesis (Sapir's term; see also Whorf 1932; 1956, 133; Kari 1989, 428)[1] of discontinuous strings of prefixes, a stem, and a suffix. These strings apply simultaneously and are, in the terms of Bauer (1988), synaffixes. In multiply derived verbs there has been a stacking of discontinuous strings, with precise interdigitation of the prefixes within the templatic structure of the verb theme.

There is adherence to a basically rigid linear surface ordering of the prefixes. The most frequently occurring prefixes appear as cumulative morphs. Zero morphemes and zero derivations are common and essential ingredients, while reduplication is not present as a grammatical process.

Figure 1 is a model of Ahtna word formation expressed as a flowchart. Twelve steps are distinguished, ordered from the abstract verb theme to the actual phonetic form. A single derived verb form, *nik'a'sngi'aas* 'we used to lift it up (n-class object such as ball or coiled rope)', is presented at the right to illustrate nine of the steps of the model.

Symbols on the flowchart are as follows: the abstract representation of verb theme, base, and underlying form are in parallelograms on the vertical line; obligatory derivations are in boxes on the vertical line; optional derivations are in circles to the right of the vertical line.

This model posits that affixes are added to verb themes in nine hierarchically ordered cycles (steps 1–9). Steps 2, 5, and 6 can optionally apply more than once and thus have a second line returning to the circle. The term *phonology* is placed to the right of steps 7 through 9 to symbolize cyclic alternation between morpheme insertion and the application of phonological rules (see (11) below).

There are four general divisions in the model, *lexicon* (steps 1–2), *derivation* (3–6), *inflection* (7–8), and *postinflectional lexicon* (PIL) (9). The Ahtna dictionary contains all the verb themes recorded to date (a total of 1386), but only a selection of the many possible derivatives of each theme. In addition, the dictionary contains all verbal affixes that are entered both as single morphemes and also, as is characteristic of Athabaskan morphology, as they occur in *strings,* in combination with other affixes. For example, the string in figure 1, *ni* + *k'a#* (i mom) 'up vertically' is listed under ni 1 in the dictionary. (Entries in the *Ahtna Athabaskan Dictionary* are alphabetized by the initial phoneme of a root or an affix.)

The symbol # denotes the disjunct boundary. The symbol + represents a morpheme boundary (also see table 2 in section 3 below). Verbal complements and postpositions that appear as separate words in a theme are separated by a space (word boundary). The symbol G indicates that the theme can take gender marking prefixes. An assumption of this approach is that at steps 1 or 2, there is an abstract notation for transitivity (±O), incorporation (inc), gender (G), but that specific derivational or inflectional prefixes are inserted in verbs at one of the later steps.

2. VERB THEMES AND THEME FORMATION

A verb theme entry consists of a root, a listing of thematic prefixes, and a marking for transitivity. Each theme also has a theme category label and a translation. Ahtna verb themes are assigned to twelve verb theme categories

Figure 1. A Model of Ahtna Word Formation

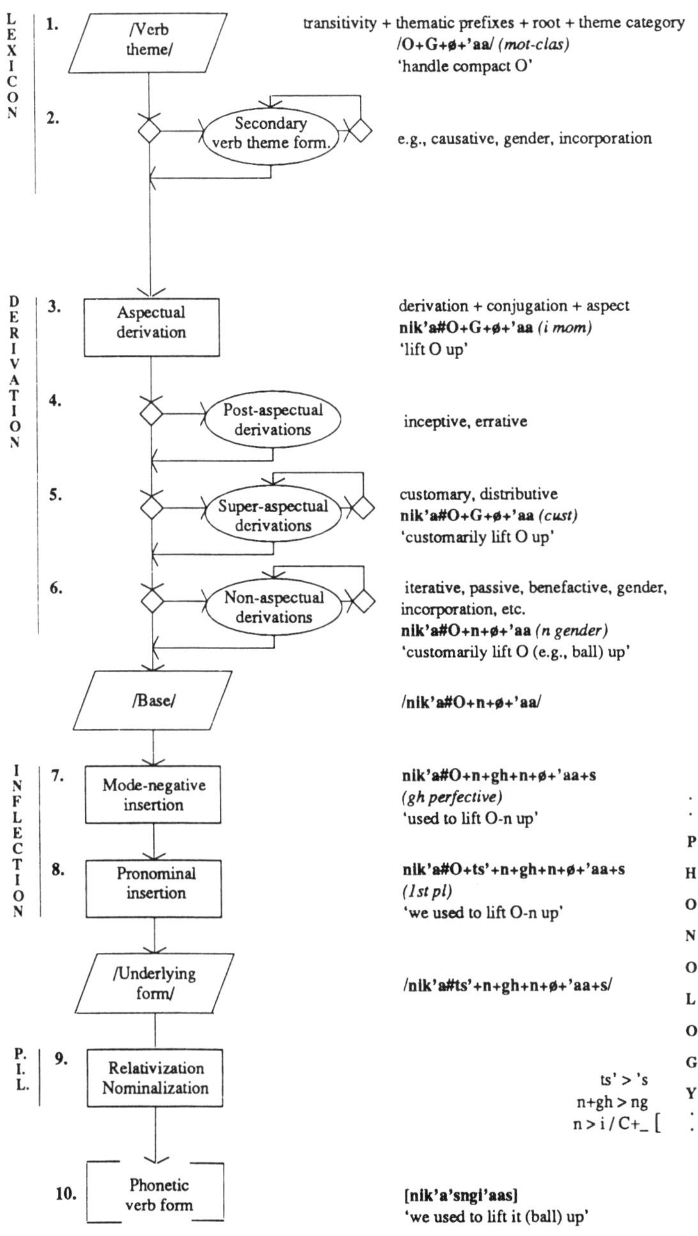

(Kari 1979). A verb theme category is a broad group of verb themes that has an identifiable semantic relationship and a common structure in the most basic derived verb forms. Verb theme categories have characteristic derivational potential—that is, the most homogeneous and productive theme categories, such as motion, successive, and extension, have sets of productive derivational strings common to that category. The Ahtna conjugation patterns and aspects are partly predictable from the categorization of the theme.

The symbols and prefixes cited before the root in verb theme entries convey information about thematic prefixes, transitivity or valence, the presence or absence of gender marking, and the relative order of these elements. Thematic prefixes are part of the structure of the theme and thus must be listed in the dictionary entry of the verb theme. They occur in all derived forms of the theme and cannot be explained as having been added by a productive derivational or inflectional process. The four classifiers—Ø, ł, D, and l—are always cited before the verb root.

To illustrate these concepts, consider one operative theme and one motion theme with two derivatives.

[1]	O + D + naan[2]	'(op) drink O'
	yatnaan'	'(durative) he drank it' /y + gh + n + 0 + D + naan + '/ /3ob + mode + perf + 3sb + cls + root + vsf/
	l + tset (mot)	'(sg) runs'
	'iltset	'(n momentaneous) he arrived running' /n + n + 0 + l + tset + n/ / mode + perf + 3sb + cls + root + vsf/

Operative themes are marked by a zero derivation in the durative aspect, which means something like 'verb performed over a span of time'. Motion themes are marked by a zero derivation in the momentaneous aspect, which means 'arrive'. There are interesting and significant distributional patterns with certain derivations: for example, motion themes can never take the durative aspect; the zero derivation 'arrive' cannot apply to operative themes. In addition to the categorized verb themes, uncategorized verb themes are posited to occur at step 3 of figure 1. The theory of Athabaskan verb theme categories has proved to be useful for grouping sets of derived verb forms, for determining the structure and meaning of the abstract verb theme, as well as for understanding Ahtna verb stem variation and aspect. See also Axelrod 1990, a detailed study of verb theme categories and aspect in Koyukon.

Frequently more than one verb theme is derived from the same root. A step for secondary verb theme formation is presented in step 2 in figure 1. In the terms of Fortescue (1990, personal communication) theme formation represents "true derivation." It is usually possible to recognize that one theme is more basic—that is, it is simpler in structure and broader in meaning, while other themes are more marked in structure and more restricted in meaning. Some attempt has been made to order themes in an entry to show theme/cotheme and theme/subtheme relationships. For example, subthemes with an incorporated subject or object (inc) are always placed after a more basic theme without an incorporate. The ordering of larger sets of themes, however, is not clear-cut. For example, with *(y)aa°* ('sg goes') are listed eighteen themes, the first of which is the most productive and general in meaning. The other themes are more restricted in meaning. Some are subthemes derived from the basic theme, while others are not derivable by any general rule of theme formation. In this case, the order of the eighteen themes conveys only a general notion of relationships between themes.

In the dictionary the abbreviation *ts* is used for theme formation strings. These are productive or semiproductive strings of prefixes that form predicates. My preliminary search has yielded fifty-four theme formation strings in Ahtna. For example, a half dozen transitive themes meaning 'follow O' (themes that include 'swim after O', 'paddle after O', 'chase O', '(sg) goes following O') are derived from intransitive themes and contain the n-qualifier prefix. Thus, a theme formation string, O + n 'follow O', can be extrapolated and entered in the dictionary as a theme formation string.

Some productive theme formation strings can become lexicalized in a subset of verb themes. For instance, in Ahtna a theme marked with *G* has gender prefixes inserted at step 6 in figure 1. The d-qualifier prefix is used to mark the gender of nouns such as wood, fire, spans of time, and words. On the other hand, certain themes in Ahtna have a lexicalized gender prefix. All verbs referring to smoke or fire have a thematic *d:* d + Ø + let 'fire smolders, smudge fire burns'. This *d* is inserted by a theme formation string: d 'thematized gender'.

Valence alternations and transitivity play an important role in theme formation. The causative is the single most prominent theme formation string. Hundreds of subthemes with the string O + ł are found, for example:

G + Ø + taan	'elongated object is in position'
O + G + ł + taan	'keep elongated O in position

Conversely, passive changes a transitive theme to intransitive. A typology of twenty-six patterns is presented in Kari (1990:47–49).

A theme marked with O is transitive; a theme without O is intransitive. By convention the abbreviations *O, P, I, comp,* and *inc* are cited in both the theme structure and the theme gloss. Both transitive and intransitive themes can occur with a thematic postposition or with a complement. The *k'* ('indefinite') prefix can appear as an inflectional direct object (in themes with O), or as an indefinite subject (symbolized as *I*), or it can be thematic. Similarly, *qo* 'area' can be a direct object, a subject, or it can be thematic.

Incorporated stems occur in a position in the disjunct portion of the verb complex, apparently in all Northern Athabaskan languages. In Ahtna about 13 percent (177) of all verb themes take one or more incorporated stems in this position in the verb complex. In [2] seven theme formation strings for verbs with an incorporated stem are illustrated. Each has a different transitivity pattern. Each example has a theme formation string, a theme, a derivative, the underlying form of the derivative (including zero morphemes), and an approximate gloss of the underlying morphemes.

[2] **a.** inc # Ø *(ts)* derived intransitive with incorporate as subject
ta # d + Ø + taan 'water drips'
natadghitaan 'water dripped down'
/na + ta # d + gh + n + Ø + Ø + taan + n/
/down + water # thematic + mode + perf + 3sb + cls + root + vsf/

b. inc # Ø *(ts)* derived intransitive with incorporate of manner or instrument
łi # Ø + yaa° '(sg) goes hunting with dogs'
tiłiniyaa 'he went out hunting with dogs'
/ti + łi # n + n + Ø + Ø + yaa + n/
/out + dog # mode + perf + 3sb + cls + root + vsf/

c. P + inc # *(ts)* derived intransitive with thematic instrumental incorporate and thematic postposition
P + qe # ł + qay 'strike P with the foot, kick P'
iqełqas 'he kicked him once'
/y + qe # z + Ø + Ø + ł + qay + ?/
/3pob + foot # perf + mode + 3sb + cls + root + vsf/

d. inc # Ø *(ts)* derived transitive with incorporated object (regular O is absent)
inc # G + Ø + taan 'handle (inc) elongated object'
nixałnitaan 'he stopped the sled'
/ni + xał # n + n + Ø + Ø + taan + n/
/stop + sled # mode + perf + 3sb + cls + root + vsf/

e. P + inc #ł *(ts)* derived transitive with incorporated object and thematic postpositional object
P + na + se #ł + k'el 'tear skin off P'
inasełk'el 'he tore the skin off of it'
/y + na + se # z + Ø + Ø + ł + k'el + n/
/3ob + ? + skin # mode + perf + 3sb + cls + root + vsf/

f. inc # O + G + Ø *(ts)* derived transitive with incorporated subject
inc # O + G + Ø + taan '(inc) causes elongated O to move'
qetaydeztaan 'water caused it (y, log) to drift ashore'
/qe + ta # y + d + z + Ø + Ø + Ø + taan + n/
/ashore + water # 3ob + gender + mode + perf + 3sb + cls + root + vsf/

g. inc # O + ł derived transitive with incorporate of manner or instrument
łi # O + ł + tae 'hunt O with dogs'
niłi'niłtaen 'he cornered something with dogs'
/ni + łi # k' + n + n + Ø + ł + tae + n/
/stop + dogs # indef + mode + perf + 3sb + cls + root + vsf/

Verb theme formation is a promising area for future research in Athabaskan languages. I anticipate a better understanding of the "syntax of lexcial word formation" (Hale 1989) or "true derivation" (Fortescue 1990)—for example, the ways in which valence changes and incorporation intersect with other theme formation processes; refinements in the morphological and semantic relationships between sets of themes, and a better understanding of the relationship between productive and lexicalized derivations.[3]

3. FOUR PATTERNS OF DERIVATION

As noted in figure 1, the abstract verb theme lacks mode and aspect marking and other derivational and inflectional material. Information is supplied to verb themes by the addition of prefixes and suffixes in a series of derivations. This powerful feature of Athabaskan word formation is what Fortescue (1990) terms extended derivation; he also suggests a principle of the "centrifugal application of expression rules." In my model I distinguish four types of derivation in Ahtna that give form to the underlying verb base: aspectual, postaspectual, superaspectual, and nonaspectual. This results in the verb base, which is defined as the derived word, without the array of inflectional prefixes that mark mode, subject, and object. Note that the verb base is employed in the entry structure of Young and Morgan (1980; 1987) and is alphabetized by the leftmost morpheme. The verb base can be thought of as a boundary between derivation and inflection.

A verb theme must take one aspectual derivation to gain some specific meaning. This derivation adds a set of prefixes and stem suffixes that mark mode and aspect. If we compare, for example, a theme and some of its possible derivatives, the distinctions between theme, derivation, verb base, and derived verb form (or derivative) can be isolated.

[3] verb theme: O + G + Ø + 'aa (*mot-clas*) 'handle compact O'

derivation1:	ni + k'a#i (*ads: i mom*)	'up vertically'
verb base:	/ni + k'a#O + G + i + (i mom) + Ø+'aa/	
verb form:	nik'ayi'aan	'he lifted it (hat) up'
derivation2:	P + la + q'e# (*ads: gh mom*)	'into the hand of p'
verb base:	/P + la + q'e#O + G + (gh mom) + Ø + 'aa/	
verb form:	ilaq'eyghi'aan	'he handed it (hat) to him'

The examples in [3] have as inflectional prefixes a third person singular subject (Ø = he, she, it) and the perfective mode, which is marked differently in each verb. Several basic distinctions in derivational processes in Ahtna have been found. Most derivational strings are mutually exclusive—that is, it is not possible to combine 'up vertically' and 'into the hand of P' into a single derivation. Furthermore, most (but not all) derivational strings require the same mode and aspect prefixes in all derivatives. In [3] 'up vertically' always has an i-perfective prefix and the momentaneous aspect and 'into the hand of P' always has a gh-perfective prefix and the momentaneous aspect.

The momentaneous is one of twenty-two morphologically distinct aspects in Ahtna that are detected in Athabaskan languages by the analysis of suffixation patterns in verb stem sets—the verb stems that occur in the four modes: imperfective, perfective, future, and optative (Kari 1979; 1990; Hardy 1979).[4]

If we experiment further with the first of these examples, we can find more derivative verbs without changing these inflectional prefixes:

[4]	nik'anayi'aan	'he lifted it (hat) up again' *(iterative)*
	nik'aytez'aan	'he started to lift it up' *(inceptive)*
	nik'aynest'aan	'he mistakenly lifted it (hat) up' *(errative)*
	nik'aydit'aan	'he lifted it (hat) up for his own benefit' *(benefactive)*
	nik'anyiz'aan	'he lifted them (hats) up one at a time' *(distributive)*
	nik'ayghi'aas	'he used to lift it (hat) up' *(customary)*
	nik'aydi'aan	'he lifted it (block of wood) up' (*d*-gender)
	nik'ayni'aan	'he lifted it (berry, coiled rope) up' (*n*-gender)
	nik'aqu'aan	'he lifted it (house) up' *(qo-gender)*
	nik'a'it'aan	'it (hat) was lifted up' *(passive)*

Each of the above derivatives has combined the derivation *nik'a* 'up vertically' with one other derivation. Moreover, it is possible to form other derivatives with 'up vertically' as well as combinations of two and three other derivations, which are noted herewith:

[5]	nik'anaydi'aan	'he lifted it (block) up again' *(iterative, gender)*
	nik'anaydit'aan	'he lifted it (block) up again for his own benefit' *(iterative, benefactive)*

nik'anayghi'aas	'he used to lift it (hat) up over and over' *(iterative, customary)*
nik'anaydghi'aas	'he used to lift it (block) up over and over' *(iterative, gender, customary)*
nik'aniidez'aan	'he lifted them (blocks) up one at a time" *(distributive, gender)*
nik'aniidest'aan	'he lifted them (blocks) up one at a time for his own benefit' *(distributive, gender, benefactive)*
nik'anaynest'aan	'he mistakenly lifted it (hat) up again' *(iterative, errative)*

Thus we find enormous derivational productivity that we must address in the model as well as the format of a dictionary. Young and Morgan (1980) demonstrate that it is possible, in a noncomputerized book, to list a large selection of verb bases in an Athabaskan language.

These facts have led us to posit that the first obligatory derivation that applies to a verb theme is an aspectual derivation (step 3 in figure 1). An aspectual derivational string, such as *nik'a # (i mom)* 'up vertically', is a bundle (or formula) of discontinuous prefixes and suffixes. The disjunct derivational prefixes *ni* + *k'a* are added, and the set of potential inflectional affixes for mode and aspect is indicated by the i-momentaneous marking—that is, there will be an i-prefix in the conjugation zone and a bundle of four aspect suffixes. In other words, stem sets reveal aspect and from these we can recognize the bundle of underlying suffixes that attach to the root. The two momentaneous suffixation patterns in Ahtna are shown here:

[6]						
	CVV roots:	s	n	ł	ł	
	CV(V)C roots:	L	n	ł	L	(L = vowel lengthening)

More than 250 of these mutually exclusive aspectual derivational strings (ADS) have been found in Ahtna to date. Most of these strings contain one to four prefixes, and there are a few with six and seven prefixes. There are six zero derivations in Ahtna with no prefix. The ADSs are listed at least once in the main entries by the initial sound of the leftmost prefix in the string as well as in an appendix. Aspectual derivational strings are marked [ads], and the aspect the string takes is given in parentheses: for example, *nik'a # (ads:i mom)* 'up vertically'. Many of the derivational strings are typically found with specific theme categories. For example, 'up vertically' and 'into the hand of P' can be added to many motion themes. Also the productivity of a verb theme can be measured by the number of ADSs that can apply to it. For example, the theme 'handle compact O' (in figure 1) is one of the most productive themes in any Athabaskan language.

The simplest aspectual derivational strings, the six that have no prefix plus several others, are fundamental to the typology of aspects. These primary aspectual strings (PAS) (Kari 1979, 64–76) are diagnostic of some of the theme categories and form links between the semantics of groups of verb themes, the distribution of morphemes for conjugation and aspect, and fundamental meaning contrasts between aspects such as durative, conclusive, and momentaneous. (Two of these PASs were illustrated above in [1].)

Another feature of this theory is the status of the uncategorized verb theme. These are defective themes in that they have a specific ADS for mode and aspect in the underlying form. Referring back to figure 1, an uncategorized theme is at step 3 in its underlying form. About 12 percent of the 1368 Ahtna verb themes are treated as uncategorized, and a similar percentage has been found in Koyukon. For example, *O + u + Ø +* niik 'grab O' is treated as *u:s mom,* an uncategorized *s*-momentaneous. All derivatives are s-momentaneous, and other ADSs are not possible. Since theme categories are general morphosemantic classes of verbs, this type of theme represents a lexicalization of the ADS as a word formation mechanism.

Two strings in Ahtna, the inceptive and the errative, have a slightly different status than the ADS. I have termed these postaspectual derivational strings.

[7] nik'aytez'aan 'he started to lift it up'
nik'aynest'aan 'he mistakenly lifted it (hat) up'

In these two cases t (s) and n (s) D are added after an ADS. The tense-mode prefixes shift, however, stem suffixation is not altered. (In Kari 1979, 92–93 I termed these supermomentaneous strings.)

It is relevant here to compare a single cognate string in Ahtna and Navajo, the inchoative. In Ahtna the inchoative is a string *P # d + n (i mom).* It is found only as an ADS (e.g., qetnibaen 'he is beginning to swim', k'etnitnaan' 'he is beginning to drink something'). It is not postaspectual like the inceptive and errative because it cannot be combined with another ADS. However, according to Young and Morgan (1987, 187–88), the Navajo inchoative string, which is quite close to the Ahtna string in structure and in meaning, *P # 'i + n* (ii mom), is what they call a subaspect. The Navajo inchoative can co-occur with other ADSs (e.g., habi'niigeed 'I started to dig it out'). This form is built on a more basic momentaneous derivation, háágeed 'I dug it out'. Thus the Navajo inchoative offers comparative support for a step of postaspectual derivation. We see cognate strings applying at different steps in two daughter languages, which sheds light on the stacking of derivations.

The term *superaspect* was first presented in Kari (1979, 93–99) with discussion of the customary, distributive, and progressive in Ahtna and with reference to the multiple and the conative in Koyukon.

A layering of three strings can be shown in the following four examples. Note that verb stem sets are listed in the four modes:

[8] **a.** diighiłtl'iit' 'he poured it (tea) into a container'
/di # y + gh + n + Ø + ł + tl'iit' + n/
/into # 3ob + mode + perf + 3sb + cls + root + vsf/
(gh momentaneous) tl'iit tl'iit' tl'eł tl'iit

b. dinyiłtl'iit' 'he poured it into (pl) containers'
/di + n # y + z + Ø + Ø +ł + tl'iit' + n/
/into + dist # 3ob + mode + perf + 3sb + cls + root + vsf/
(distributive) tl'iit tl'iit' tl'iit tl'iit

c. diighiłtl'et 'he customarily poured it into it'
/di # y + gh + n + Ø +ł + tl'iit' + s/
/into # 3ob + mode + perf + 3sb + cls + root + vsf/
(momentaneous-customary) tl'et tl'et tl'et tl'et

d. diniighiłtl'iit 'he customarily poured it into containers'
/di + n # y + gh + n + Ø +ł + tl'iit' + s + E/ (E = vowel expansion)
/into + dist # 3ob + mode + perf + 3sb + clas + vsf + vsf/
(mom − dist − cust) tl'iit tl'iit tl'iit tl'iit

The verbs in [8b] and [8c] have one superaspect added on top of the ADS. The example in [8d] is doubly derived—by both the distributive and the customary. Each example has a different stem set, which is an indication of distinct stem suffixation in each aspect or superaspect.

On the other hand, when the *na-* 'iterative, again' prefix is introduced, the tense-mode prefixes do *not* change (e.g., *nik'anayi'aan* 'he lifted it (hat) up again', *ilaq'enayghi'aan* 'he handed it (hat) to him again'). *Na-* 'iterative' does not require its own perfective prefix. Thus, the 'iterative' can be viewed as a *nonaspectual derivational string* (NDS) (step 6 in figure 1) in that it does not alter conjugation and aspect. These strings are marked as [*nds*] in the main entries.

Fifteen nonaspectual derivational strings have been found in Ahtna. As shown in [4] and [5] above, many of these NDSs can co-occur, which can create numerous derived verb bases. Indeed, the principle seems to be that lack of selection of conjugation prefixes and aspect suffixes facilitates this recursion. The NDSs are illustrated in table 2. At the top of this table is a list of the affix positions and zones in the Ahtna verb complex, with their abbreviations. Each prefix in the NDS is placed on table 2 in its position to convey how the prefixes can interdigitate or accumulate within the linear order of the verb complex. The insertions of incorporated stems and gender prefixes are also treated as nonaspectual derivations. Some other derivations such as the passive and reciprocal have been treated as NDSs, but might also be argued to be inflectional processes. Also I should point out that I can't make any

Table 2
Ahtna Nonspectual Derivational Strings

11		10	9	8	7	6	5						4						3				2	1	stem	
B	A	C B A					F	E	D	C	B	A	F	E	D	C	B	A	D	C	B	A				
pob		der/th					pronominal						qualifier						conjugation						stem	
$3p_a$	pob	der/th	iter	dist	inc	th #	3y	dob	1p	indf	th	$3p_i$ =	area/qual	con	icp	qual	qual	qual %	trn	spn	mode	prf	subj [	clas	root + vsf	
																								D/ł		passive
																	Ø									Ø-gender
																	n									n-gender
																d										d-gender
					da											d										verbally
													qo													area gender
																d								D/ł		reflexive
	Ø +	pp														(d)								D/ł		indirect reflexive
																d								D/ł		benefactive
		xa														d								D/ł		for oneself
								nił																D/ł		reciprocal
		na																						(D/ł)		iterative
					kin'											d								ł		pretending to V
P					kin'											d								ł		pretending to V at P
					inc																					incorporate insertion

Table 2 (*continued*)
Ahtna Nonaspectual Derivational Strings

	##	word boundary
	+	morpheme boundary
11B	$3p_2$	second third person plural subject
11A	pob	postpositional object
10C–A	der/th	derivational/thematic
9	iter	iterative
8	dist	distributive
7	inc	incorporate
6	th	thematic
	#	disjunct boundary
5F	3y	third person plus *y*
5E	dob	direct object
5D	1p	first person plural subject
5C	indf	indefinite object-subject
5B	th	thematic
fA	$3p_1$	first third person plural subject
	=	pronominal-qualifier boundary
4F	area/qual	areal subject-object/q-qualifier
4E	con	conative
4D	icp	inceptive
4C	qual	d-qualifier
4B	qual	n-qualifier
4A	qual	gh/z-qualifiers
	%	qualifier-conjugation boundary
3D	trn	transitional
3C	spn	s-perfective-negative
3B	mode	mode
3A	prf	perfective
2	subj	subject
	[	(C)STEM boundary
1	clas	classifier
0	root	root
1–3	vsf	verb suffixes 1–3

NOTE: This table follows Kari (1989; 1990, 40–41).

particular case for the ordering of steps 4 through 6 of figure 1 internal to one another.[5]

4. INFLECTION

In the Athabaskan literature there is no consistent and precise policy regarding the parameters of inflection. In Ahtna I analyze twenty-four distinct prefix-suffix combinations to mark mode negativity (e.g., s-perfective, i-perfective, perfective-negative, optative, optative-negative). Intransitive verbs inflected for six subjects and mode can typically appear in forty-eight-member paradigms. Transitive verbs can take up to thirteen objects and can read out to paradigms of over five-hundred members. Through the course of steps 3 through 5 in figure 1 there is a filtering or winnowing down of sets of conjugation prefixes and aspect suffixes to give rise to the myriad of inflectional choices that we can assume are specified by the phrase structure.

I have separated mode-negative insertion and subject-object insertion into two steps in figure 1. I treat mode negativity in Ahtna as being marked by eight prefixes that occur in six positions as well as by nine suffixes in two suffix positions. Mode-negative conjugations are marked by discontinuous strings of prefixes and suffixes that I assume apply simultaneously, as in the following third person progressives:

[9]	*prog*	gh + ł	aqaeł	'he is going in a boat'
	prog-neg	z + gh + ł + e	asquaele	'he is not going in a boat'

Subject and object inflection (including postpositional objects) is marked in Ahtna by thirty-two prefixes in nine distinct positions. Many of these prefixes are the same abstract morpheme occurring in separate positions. Most of the subject-object affixes are single autonomous prefixes. (However a discontinuous pronoun can be found in some languages—e.g., Sekani *s-ìd* '1st dual'; Hargus 1988). Also in Northern Athabaskan languages the '3rd pl' subject occurs in a "floating position" depending on the presence or absence of the *y* '3 sg object', a very interesting problem in the linearization of surface morphemes (Kari 1989, 443).

It might be suggested for Ahtna that mode-negative and pronominal prefixes are added at a single step. However, in many Athabaskan languages, such as Navajo, there is radical allomorphy in the subject pronoun sets in perfective versus nonperfective paradigms. For this allomorphy I am attracted to the idea of assigning mode at one step and then adding the appropriate form of the pronoun at a later step. For example, a first person singular nonperfective and perfective of 'dig O' in Navajo might be derived thus:

[10] 1 O + Ø + geed (mot) 'dig O'
3 ha#O + (gh) + Ø + geed 'dig O out' gh-mom
7 ha#Ø + Ø + gééd O-imperf ha#Ø + gh + n + Ø + geed gh-perf
8 ha#sh + Ø + géėd 1sg ha#gh + n + í + Ø + geed 1sg
haashgééd 'I am digging it out' háágeed 'I dug out'

Here two different first person singular pronouns (*sh* or *í*) are added at step 8, eliminating what I treated as a nonphonological pronoun readjustment rule (or sh-deletion rule; Kari 1976, 172–73). Fortescue (1990) attaches inflectional affixes and gender agreement via "expression rules."

5. POSTINFLECTIONAL LEXICON

Rice (1985) has observed that nominalized verbs in Slave must be formed by a word formation process that applies after regular inflection. This holds true for Ahtna nominalized and relativized verbs as well.

From these examples of 'cut O' we find that verb suffixes that relativize or nominalize (*-i* 'nonhuman', *-en* 'sg human', *-ne* 'pl humans') can be built on virtually any multiply derived form, in various aspects and inflections.

[11]	k'et'aasen	'the one who is cutting' *(relativized durative)*
	'ele' k'est'aazen	'the one who isn't cutting' *(relativized durative, negative)*
	k'et'asne	'the ones who customarily cut' *(relativized customary)*
	st'asi	'that which has been cut once' *(relativized passive, semelfactive)*
	at'aats'i	'that which has been cut repeatedly' *(relativized passive, durative)*
	'ele' qay'tnit'asi	'that which you did not cut into pieces' *(relativized momentaneous, perfective-negative)*
	tl'ogh u'eł t'aasi	'scythe; *lit. 'with it grass is cut' (nominalized durative, passive)*
	dinaat'aats'i	'diced meat; *lit. 'that which has been repeatedly cut into (container)' (nominalized momentaneous, passive)*

A level of postinflectional lexicon (PIL) in step 9 of figure 1 addresses the fact that nominalization/relativization can occur following various preceding routes of derivation and inflection. This reflects Fortescue's (1990) term, *recycling back into the fund,* a process that is notoriously flexible in Eskimo languages, and that occurs in Athabaskan under more delimited circumstances.

There is also a phonological argument that relative suffixation follows negative suffixation in Ahtna. Contrast the first two examples in [11] 'cut O' with the basic positive and negative in [12].

[12]	k'et'aas	'he is cutting'
	'ele' k'est'aaze	'he isn't cutting'

The negative suffix *e* triggers voicing of the stem final fricative *s,* whereas the relative suffix *i* does not. Derivations of the first two examples of 'cut O', a positive and a negative, attest to level ordering of these processes: (1) e (negative) insertion and (2) fricative voicing, followed by (3) i (relative) insertion and (4) e (negative) deletion.

[13]			
		/k' + t'aas/	/k' + t'aas/
	neg insert	—	k' + s + t'aas + e
	fric voic	—	k' + s + t'aaz + e
	rel insert	k' + t'aas + en	k' + s + t'aaz + e + en
	e-del	—	k' + s + t'aaz + en
	ultimately	[k'et'aasen]	[k'est'aazen]
		'the one who is cutting'	'the one who isn't cutting'

6. REVIEW OF THE MODEL OF AHTNA WORD FORMATION

Table 3 is a summary of the formal distinctions in steps and types of strings presented in figure 1.

To review the model, I present in tables 4 and 5 several sample derivations. In table 4 the separate steps are contrasted. The numbers on the left of the table refer to the steps in figure 1. The table has four derivatives of four different verb themes with the root *taan* 'classify elongated object'. Morphemes that have been added at a step are underlined.

The themes in columns A and B at step 1 are the basic intransitive stative-classificatory and transitive motion-classificatory themes, both of which can occur in many thousands of derivatives. Secondary theme formation is illustrated in column C at step 2 by a subtheme with an incorporated stem *(inc)* as direct object, 'handle (inc) elongated object'. Also at step 2 in column D, the theme 'steer O' has three thematic prefixes beyond that of the basic transitive theme. It has a theme formation string of the shape *x # gh* that applies to themes that are held, attached, constrained, or tethered at one end (Kari 1989, 441–42).

Each of the themes has an aspectual derivation apply at step 3. The theme in A has a zero derivation (with no overt derivational prefix) and the s-neuter aspect whereas the three other themes have derivations with a disjunct prefix and a specific aspect. In this model I posit that derivational prefixes and an array of prefixes and suffixes for conjugation and aspect are added at step 3, but that a specific set of prefixes and suffixes for mode is not selected until step 7. The theme in column B is shown at step 4 taking a postaspectual derivation, the inceptive. This adds *t (s-perfective)* to the verb while the aspect remains momentaneous. The theme in column C is altered at step 5 to illustrate a superaspectual derivation, the customary. In this case, customary stem suffixation will supplant the momentaneous suffixation that had been added to this verb at step 3. Three nonaspectual derivations are presented at step 6. In column A, a d-prefix is added because a subject that is wooden and takes d-gender is presumed (e.g., 'stick is . . . '). In column C, the stem *xaɫ* 'sled' is used here to illustrate one of a list of potential incorporated stems ('stick', 'gun', 'cane', 'snowshoe') that could appear in this subtheme. In

Table 3
Properties of Strings of Morphemes

Step

1–2 Theme formation strings (TS)
- a. create predicates, assign valence/transitivity
- b. lack specific prefixes/suffixes for mode/aspect
- c. some recursion is possible

3 Aspectual derivational strings (ADS)
- a. obligatory derivation
- b. assigns a set of prefixes/suffixes for mode/aspect
- c. all ADSs are mutually exclusive
- d. primary aspectual strings, the simplest ADSs, are diagnostic of theme categories
- e. uncategorized verb themes are ADSs that have been lexicalized

4 Postaspectual derivational strings (PDS)
- a. inherit an ADS
- b. add one or more derivational prefixes and shift mode prefix but do not alter the aspectual suffixation of the ADS

5 Superaspectual derivational strings (SDS)
- a. inherit an ADS
- b. add zero or one derivational prefix, shift the mode prefix, and supplant the suffixation of the ADS
- c. recursion of SDS is possible

6 Nonaspectual derivational strings (NDS)
- a. inherit an ADS
- b. add one or more derivational prefixes or an incorporated stem, but do not shift mode prefixes or aspectual suffixes assigned by ADS, PDS, or SDS.
- c. recursion of NDS is possible

7–8 Inflectional strings
- a. insert strings of mode-negative prefixes and aspect suffixes appropriate to ADS and other strings and to phrase structure
- b. insert individual subject-object pronouns appropriate to phrase structure

9 Relativization/nominalization (postinflectional lexicon)
- a. inherit and recycle all derivational affixes by ADS and other strings as well as inflectional affixes and phonology appropriate to inflection
- b. add a suffix in one of the rightmost positions in the verb complex

column D, the iterative derivation is shown, which introduces a disjunct prefix, *na*. The underlying verb bases for the four verbs are given between steps 6 and 7. Here all derivational prefixes are specified, and the aspects have been assigned, but the particular prefix-suffix selections for mode and person have not yet been determined. Specific prefixes and suffixes for mode are added to each verb at step 7. Note that a negative form is shown in column C. At step 8 subject and object pronoun prefixes are selected. In step 9, after

Table 4
Four Verb Themes and four Derivatives

Step	A	B	C	D
1.	/G+Ø+taan/(stat-clas) 'elongated-O is'	/0+G+Ø+taan/(mot-clas) 'handle elongated O'		
2.			/inc+Ø+taan/ (mot) 'handle inc. elongated O'	/x#O+n+gh+Ø+taan/ (mot) 'steer O'
3.	G+Ø+Ø+taan (s neu) 'elongated O is'	na#O+G+Ø+taan (gh mom) 'put elongated O down'	ni+inc#Ø+taan (n mom) 'stopping inc'	łu+x#O+n+gh+Ø+taan (per) 'steer O around'
4.		na#O+t+Ø+taan (inceptive, s-perf) 'start to put elongated O down'		
5.			ni+inc#Ø+taan (customary) 'customarily stop inc'	

6.	d+Ø+taan (d. gender) 'elongated d-O (wood) is'		ni+xał#Ø+taan 'sled' 'cust. stop sled'	łu+na+x#O+n+gh+Ø+taan (iterative) 'steer O around again'
	/d+Ø+taan/	/na#O+t+Ø+taan/	/ni+xał#Ø+taan/	/łu+na+x#O+n+gh+Ø+taan/
7.	d+z+Ø+taan+n (s-imperf. neuter) 'elongated d-O is'	na#O+t+z+Ø+taan+n (s-perf) 'started to put elongated O down'	ni+xał#z+Ø+taan+s (O-imperf -neg) 'not cust. stops sled'	łu+na+x#O+t+n+gh+gh+Ø+taan+ł (future) 'will steer O around again'
8.	d+z+Ø+Ø+taan+n (3 sg.) 'it d-O is'	na#k'+t+z+i+Ø+taan+n (indef + 2 sg.) 'you started to put something down'	ni+xał#z+es+Ø+taan+s+e (1 sg-neg) 'I don't cust. stop sled'	łu+na+x#y+t+n+gh+gh+Ø+Ø+taan+ł (3y + 3 sg) 'he will steer it around again'
9.	d+z+Ø+Ø+taan+n+i 'that which is'			
	/d+z+taan+n+i/ e Ø	/na#k'+t+z+i+taan+n/ y'i Ø	/ni+xał#z+es+taan+s+e/ ii tiige	/łu+na+x#y+t+n+gh+gh+taan+ł/ ii ng a tiił
10.	[deztaani]: 'that which is (wood)'	[nay'tizitaan] 'you started to put something (gun) down'	[nixałiistiige] 'I don't cust. stop a sled'	[łunaxiitngatiił] 'he will steer it around again'

Table 5
Three Derivatives of 'steer O'

Step	A	B	C
1.		/O + Ø + taan/	
2.		/x#O + n + gh + taan/	
3.	łu + x#O + n + gh + Ø + taan	sta + x#O + n + gh + Ø + taan	qe + x#O + u + n + gh + Ø + taan + gh
4.		sta + x#O + n + gh + D + taan + n	
6.	łu + na + x#O + n + gh + Ø + taan	sta + na + x#O + n + gh + D + taan	qe + na + x#O + u + n + gh + Ø + taan
7.	łu + na + x#O + n + gh + n + i + Ø + taan + n	sta + na + x#O + n + gh + z + D + taan + n	qe + na + x#O + u + n + gh + z + Ø + taan + n
8.	łu + na + x#ts' + n + gh + n + i + taan + n	sta + na + x#ts' + n + gh + z + D + taan + n	qe + na + x#ts' + u + n + gh + z + taan + n
10.	[łunax'snginitaan] 'we were steering it around again'	[stanax'sngestaan] 'we got lost steering it again'	[qenaxts'ungeztaan] 'we managed to steer it to a place again'

inflection has taken place, an i-relative suffix is added to the verb in column A. The underlying forms and output of phonological rules are given between steps 9 and 10.

By way of further review, table 5 presents three other derivatives of the theme 'steer O'. In this table three different ADS apply at step 3, one PDS applies at step 4, and the same derivations apply at steps 6, 7, and 8. The morphemes added at each step are italicized.

Since 'steer O' has three thematic prefixes plus an object slot, this is an appropriate theme with which to illustrate the twofold principles of interdigitation and accumulation. We assume here that 'steer O' is based on a simpler transitive theme shown here at step 1 and that *x # gh* are added at step 2. However, the n-prefix in the theme 'steer O' is not accounted for by a productive theme formation string. At step 3 three different ADS are exemplified. In columns A and B prefixes are added only in the leftmost position. In column C the string *qe # u + gh* (ss mom) 'arriving with difficulty at a destination' contains a disjunct prefix and two conjunct prefixes. The u (conative) prefix is placed between the object slot and *n*. However, both the theme and the string have the same prefix, the *gh* 'qualifier', which occurs in position 4A of the verb complex. Only one *gh* is overtly marked, a typical example of a cumulative morph. Similarly, at step 4 in column B, the errative string *n + D* contains an n-qualifier prefix, whereas the theme already contains the same *n* prefix. The three subsequent steps, 6, 7, and 8, are the same: iterative, perfective-positive (A is an n-perfective, whereas B and C are s-perfectives), and first person plural subject.

Although it is not relevant to this paper, details about the phonology of the three forms in table 5 could be presented. For example, the s-form of the mode prefix in column B is a sure test that the errative derivation has applied at step 4. In this case the *n* is cumulative, the z-mode prefix has devoiced before *D*, and the *D* has been deleted. In Athabaskan languages circuitous accounts of arcane phonetic or morphological detail are routine. It also appears that several boundaries internal to the verb complex are needed to account for certain morphophonemic alternations (Kari 1989; 1990, 650–69).

7. DISCUSSION

There is no space here to discuss the recent literature on Athabaskan word formation. Briefly, the model presented in Kari (1990) for Ahtna treats several aspects of the Athabaskan verb complex and word formation that have not been addressed in the early or recent sources.

It seems that the most appropriate characterization of word formation for an Athabasakan language involves the stacking and interdigitation of strings of affixes within the underlying verb theme. Access to the underlying template of the verb complex must be available. Strings of morphemes, either verb themes or derivational or inflectional strings, are entered in the lexicon to reflect their mutual order, just as in *Ahtna Athabaskan Dictionary*.

The verb complex is treated as a fully specified morphological template. The surface and underlying order in the Ahtna verb complex has been analyzed to a greater degree than in other languages, and specific subpositions in the verb complex are explicitly pursued and formalized. If consistent criteria are applied, most Athabaskan languages have twenty and more distinct prefix positions. Morpheme insertion rules can't waffle when it comes to the interesting ordering relationships within, for example, the qualifier zone. We need to recognize all distinct positions and subpositions in the verb complex to account for stringlike morpheme insertion with accuracy and flexibilty.

The stringlike nature of Athabaskan word formation is formally recognized and is present at most steps of the model. Prefixes and suffixes are assumed to apply simultaneously and to interdigitate or, if they are repeated, to accumulate as cumulative morphs. In contrast, Randoja (1989) treats most morpheme insertion by means of the addition of individual positions of prefixes (although not in a strict right-to-left order) with some allowance for co-ocurrence by links between positions.

An attempt is made to define and then to research the hierarchical ordering of classes of derivations and morpheme insertion cycles based on several facts about the stringlike derivations, such as effect on suffixation and prefixation, and co-occurrence versus mutual exclusivity. Evidence has been presented for some distinct tiers of morpheme insertion with recursion at some steps. The morpheme insertion cycles do not directly correspond to the linear order of affixes. Here the model has a number of gray areas. In might be said that this Ahtna model has too many distinct steps—for example, inflection occurs at a single step. Also refinements in the internal ordering of steps 4 through 6 may be possible (see note 6).

The distinctions in the model—theme formation, aspectual, postaspectual, superaspectual, nonaspectual derivations, and postinflectional word formation—seem to be valid for other Athabaskan languages, such as Navajo. The Young and Morgan grammar and dictionary of Navajo (1980; 1987) provides a vast data base for the study of word formation processes. I note the following points for comparison:

1. Many of the most common theme formation strings are the same in Ahtna and Navajo. The Navajo verb lacks incorporation either in theme formation or as a derivational process.

2. Navajo has a larger battery of aspectual derivational strings, some of which are directly cognate in northern languages. The aspect system, especially as described in Hardy 1979, is probably 80 percent congruent with those in northern languages.

3. The Navajo distributive is a superaspect and is secondary to an ADS, just as in northern languages. The Navajo usitative is cognate with the custom-

ary superaspect in the north, but since it is not inflected in a full paradigm, it can be treated as a fifth mode in Navajo.

4. Navajo has several more postaspectual derivations and nonaspectual derivations than has been attested for Ahtna—for example, the seriative and inchoative (PDS) and semeliterative (NDS).[6]

5. Navajo inflection is very similar to Ahtna, but neuter verbs are inflected only in one paradigm and verb internal negative morphology is absent.

6. Navajo has a tier of postinflectional word formation for nominalizations and relativizations.

A NONCONFIGURATIONAL APPROACH TO MORPHOLOGY

Renate Raffelsiefen

INTRODUCTION

In this article I will take issue with the claim that morphologically complex words are most adequately represented in terms of hierarchically arranged elements. Most generative linguists take this to be a matter of course:

> Evidence that a labeled tree representation is necessary for affixed words is provided not only by the intuitions of native speakers concerning the internal structure of words, but also by processes which interpret these structures, be they semantic or phonological. As SPE demonstrated, for instance, the internal structure of a word may determine in part its accentual properties. [Selkirk 1982, 67]

By contrast, I will argue that morphological operations are best analyzed as functions, that is, as relations between meaningful phonological expressions in the tradition of Categorial Grammar.

Introducing and comparing the different frameworks will be the topic of section 1. In section 2 I will address a phenomenon that poses difficulty for tree representations, namely cases where one morphological operation can be shown to be sensitive to another one. Investigating such cases sheds new light on an issue that inevitably comes up as soon as one enters the realm of English word formation: the distinction between stress-neutral and stress-determining affixes.

Section 3 sets out to challenge the adequacy of tree representations from a more theoretical perspective. The configurational approach allows for the possibility of affixes to be sensitive to the entire representation of their base. However, examining morphological operations reveals the curious fact that the internal syntactic structure of complex words is never accessed by further derivation. This state of affairs is predicted if morphological operations are analyzed in terms of functions but calls for the stipulation of special constraints such as Allen's Adjacency Condition in configurational frameworks.

However, some linguists hold that internal structure is crucial to explaining the derivability of complex words. Such cases will be discussed and reanalyzed in section 4. Finally, in section 5 I compare the two frameworks with regard to inflectional morphology.

1. TREES VERSUS FUNCTIONS

1.1. Comparison of the Frameworks

The explicit representation of internal structure generally follows from the formalization of word formation rules. Consider for instance the generation of adjectives in *-ly* in the following frameworks:

I. Aronoff (1976):
Rule for *#ly*: $[X]_N \rightarrow [[X]_N\#ly]_{Adj}$
$[mother]_N \rightarrow [[mother]_N\#ly]_{Adj}$

II. Lieber (1980):
Lexical entry for *-ly*: phonological representation
semantic representation
category/subcategorization: N]A]
insertion frame: (for the derived adjective)
diacritics: level 2

Along with these entries Lieber suggests context-free rewrite rules that generate binary tree structures. Lexical terminals are inserted into these tree structures subject to subcategorization restrictions; the percolation of features defined by a set of conventions yields the following output.

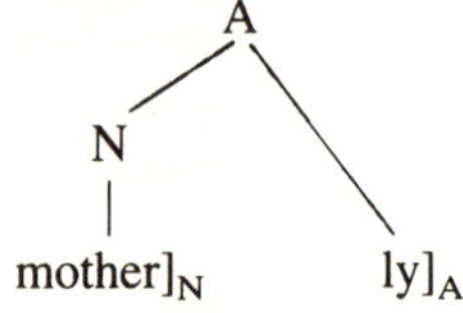

III. Selkirk (1982):
Lexical entry for *-ly*: (i) A^{af}
(ii) [N__]

The following rule is an instantiation of her set of context-free rewriting rules for affixation:

$$A \rightarrow N \quad A^{af}$$

Given lexical insertion the structure generated by the above rule will yield adjectives like *motherly*:

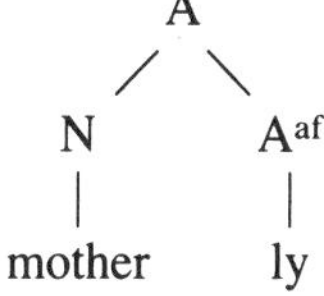

IV. Kiparsky (1982):
Insert /ly/ in environment $[[\text{N}]\ \_\_]_{\text{A}}$ at level 2.
$[[\text{mother}]_{\text{N}}\_\_]_{\text{A}} \rightarrow [[\text{mother}]_{\text{N}}\ \text{ly}]_{\text{A}}$

In spite of the differences between these rules they all yield similar outputs. They are characterized by the post-Bloomfieldian emphasis on configuration as the essence of grammatical structure. Hockett (1954) called this approach Item-and-Arrangement and contrasted it with its predecessor, the theory in which Boas, Sapir, and their students carried out their work on Native American languages, which he termed Item-and-Process.[1] Within this theory, a language is described as having a set of roots from which a set of expressions can be derived by formal processes such as affixation and reduplication. Hockett observed that this matches the dynamic rather than the static view of functions in algebra. Instead of thinking of f_{ly} as the set of ordered pairs $\langle[\text{mother}]_{\text{N}}, [\text{motherly}]_{\text{A}}\rangle$, $\langle[\text{friend}]_{\text{N}}, [\text{friendly}]_{\text{A}}\rangle$, and so on, one can think of it as a function that maps expressions from its domain, the set of relational nouns, into the set of adjectives.[2]

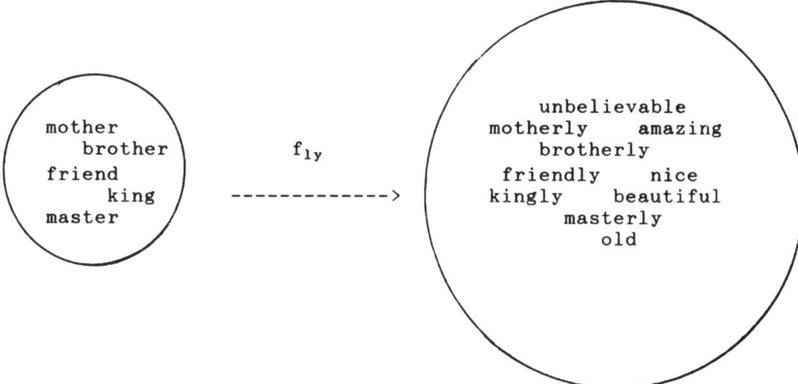

Note that Aronoff's rule for *-ly* looks something like this, but while his rule yields a configuration as output, the function f_{ly} simply maps expressions from one set into another.

The essential question raised in this paper is whether it is adequate to categorize expressions such as *motherly* as plain adjectives on a par with expressions such as *nice*. Such a categorization derives some plausibility from the observation that morphologically complex words appear to be in the same syntactic classes as monomorphemic words since they follow the same pattern. Harris addresses this issue in the following passage (Where *An* stands for deadjectival nominal suffixes, *Na* stands for denominal adjectival suffixes):

> In XY = Z, where a sequence of two (or more) classes is equivalent to some other class, we may say that Y changes the utterance position of X into that of Z. This way of talking is useful when Y is in some sense secondary to X, e.g. when Y never occurs except in this equation, whereas X occurs in various other equations, too. Thus in A An = N (*darkness* substitutable for *dawn*), or N Na = A (*boyish* substitutable for *large*), it is convenient to say that the addition of An permits A to occur in N position, or that Na changes N into A as regards utterance position. [Harris 1951, 275; all footnotes omitted]

Interestingly, Harris notes that for any "sequence of morphemes" in any given language one will usually be able to find "single morphemes" that are syntactically equivalent to that sequence (e.g., *dark* + *ness* = *dawn, boy* + *ish* = *large*) (Harris 1951, 264). This syntactic equivalence has been posited as a defining characteristic for derivational morphology by others (cf. Nida 1949) and plays a central role in the Lexicalist Hypothesis (cf. Chomsky 1970, esp. pp. 196ff.). The most straightforward way to express the syntactic atomicity of complex words is to assign atomic categories to them that do not reflect their derivational history.

When complex words are represented by atomic categories, the type of equations formulated by Harris becomes superfluous. How does it follow from treating morphological operations as functions that expressions such as *motherly* are categorized as adjectives rather than denominal adjectives? The answer lies in the procedure for computing the category of affixes. Following the tradition of Categorial Grammar,[3] categories of affixes are obtained by removing an occurrence of an expression of known category from another expression of known category; the remaining expression will be a function the category of which is determined by the categories of the whole expression (its range) and the subexpression (its domain).[4] For example, suppose we know that the category of *motherly* is A,[5] and that the category of *mother* is N. Then we can compute the category of *-ly* to be a function from nouns to adjectives and assign the category N\A (read: N under A) to it. The affix *-ly* is thus categorized as an incomplete expression that when combined with an expression of category N yields an expression of category A.

[2]	mother	ly	→	motherly
	N	N\A		A

The cancellation of the argument category indicates that expressions such as *motherly* are simply categorized as adjectives and not as denominal adjectives.

On this view affixes or morphological operations in general exist only in their capacity of relating expressions to each other but are not independently identifiable lexical items. Hence, English speakers may relate <long, length>, <warm, warmth>, and <true, truth>, but will probably fail to relate <foul, filth>, <whole, health>, <slow, sloth>, even though all nouns presumably contain the same suffix.

Finally, a word is in order with regard to the issue of productivity. If the domain of a morphological operation can be sufficiently characterized in syntactic, phonological, and/or semantic terms the operation is productive. For instance, the domain of f_{able} is the set of transitive verbs,[6] the domain of f_{ize} is the set of adjectives that end in a sonorant and have no stress on their final syllable, and so forth. If the domain of a morphological operation cannot be generally specified, it is fossilized. I will tentatively suggest that such operations be represented in terms of listed ordered pairs.

1.2. Why Preserve Internal Syntactic Structure?

The lack of internal syntactic structure resulting from the formal procedure for deriving complex expressions is of course subject to empirical verification. Arguments in favor of preserving internal structure are of three different types, they relate (1) to phonology, in particular the placement of stress, (2) to semantic interpretation, and (3) to morphological operations that depend on word-internal structure of the base.[7]

The first two arguments are actually only valid within a theoretical framework in which phonology and semantics are interpretive components that are subsequent to morphological and syntactic operations. If an operation is *simultaneously* a syntactic, semantic, and phonological operation, these arguments do not apply.

The claim that there is a direct correspondance between syntactic and semantic rules is at the core of Categorial Grammar. If morphological functions relate meaningful expressions, then the semantic operation associated with a morphological operation can be inferred on the basis of knowing the meaning of related expressions. Hence *-ly* is a function that maps expressions that refer to relational-noun-type denotations into the set of expressions that refer to adjective-type denotations.[8]

Cases that show a mismatch between syntactic and semantic structure (e.g., *theoretical grammarian*) have been the center of much debate (cf. Pesetsky 1985; Sproat 1985). Spencer (1988) argued convincingly that many such formations are best analyzed as cases of analogical back-formation. The claim that semantics is compositional applies only to productively derived formations. Back-formation is to my knowledge never genuinely productive;[9] hence it is outside the domain of the compositionality principle.

Parallel with treating affixes as syntactic and semantic functions, they will also be looked upon as functions with respect to phonology. Hence, the phonological operation associated with a morphological function is also inferred on the basis of relations between fully specified phonological expressions that include the representation of prosodic structure. The exact nature of such representations is determined by a theory of phonology; I will use orthographic symbols to represent phonological structure (e.g., <mother, motherly>). Regarding affixes as relations rather than as lexical items allows affixation to be treated on a par with morphological operations such as reduplication or umlaut.

Empirical evidence does not support an ordering that requires all morphological operations to precede all phonological operations, since morphological rules can often be shown to be sensitive to features of phonological surface structure. Once the ordering between a morphological and a phonological component is abandoned it is no longer necessary to preserve internal syntactic structure in order to account for stress. If morphological operations relate fully specified phonological expressions, then so-called cyclic effects follow from the preservation of prosodic structure of the base.

I have argued that arguments for representing internal syntactic structure that relate to phonology or semantics are only cogent within a theory that includes the notion of ordered grammatical components. I conclude that Selkirk does not provide any substantive evidence to back her claim in the passage cited in my introduction. In contrast to her theory-dependent arguments, those concerning word-internal structure-dependent morphological operations have more empirical support. If it can be shown that the attachment of a certain affix depends on the presence or absence of a particular syntactic category within its base, this would convincingly demonstrate that internal structure needs to be preserved, regardless of the overall architecture of the grammar. In section 4 I will discuss several analyses that claim the existence of such affixes. I hope to show that the relevant data can be reanalyzed in a way that does not require the retention of internal syntactic structure. Further, I argue that structureless representations have explanatory force that structured representations lack.

2. EVIDENCE FOR COMPOSED FUNCTIONS

The inadequacy of configurational approaches to nonconcatenative processes is well known. I will therefore turn to a different type of evidence that favors analyzing morphological operations in terms of functions. This evidence concerns cases where one morphological operation can be shown to be sensitive to another one.

2.1. The German Suffix *-chen*

The diminutive suffix *-chen* maps nouns of any gender into neuter nouns.

[3]	das Kind	'the child'	das Kindchen
	die Liste	'the list'	das Listchen
	der Film	'the film'	das Filmchen

If the base contains a back vowel, that vowel will be umlauted:

[4]	das Rad	'the wheel'	das Rädchen
	der Hund	'the dog'	das Hündchen
	die Frau	'the woman'	das Fraüchen
	das Tor	'the gate'	das Törchen

Within an Item-and-Arrangement framework this fact is usually accounted for by assuming that nouns with back vowels have separate allomorphs with front vowels when they combine with suffixes like *-chen*. This analysis has been criticized because it posits the existence of forms such as *Räd* and *Hünd,* which never occur in isolation. The alternative would be to first generate a form like *Hundchen* and then umlaut the stem vowel by a subsequent phonological operation. This view is problematic as well, since umlaut in Modern German is clearly a morphological rather than a phonological process.

Clearly, there is a direct correlation between the attachment of the suffix and the change of the stem vowel in the base. Whether or not the stem vowel of the base will be umlauted is determined by the suffix; speakers of German learn that the suffixes *-chen, -lein* (*Hund, Hündlein*), *-ern* (*Holz* 'wood,' *hölzern* 'wooden'), and others cause umlaut, whereas other suffixes will not affect the stem vowel. Within the present framework I suggest an analysis in terms of functional composition, requiring functions such as *-chen, -lein,* and *-ern,* to compose with the umlaut function. The umlaut function will be defined as follows:

[5] f_{umlaut} is the function fronting the last stressed vowel in any expression belonging to the syntactic categories N, V, or A. In case this vowel is already fronted, f_{umlaut} reduces to the identity function.

The composed function maps expressions such as *Rad* directly into the related diminutive expression *Rädchen.*

In the literature on umlaut, it has often been observed that certain affixes always trigger umlaut, others never trigger umlaut, and a third group is said to somewhat idiosyncratically show umlaut in some cases. For instance, Wellmann (1975) claims that *-chen* triggers umlaut in 90 percent of the cases. However, the exceptions appear not be random. Wellmann notes for instance that deadjectival formations such as *Dummchen* (from *dumm* 'stupid') and *Altchen* (from *alt* 'old') do not show umlaut. But these nouns differ from the ones listed in [4] in that they relate to an adjective. Such formations are not productive in German but need to be listed.

Another group of examples are appellative nouns, such as *Mamachen* ('sweet Mom'), *Muttchen* ('sweet Mom'), *Papachen* ('sweet Dad'), *Tantchen* ('sweet aunt'), as well as names, such as *Lottchen* (*Lotte* 'fem.name'), *Ruthchen* (*Ruth* 'fem. name'), and *Ralphchen* (*Ralph*, 'masc. name'). These forms fail to show umlaut because proper nouns are not in the domain of the umlaut function as defined in [5].[10]

Finally, there are formations such as *Frauchen* that do not result from application of the diminutive function *-chen*, as can be inferred from their meaning. Thus, *Frauchen* means 'female owner of a dog', which contrasts with *Fräuchen*, which means 'little woman'. On my analysis the fact that the stem vowel in the form *Frauchen* is not umlauted correlates directly with its lack of compositionality.[11]

2.2. Productivity and Stress in English

The cases to be discussed in this section all share a remarkable property: by and large, fossilized operations have developed perfect productivity under specific circumstances. These circumstances can be straightforwardly explained if morphological operations are analyzed in terms of functions that relate phonological expressions, but appear rather mysterious from a configurational perspective.

The data cannot be explained satisfactorily without taking stress into account. The distinction between stress-neutral and stress-determining morphological operations has long been a central topic in English morphology. This distinction is at the heart of level ordering, where it has been connected with the order of affixes (cf. Siegel 1974 and contributions within the framework of Lexical Phonology for a more recent adaptation of this proposal). In the following case studies I will investigate this distinction from the perspective of productivity, thereby establishing a parallelism between several seemingly unrelated developments in English.

2.2.1. The Stress-Shifting Nominalization

The process that converts dissylabic verbs into nouns by shifting the stress is in general rather fossilized:

[6]	<accént, áccènt>	*<accóunt, áccòunt>
	<addréss, áddrèss>	*<arrést, árrèst>
	<allóy, állòy>	*<allúre, állùre>
	<abstráct, ábstràct>	*<advánce, ádvànce>
	<conflíct, cónflìct>	*<consént, cónsènt>
	<contést, cóntèst>	*<concérn, cóncèrn>
	<constrúct, cónstrùct>	*<contról, cóntròl>

<decréase, décrèase> *<deféat, défèat>
<discárd, díscàrd> *<disgúst, dísgùst>
<discóunt, díscòunt> *<disdáin, dísdàin>
<expórt, éxpòrt> *<exháust, éxhàust>
<misprínt, mísprìnt> *<mistrúst, místrùst>
<survéy, súrvèy> *<surpríse, súrprìse>

The starred relations are not even marginally acceptable and yet there is no criterion that formally distinguishes them from the well-formed pairs. It appears that a noun derived by the stress shifting operation will only be readily accepted if the speaker is familiar with it. Consequently the acceptable relations in [6] have to be listed. However, while generally idiosyncratic, the stress-shifting function has found a niche where it appears to be fully productive: the set of verbs that are prefixed with *re-*:

[7] <fill, refíll> <refíll, réfìll>
<do, redó> <redó, rédò>
<make, remáke> <remáke, rémàke>
<load, relóad> <relóad, rélòad>
<paint, repáint> <repáint, répàint>
<play, repláy> <repláy, réplày>
<count, recóunt> <recóunt, récòunt>
<print, reprínt> <reprínt, réprìnt>
<run, rerún> <rerún, rérùn>
<take, retáke> <retáke, rétàke>

The stress-shifting process is sensitive to *re-* prefixation rather than the mere presence of word-initial *re-*:[12]

[8] *<rebúke, rébùke>
*<regrét, régrèt>
*<repéat, répèat>
*<requést, réquèst>
*<resúlt, résùlt>
*<rewárd, réwàrd>

The sensitivity of the stress-shifting function to f_{re} is most naturally analyzed if f_{re} is specified as the domain of this function:

[9]
$$f_{re} \xrightarrow{f_{[-\acute{-}]_V \rightarrow [\acute{-}\grave{-}]_N}} f_{[\,]_V \rightarrow [r\acute{e}\grave{-}]_N}$$

The stress-shifting function differs, for instance, from f_{ly} in that f_{ly} relates expressions whereas the stress-shifting function relates functions or sets of ordered pairs, respectively. In particular a subset of f_{re}, namely the ordered pairs whose first coordinate is monosyllabic, is the domain of the stress-shifting function, whereas its range is the corresponding composed function. On this analysis the relations as stated in [7] needs to be revised as follows:

[10] <<fill, refíll>, <fill, réfìll>>
<<do, redó>, <do, rédò>>
<<make, remáke>, <make, rémàke>>

The verbs in [8] are underived and therefore are not included in the domain of the stress-shifting function. A few cases such as <rejéct, réjèct> need to be listed along with the relations in [6]. The semantic relation between verb and noun is somewhat idiosyncratic in the listed pairs. Hence, *réjèct, rébel, cónvìct, pérvèrt,* and others denote persons, a possibility excluded with regard to forms that are part of the function stated in [9]. Productively derived forms invariably refer to the result of the verbal action, if possible to a material associated with the result. Hence, nouns like *rémìx* and *récòok* will be interpreted as referring to substances but never to persons.

Finally, note that these data constitute a paradox, given the notion of ordered levels within Lexical Phonology. Within that framework the process converting verbs to nouns with concomitant stress shift has been assigned to level 1 (cf. Kiparsky 1982, 12ff.), whereas the process of *re-* prefixation takes place at level 2.

2.2.2. The English Suffix *-ation*

Suffixing *-ation* to verbs is not a productive process in modern English since it is impossible to specify a domain for this suffix other than listing the individual verbs. The following examples show that acceptance of such forms relies on token familiarity, which indicates that they are fossilized:

[11]

<perturb, perturbation>	*<disturb, disturbation>
<embark, embarkation>	*<remark, remarkation>
<explain, explanation>	*<remain, remanation>
<declare, declaration>	*<compare, comparation>
<inspire, inspiration>	*<desire, desiration>
<preserve, preservation>	*<deserve, deservation>
<expire, expiration>	*<retire, retiration>
<adore, adoration>	*<ignore, ignoration>
<obscure, obscuration>	*<secure, securation>
<converse, conversation>	*<rehearse, rehearsation>
<accuse, accusation>	*<abuse, abusation>
<invite, invitation>	*<delight, delightation>
<consult, consultation>	*<insult, insultation>
<indent, indentation>	*<invent, inventation>
<present, presentation>	*<dissent, dissentation>

<adapt, adaptation>
<quote, quotation>
<import, importation>
<infest, infestation>
<permute, permutation>
<derive, derivation>
<starve, starvation>

*<adopt, adoptation>
*<vote, votation>
*<support, supportation>
*<invest, investation>
*<pollute, pollutation>
*<arrive, arrivation>
*<carve, carvation>

Again, it is remarkable just how bad the nouns in the starred relations sound. Unacceptability of these nouns cannot be generally linked to blocking, as several verbs lack a derived nominal other than X-ing (e.g., *carve, ignore,*[13] *remain, secure, deserve*), whereas others coexist with their alleged blockers (e.g., *adaptation, adaption*).

While it is generally fossilized, there is one case where suffixation with *-ation* is accepted without fail, namely in combination with the suffix *-ize:*

[12] <urbanize, urbanization>
<radicalize, radicalization>
<randomize, randomization>
<westernize, westernization>

Acceptability of formations does not depend on familiarity with the noun in question; rather, all formations are accepted in case suffixation of *-ize* is approved of:

[13] <emotionalize, emotionalization>
<essentialize, essentialization>
<fragmentalize, fragmentalization>
<superficialize, superficialization>
<proletarianize, proletarianization>

The following data show that it is the suffix rather than the sound sequence [aIz] that is responsible for productivity in such cases:

[14] *<ostracize, ostracization>
*<baptize, baptization>
*<analyze, analyzation>
*<apologize, apologization>
*<recognize, recognization>
*<fantasize, fantasization>
*<criticize, criticization>
*<exorcize, exorcization>
*<aggrandize, aggrandization>
*<sympathize, sympathization>
*<exercise, exercisation>
*<surprise, surprisation>

*<advertise, advertisation>
*<emphasize, emphasization>

The analysis of these data is straightforward: *-ation* belongs to the set of functions that map functions to functions rather than expressions to expressions:

[15] $f_{ize} \xrightarrow{f_{ation}} f_{ization}$

Consequently the well-formed relations in [13] will be listed, confining the productive power of *-ation* as depicted in [15]. Accordingly, the ordered pairs in [12] and [13] need to be revised:

[16] <<urban, urbanize>, <urban, urbanization>>
<<emotional, emotionalize>, emotional, emotionalization>>

The reader may be aware that forms like *urbanization* constitute another ordering paradox (cf. Aronoff 1976, 84ff.; Aronoff and Sridhar 1983).

2.2.3. The English Suffix *-ity*

Like the preceding two morphological processes, *-ity* is fossilized in general:

[17]
<rancid, rancidity> *<candid, candidity>
<rapid, rapidity> *<vivid, vividity>
<antique, antiquity> *<unique, uniquity>
<diverse, diversity> *<inverse, inversity>
<clear, clarity> *<dear, darity>
<modern, modernity> *<western, westernity>
<dual, duality> *<cruel, cruelity>
<obscene, obscenity> *<pristine, pristinity>
<profane, profanity> *<arcane, arcanity>
<vain, vanity> *<plain, planity>
<sexual, sexuality> *<casual, casuality>
<vital, vitality> *<usual, usuality>
<feminine, femininity> *<genuine, genuinity>
<curious, curiosity> *<hideous, hideosity>
<domestic, domesticity> *<enthusiastic, enthusiasticity>
<nervous, nervosity> *<vicious, viciosity>

In addition, the suffix *-ity* is very sensitive to various euphonic restrictions. For instance, polysyllabic adjectives ending in [t] never occur with *-ity: *remotity, *acutity, *ineptity, *arrogantity,* and so on.[14] Such negative restrictions are atypical for productive processes.

While formations containing the suffix *-ity* often appear to be listed rather than productively derived, there is one domain, adjectives derived by f_{able}, where *-ity* can in fact be shown to outdo its generally much more productive rival *-ness*.[15]

[18] <bridgeable, bridgeability>
<recognizable, recognizability>
<disciplinable, disciplinability>

The ungrammaticality of forms such as **terribility* and **horribility* suggests that *-ity* is not just sensitive to the phonological structure of the adjective ending. Rather, the suffix *-ity* can be shown to be truely productive only when combined with the productive function *-able,* which maps transitive verbs to adjectives. On the basis of these observations the analysis of the function *-ity* is straightforward: its domain is the function f_{able}, and its range is the composed function $f_{ability}$[16]:

[19]
$$f_{able} \xrightarrow{f_{ity}} f_{ability}$$

This function relates sets of ordered pairs, such as the following:

[20] <<bridge, bridgeable>, <bridge, bridgeability>>
<<recognize, recognizable>, <recognize, recognizability>>
<<discipline, disciplinable>, <discipline, disciplinability>>

The unacceptability of forms such as **remarkability, *considerability, *agreeability, *decayability,* and **laughability,* comes as no surprise under this analysis. Adjectives like *remarkable* and *considerable* are not productively derived, since they do not relate to transitive verbs. Accordingly, the meaning of these formations is not compositional.

The same is true for expressions such as *honorable, comfortable, fashionable, personable,* and others that relate to nouns. Such unproductive formations lack compositionality of meaning. Marchand noted that suffixation of *-ity* to these forms is uncommon as well. These observations fit neatly into the analysis presented here: $f_{ability}$ is a function from transitive verbs to nouns, and hence applies neither to intransitive verbs nor to nouns. Note that deriving the expression *fashionability* from the transitive verb *fashion* appears to be acceptable.[17]

Again, this analysis is at odds with the characterization of these affixes in terms of level ordering. Since *-ity* is a level-1 affix, it should only attach to "level-1" *-able,* (forms such as *derivability* and *approachability* constituting "ordering paradoxes"). However, I claim that the domain of *-ity* is actually the "level-2" *-able.*

Finally, I would like to compare my analysis with the somewhat similar work by Guerssel (1983), who defines a function *-able* that maps transitive verbs into a subset of adjectives he categorizes as A^{able}. This set also includes underived items such as *possible* and *terrible*. He then proceeds to specify the function *-ity* so as to select any form headed by *-able*. As a consequence *-ity* can either compose with the function *-able* and then combine with a transitive verb, or *-ity* can apply to an adjective that belongs to the set A^{able}. Guerssel will therefore derive forms such as *possibility* in the same way as forms like *predictability*. The difference between these two derivations is that only the latter can also proceed in an associative fashion.

By contrast my analysis is nonassociative since I only generate ordered pairs such as <predict, predictable>, and <predict, predictability>, but not <predictable, predictability>. While it might appear to be a serious drawback of my analysis compared to Guerssel's that I treat forms such as *possibility* as primitive, it seems clear that any rule that allows the derivation of *possibility* from *possible* must also allow the derivation of *terribility* from *terrible*. Furthermore Guerssel defines a new category of adjectives that not only leads to a proliferation of syntactic categories but also necessitates a statement in the grammar to the effect that A^{able} in other respects acts just as any other adjective.

2.2.4. Conclusions

Marchand noted that forms in *-ableness* are usually older than their rival forms in *-ability*, which gained currency chiefly in the nineteenth century or later. This suggests that the function in [19] developed around that time. One might ask whether it is possible to specify the conditions that were conducive to this development.

To begin with one can state formal conditions under which composition of functions can take place. Why is it possible to develop functions such as [9], [15], and [19] but not the following:

[21] $$* \quad \begin{array}{l} \;\; f_{ity} \\ f_{ize} \longrightarrow f_{izity} \end{array}$$

E.g., *<<urban, urbanize>, <urban, urbanizity>>

The possibility that a composed function f_{izity} may develop is not allowed, as two functions may compose if and only if the range of one matches the domain of the other:

[22]
$$\begin{array}{ccc} & f_{ity} & \\ & \text{Ⓐ} \rightarrow N & \\ f_{able} & & f_{ability} \\ TV \rightarrow \text{Ⓐ} & \longrightarrow & TV \rightarrow N \end{array}$$

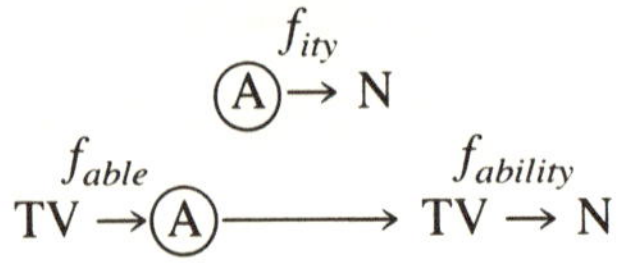

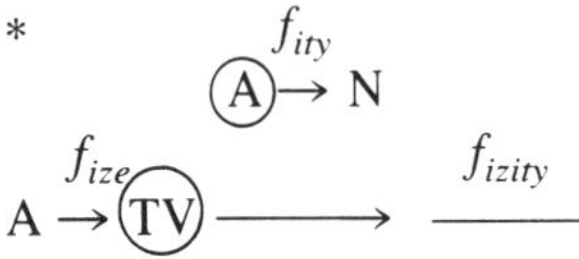

The condition only makes sense in diachronic perspective. Formally, it can be stated as follows:

[23] If f_g is a function from X to Y, and f_h is a function from Y to Z, where X, Y, and Z are syntactic categories, then f_h may develop into a function whose domain is f_g and whose range is a composed function with the domain X and the range Z.

The cancellation of the category Y in [23] shows the affinity between functional composition and functional application as illustrated in [2]. The difference between these rules is that composition as defined in [23] is a rule of historical reanalysis whereas application is a synchronic rule of the language.

Crucially, the domain of f_g or the range of f_h may not matter with regard to the question whether a composed function may develop. Evidence in favor of this claim can be inferred from the behavior of f_{ation}. According to [23] the domain of f_{ize} may no matter with regard to the question whether composition may take place, as long as there is a productive and compositional operation. In fact, there is a separate function f_{ize} that, subject to phonological restrictions,[18] applies to proper names:

[24] <Reagan, Reaganize>
<Thatcher, Thatcherize>
<Carter, Carterize>
<Finland, Finlandize>

As expected on the basis of the definition given in [23], *-ation* is just as productive with regard to this domain as it is with regard to the function in [12].

Apart from this general syntactic condition of functional composition, there appears to be a language-specific phonological condition that determines potential productivity of functions in English:

[25] In order for a morphological operation to be productive the stress in the expressions to be related must match. That is, stress may not shift within the base of a derived form, nor may relative prominence relations be affected.

This hypothesis is natural in that it links transparency of form to productivity. It is language-specific in that it will obviously not hold for languages where stress is always fixed on a particular syllable due to its position in a word. However, the hypothesis might still be universal for languages where stress has similar properties as in English.

The observation that stress-determining affixes quite generally lack productivity is not new, though generally presented as coincidental:

> The reader will have noticed that affixation at stratum 1 is by and large less productive than affixation at stratum 2. This also correlates with the fact that there are fewer lexical exceptions, and fewer cases of semantic opacity in words derived at stratum 2. . . . If this is a correct observation, it merits further study. [Mohanan 1986, 57]

If stress neutrality is in fact a necessary, though certainly not a sufficient, prerequisite for productivity, a stress-shifting affix may be productive only in combination with a stress-neutral one. Hence productive stress-determining affixes will always be outside stress-neutral ones. On this view the lack of productivity of *-ation* in [11] is directly linked to the fact that it causes the stress in its base to shift due to a stress clash. On the other hand, in combination with the suffix *-ize* it will never affect the stress within the base and hence may become productive:

[26] <indént, ìndentátion> ↔ <úrban, ùrbanizátion>
<pertúrb, pèrturbátion> ↔ <emótional, emòtionalizátion>

The same is true of *-ity* in [20] versus [17]. Curiously, the condition stated in [25] also holds true of the operation in [9], even though shifting stress is exactly what this operation is supposed to do.

If these analyses hold water then this would deal a fatal blow to level ordering in English morphology. Not only are there many exceptions to the rule that stress-neutral affixes must always be outside stress-determining affixes in English, but exactly the opposite is true once productivity is taken into consideration.

Finally, the sensitivity of the suffix *-ity* to the suffix *-able* cannot be expressed in a configurational framework: "One property distinguishing Affix from Root or Word is that it is always sister to a nonaffix category type in word structure" (Selkirk 1982, 124). This only leaves the possibility of specifying a complex suffix *-ability* along with the suffix *-able*. Such an analysis is inadequate in that it fails to express the fact that for every nominal derived by suffixing *-ability* there exists a related adjective in *-able*. This state of affairs contrasts with cases where composed suffixes are synchronically primitive rather than derived. One such case is German *-igkeit,* which is a complex affix because intermediate forms with just *-ig* need not exist:

[27]	dicht	'dense'	*dichtig	Dichtigkeit
	dreist	'cheeky'	*dreistig	Dreistigkeit
	eng	'narrow'	*engig	Engigkeit
	fest	'firm'	*festig	Festigkeit

feucht	'moist'	*feuchtig	Feuchtigkeit
glatt	'smooth'	*glattig	Glattigkeit
hell	'light'	*hellig	Helligkeit
leicht	'easy'	*leichtig	Leichtigkeit
matt	'exhausted'	*mattig	Mattigkeit
müde	'tired'	*müdig	Müdigkeit
nett	'nice'	*nettig	Nettigkeit
neu	'new'	*neuig	Neuigkeit
rauh	'rough'	*rauhig	Rauhigkeit
schnell	'fast'	*schnellig	Schnelligkeit
zäh	'tough'	*zähig	Zähigkeit

From a configurationalist's perspective the coming into being of composed affixes must be rather mysterious in the first place. The question is how affixes in a configuration such as [28] ever result in a single item since they do not even form a constituent.

[28]

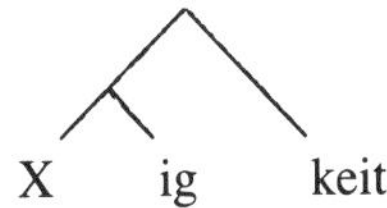

However, given that suffixes are analyzed as functions, such developments are natural. A function and its argument will in historical perspective often "freeze," as can be seen from expressions such as *another, together, alone, along,* and many others. Accordingly one might also expect to find fossilized functions consisting of composed affixes.

2.2.5. Empirical Consequences: *recognizability* versus **inventivity*

Anticipating the discussion in the following section we may note that the data discussed in the case studies above could be cited in defense of internal structure preservation. On this view, *-ity* would be characterized as a suffix that needs to look inside its base: it will only attach if the base is deverbal, thereby violating subjacency.

[29] $[[[]_V \text{ Suf}]_A \text{ -ity}]_N$

This type of analysis would be similar to mine in that expressions such as *vulnerability* and *personality* are listed, restricting the generative power of [29] to yield forms of the type *drinkability*. However, these two analyses are radically different: one refers to items inserted into a particular position in a syntactic tree; the other is formulated in terms of functional composition. Crucially, given functional composition, the category V may not matter since it constitutes the domain of f_{able} (cf. [23]).

Empirical evidence distinguishing between the two analyses can be obtained by looking at cases that match the structure in [29] but fail to satisfy the conditions stated in [23] and [25]. Such evidence exists: the suffix *-ive* applies to verbs and yields adjectives, thereby satisfying the requirement of the configurational analysis stated in [29]. However, it turns out that only about fifteen out of hundreds of adjectives resulting from the application of *-ive* to a verb (excluding cases like *passive* and *primitive*) will serve as a base for the suffix *-ity* (note the unacceptability of forms such as **inventivity, *intuitivity, *dispersivity, *innovativity, *caressivity, *abusivity*).[19] This ratio needs to be compared with the perfect productivity of cases involving the structure [verb]-*able-ity*.

Since the categories of the functors f_{ive} and f_{ity} satisfy the syntactic condition stated in [23], the failure of *-ivity* to be reanalyzed as a composed function must be due to the prosodic condition in [25]. This analysis seems to be right on track since even though the suffix *-ive* is stress-neutral, a combined suffix *-ívity* will now allow its base to preserve stress:

[30] *<<invént, invéntive>, <invént, ìnventívity>>
*<<abúse, abúsive>, <abúse, àbusívity>>
*<<ínnovàte, ínnovàtive>, <ínnovàte, ìnnovatívity>>

In fact, suffixation of a composed suffix *-ivity* necessarily causes a stress clash since the suffix *-ive* will only attach to verbs with stress on their final syllable.

If this analysis is correct then it argues further against a model in which affixation is an autonomous process yielding structures that are subsequently phonologically interpreted.

3. THE INVISIBILITY CONSTRAINTS, OR BLINDFOLDS FOR AFFIXES

A number of constraints have been formulated within formal morphology to the effect that internal morphological structure should not be accessible for further morphological operations. Siegel (1978) argues this point with the following example:

[31]

$*_A$[un$_A$[dis$_A$[honest]]]	$_A$[un$_A$[[distract]ing]]
$*_A$[un$_A$[dis$_A$[courteous]]]	$_A$[un$_A$[[distinguish]ed]]
$*_A$[un$_A$[dis$_A$[loyal]]]	$_A$[un$_A$[[discover]able]]

She accounts for the ungrammaticality of the examples in the lefthand column by the following constraint:

[32] Words in *un* are thrown out if the morpheme *dis* is uniquely contained in the cycle adjacent to *un*. [1978, 192]

Siegel generalizes this constraint, claiming that her observation holds for any two adjacent morphemes:

[33] No word filter may involve A [affix] and SP [base that exhibits a certain property] unless SP is uniquely contained in the cycle adjacent to A. [ibid]

Siegel's example is not convincing because the "morphemes" *dis* in *dishonest* and *dis* in *distracting* seem not to have much in common beyond their phonetic form. Also her formulation of the Adjacency Constraint is awkward, being stated in terms of a filter rather than in terms of word formation. A better formulation of this constraint was independently developed by Allen, who called it the Adjacency Condition:

[34] No rule of word formation can involve X and Y, unless Y is uniquely contained in the cycle adjacent to X. [1978, 155]

This condition can be illustrated as follows:

[35] $[[[\ldots]_{Y'}\ldots]_{Y}\ldots]_{X}$

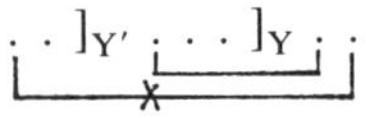

Allen's Adjacency Condition reflects Siegel's Adjacency Constraint, although it is specified as a constraint on word formation rather than on word filters. But it is still specified negatively: it does not say what a rule of word formation can or must involve. Allen agrees with Siegel in interpreting the Adjacency Condition as a filter that has the function of throwing out words that violate it.

In her discussion, however, Allen gives the impression that she interprets the Adjacency Condition positively in terms of what material affixes may refer to:

> A morphological theory which countenances rules and conditions on rules which refer to *internal* bracketings is more powerful, i.e. permits a greater range of analyses, than a theory in which rules and their conditions can make references only to 'external' bracketings, or more exactly, to the level of bracketing which is structurally adjacent to the level at which the rule or condition is operative. [1978, 154]

Given this interpretation the Adjacency Condition says virtually the same as the Atom Condition formulated by Williams:

[36] A restriction on the attachment of af_x to Y can only refer to features realized on Y.

Williams does not interpret the Atom Condition as a condition on filters but rather on word formation implemented by means of Feature Percolation.

Subsequently Lieber improved William's Feature Convention by dropping the Righthand Head rule, which seems to be problematic for other languages and even for a few cases in English. She states that derived words adopt all the features of their outermost morphemes, formulated as the following convention:

[37] Feature Percolation Conventions:

Convention I: all features of a stem morpheme including category features percolate to the first non-branching node dominating that morpheme.

Convention II: all features of an affix morpheme including category features percolate to the first branching node dominating that morpheme. [1981, 49]

The following example from German will illustrate how this convention works:

[38]

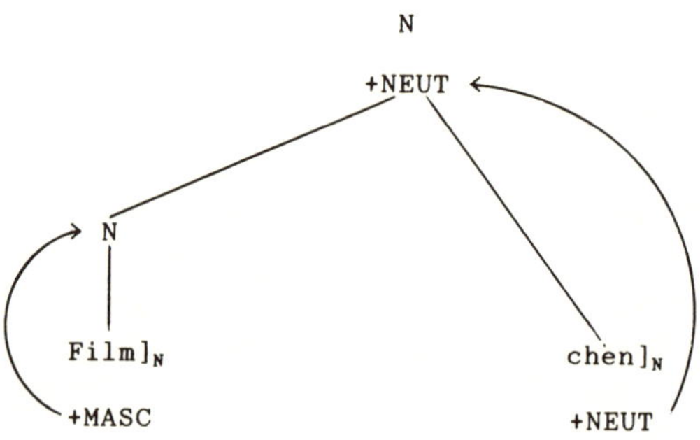

As mentioned above words derived with the diminutive *-chen* are neuter regardless of the gender of the base to which *-chen* attaches.

> Notice that this state of affairs is not an a priori necessary one: it is at least conceivable that words should receive the category of their outermost affix, but the gender of an inner morpheme. This possibility seems never to occur, however. [1980, 49]

Hence Lieber considers this convention a necessary part of her theory. As a consequence of this formulation, Lieber's convention makes the same predictions as did Siegel's or Allen's original constraints: the internal composition of a derived form is always irrelevant to further composition. Other proposals to the effect that internal structure becomes inaccessible to further derivation are erasure conventions in Lexical Phonology. Pesetsky's Bracket Erasure Convention (1979) differs from Mohanan's Opacity Condition (1982) and Kiparsky's Bracket Erasure (1982) with regard to whether brackets along with morphosyntactic labels should be erased after each morphological operation or at the end of a stratum.[20] Botha's Morphological Island Constraint is also intended to restrict access to word-internal structure:

[39] The individual constituents of the complex words formed by means of WFRs lose the ability to interact with inflectional, derivational and syntactic processes. [1981, 46]

In this context, One might also mention Lapointe's Generalized Lexical Hypothesis, which says that no syntactic rule can refer to a morphological feature or category (1980). This hypothesis, which is inspired by Chomsky's Lexicalist Hypothesis (1970), is weaker than those previously mentioned in that Lapointe renders internal structure of derived forms only invisible to syntactic but not derivational and inflectional processes. On the other hand, his as well as Botha's formulation are too strong, since at least features such as case ought to be accessible in the syntax.

In spite of the fact that the various constraints, conditions, and conventions presented above make slightly different predictions in a few cases, they all reflect the same observation: that there are no processes that are sensitive to word-internal structure. The proposed constraints describe the facts but fail to explain them. None of the authors mentioned so far directly confronts the central problem, and consequently each redescribes it in terms of constraints based on specific examples. They fail to address the question as to why internal structure of derived words should be inaccessible to further derivation. Why should only the features of the outermost affix be relevant, or alternatively, why should internal structure be erased? Devices such as Bracket Erasure do not follow from anything; they are rather merely stipulative. A theory must account for an empirical observation in its architecture rather than in the form of descriptively true but explanatorily unsatisfactory ad hoc statements. Analyzing affixes as functions renders superfluous all the constraints aiming at rendering internal structure invisible. Invoking cancellation is not yet another constraint stipulated in the grammar, but follows from the notion of a function. The invisibility of internal structure is hereby explained, since there is no internal structure once composition is effected.

4. DISCUSSION OF PUTATIVE COUNTEREXAMPLES

The claim that internal structure need not be represented can be refuted if such structure can be shown to be crucial for further derivation. I will argue that all the putative counterexamples can be explained without reference to internal morphosyntactic structure.

4.1. What Is Wrong with **employmental*?

Aronoff claims that there is a constraint on the operation of the denominal suffix *-al* that "depends on internal constituent structure" (1976, 54).

[40]	a.	ornament	*$orna_V$	ornamental
		excrement	*$excre_V$	excremental
		regiment	*$regi_V$	regimental
	b.	employment	employ	*employmental
		discernment	discern	*discernmental
		containment	contain	*containmental
		derangement	derange	*derangemental

This constraint links the ungrammaticality of the derived adjectives in [40b] to the presence of the verbal stem in their nominal base, saying that *-al* can be attached only in case there is no verb in the internal structure of the noun. Hence *-al* cannot attach to *employment* but can attach to *ornament.* Aronoff himself notes that there is no general constraint to the effect that *-al* may not attach to deverbal abstract nominals, as his examples *organizational, observational, preferential,* and so on show. This observation sheds some doubt on his explanation in terms of the internal syntactic structure of the noun.

According to the functional view of affixes, the derivational history of *employment* cannot be relevant, because the categorial information that *employ* is a verb is canceled as soon as *-ment* applies. Also, the category of *employ* may not matter with regard to the question whether a composed suffix *-mental* may be derived because composition only requires the range of f_{ment} to match the domain of f_{al} (cf. [23]). The category of *employ* however constitutes the domain of f_{ment} and is consequently irrelevant.

The failure of a composed suffix *-mental* to develop is due to the same dilemma that was found to be the cause for the lack of productivity of nouns in *-ivity:* since both *-mental* and *-ivity* bear initial stress they will cause a stress clash when suffixed to expressions with final stress. The dilemma lies in the fact that forms such as **emplòyéntal* are phonologically ill formed, but that resolving the stress clash by shifting the stress conflicts with stress neutrality (**èmployméntal*). As a consequence such forms will not arise.

This analysis does not rule out that there may be adjectives in *-mental* that relate to verbs as long as stress neutrality is given. Potential candidates are monosyllabic verbs or verbs with no stress on their final syllable:

[41] <judge, jùdgméntal>
<state, stàteméntal>
<árgue, àrguméntal>
<góvern, gòvernméntal>
<envíron, envìronméntal>
<devélop, devèlopméntal
<accómpany, accòmpaniméntal>

In each case where an adjective in *-mental* relates to a verb the verb satisfies the prosodic constraint specified above. The adjective *dèpartméntal* is not an exception since this expression is unrelated to the verb *depárt*.

At near sight, even the relations in [41] seem somewhat fossilized. The failure of a productive function f_{mental} to develop may be partially due to the fact that most verbs have stress on their final syllable but should probably mostly be blamed on the fact that the suffix *-ment* itself is rather unproductive.

It appears that the ill-formedness of expressions such as *employmental* does not support the claim that complex words need to be represented configurationally. Such an account fails to show the important link between the development of productive composed functions such as $f_{ability}$ and $f_{ization}$ compared to the failure to establish composed functions such as $*f_{ivity}$ and $*f_{mental}$.

4.2. What Is Wrong with **figurive* and **respectal*?

A similar case has been made in order to explain the grammaticality patterns in the following data:

[42] a. respective, supportive, exhaustive, effective
*respectal, *supportal, *exhaustal, *effectal

[42] b. *figurive, *gesturive, *culturive, *orbitive
figural, gestural, cultural, orbital

Strauss, who explicitly rejected Allen's Adjacency Condition, has provided an analysis where he describes these facts in terms of reference to internal structure. He notes that *-al* attaches to nouns, whereas *-ive* attaches to verbs, and argues that neither the nouns that serve as the base for *-al* nor the verbs to which *-ive* attaches may be derived by zero derivation. Hence, the ungrammaticality of the forms in [42] is accounted for in terms of the following constraint:

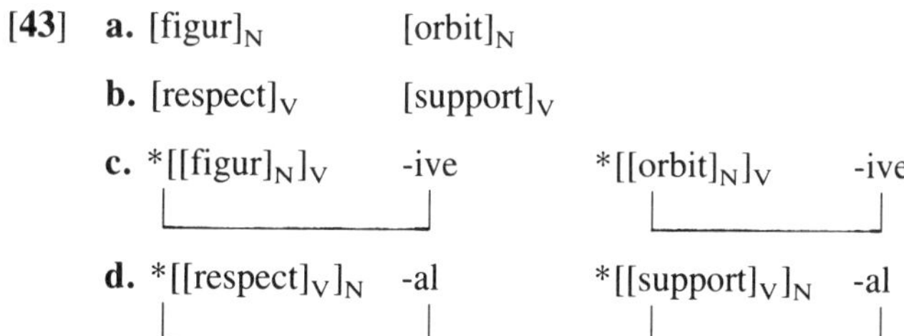

Whereas the forms in [43a] and [43b] are acceptable bases for *-al* and *-ive,* respectively, due to their lack of internal structure, configurations such as the ones listed in [43c] and [43d] are unacceptable. This analysis relies, of course, on the preservation of internal structure. These data were originally analyzed by Allen, who proposed an account in terms of level ordering. Since level ordering as a theoretical device cannot be maintained on empirical grounds, I will not go into Allen's argument but instead point out some simple, but salient, facts about the two suffixes under consideration. Looking at the total number of adjectives in English ending in *-ive,* it turns out that their base almost always ends in either [s] or [t] and has stress on the final syllable. None of the forms in [42b] fulfills both these conditions;[21] hence those forms are outside the domain of this function. The suffix *-al,* on the other hand, never attaches to nouns with main stress on their final syllable, except for monosyllabic nouns—which means that none of the forms in [42a] are in the domain of *-al.*[22]

So far Strauss's generalization seems to cover the data equally well. However, his account relies on knowledge that is irrelevant to my account, namely, knowing whether a given word is underlyingly a noun or a verb. I assume it is controversial whether most speakers have strong intuitions about whether *respect* is a noun derived from a verb or vice versa. My analysis only relies on the speaker's knowledge of the phonological structure—knowledge that is uncontroversial.

As a matter of fact, even based on their small sample of data, Allen's and Strauss's elaborate theoretical frameworks do not account for all the facts. Hence, while they take pains to explain why forms such as **reproachal, *researchal,* and **supplyal* cannot be generated due to violations of level ordering and internal structure, they fail to account for the fact that forms such as **reproachive, *researchive,* and **supplyive* are equally ungrammatical. These forms are in perfect accord with their theories and would probably be subsumed under the label Possible, but Nonoccurring. Within the categorial framework advocated here, the notoriously slippery but intuitively appropriate notion of possible but nonoccurring forms will be naturally confined: it is the set of expressions the base of which is contained in the domain of the function from which they are derived. On this view, the expressions *dismountive, exacerbative, domesticative, harassive, jubilative,* none of which is in common use are Nonoccurring but Possible. On the other hand, forms such as **remindive, *developive, *governive,* and **attachive* will not be generated because none of the verbs in question is in the domain of the function *-ive,* since none of them matches both the prosodic and segmental restrictions specified above.

4.3. What Is Wrong with **accusationize*?

Allen claims that words cannot have the following structure:

[44] $*[[[\ .\ .\ .\ ]_X\ .\ .\ .\ .\ ]_Y\ .\ .\ .\ ]_X$

This constraint rules out affixation where two or more bracketings have the same category label and is meant to explain the ungrammaticality of the following forms (Allen 1978, 209):

[45] $*[\ [\ [\text{accuse}]_V\ +\text{ation}]_N\ +\text{ize}]_V$
$*[\ [\ [\text{profound}]_A\ +\text{ity}]_N\ +\text{all}]_A$
$*[\ [\ [\text{support}]_V\ +\text{ive}]_A\ +\text{ize}]_V$

However, as noted by Allen herself, many forms are counterexamples to the constraint stated in [44]:

[46] $[\ [\ [\text{grace}]_N\ \#\text{less}]_A\ \#\text{ness}]_N$
$[\ [\ [\text{straight}]_A\ \#\text{en}]_V\ \#\text{able}]_A$

This observation prompts her to restrict the constraint to level-1 word formation. Rejecting the notion of level ordering, we feel stimulated to look for alternative explanations. The real problem with the forms in [45] is that suffixes are attached to expressions that are outside their domain. As noted earlier the domain of productive *-ize* suffixation is the set of adjectives that have no stress on their final syllable and end in a sonorant. This set of expressions includes neither the noun *accusation* nor the adjective *supportive*. The stress-shifting suffix *-al*, on the other hand, is generally unproductive, and composition with the likewise stress-shifting suffix *-ity* would not pave the way to productivity. These observations suggest that the constraint stated in [44] has nothing to do with the ungrammaticality of the forms in [45].

4.4. What Is Good about *undrinkable*?

Aronoff claims that the prefix *un-* attaches most productively to deverbal adjectives, a class that includes present and past participles and words in *-able*. In a subsequent specification of this word formation rule, he also lists adjectives ending in *-y, -ly, -ful, -al,* and *-like* as potential bases for *un-* prefixation. It has in fact been frequently noted that negative *un-* predominantly attaches to derived adjectives, which has resulted in a continuous loss of formations such as *unbroad, undeep, unbold, unglad, unstrong, unwide, unhonest,* all of which were attested in earlier stages of the language (Marchand 1966, 152). A careful look at the cases where such formations still exist shows a number of idiosyncratic restrictions on their use:

[47] *clean* versus *unclean*
unclean is usually used in the sense 'morally defiled, unchaste'
**The dishes are unclean.*

easy versus *uneasy*
uneasy refers usually to a state of physical discomfort or restlessness
**The homework is uneasy.*

clear versus *unclear*
unclear cannot be used to refer to obstructed vision **an unclear day; *Let the water run until it turns unclear.*

common versus *uncommon*
uncommon is confined to 'unusual, remarkable'
common (joint) *interests,* but **uncommon interests; the common crow* (occurring most frequently, ordinary), but **the uncommon crow; a common sailor* (without special status or rank), but **an uncommon sailor.*

ripe versus *unripe*
**The time was unripe.*

The astute reader will find analogous peculiarities in other cases, which clearly suggests that such forms are to be listed lexically. This conclusion was also reached by Zimmer on different grounds:

> . . . we must differentiate between two kinds of acceptability: acceptability in terms of a particular form (e.g., *unkind*) and acceptability in terms of a particular pattern (e.g., *un-x-able*). In terms of the linguistic behavior of individual speakers it is clearly only the second kind of acceptability which implies productivity. . . . It seems reasonable to assume that we should not try to account for all such morphologically complex forms in terms of the generative combination of smaller elements. It might be advisable rather to list some of them as lexical items on a par with monomorphemic forms—our lexicon would thus list both *true* and *untrue*. . . . On the other hand we would try to give formal definitions of classes of stems where *un*-prefixation is unrestricted; that is there would be productive rules for generating forms such as *unopenable, unweldable,* etc. In a sense only the forms generated by these restricted rules are to be considered as "grammatical"; the other forms in *un-* are neither grammatical nor ungrammatical, but "lexical."
>
> The implication of such an approach as a model for the linguistic behavior of speakers of English is that a number of forms such as *untrue, unhappy, unkind* are learned as lexical items like *true, happy, kind* while other forms in *un-* can be reasonably accounted for as the output of productive rules that should be given a place in the equipment we assume the speaker to be operating with. This does not mean that individual forms belonging to the second group may not often be acquired by repetition; what we are concerned with is the readiness with which speakers do use forms that they may never have heard before, and the readiness with which such forms are accepted. [1964, 85–86][23]

This also resolves the controversy around forms such as *uncouth, unkempt, untoward,* and *unruly.* Since they are lexically listed, there is no need to explain the nonoccurrence of their putative base. The contention that all *un*-adjectives are derived is further weakened by the existence of forms such as *ungainly, unseemly, unsightly,* where the negated form is much more common than the 'base'. The latter examples also call into question Aronoff's claim that adjectives ending in 'level-1' +*ly* tend to serve as a base for the prefix *un*. According to Marchand several cases of adjective-forming suffixes -*ly* need to be distinguished. For instance there is a suffix -*ly* that quite productively applies to relational nouns:

[48] motherly, fatherly, sisterly,
brotherly, friendly, scholarly,
masterly, kingly, princely . . .

On the other hand there is a suffix -*ly*, no longer productive, that forms adjectives from adjectives:

[49] cleanly, goodly, weakly,
lonely, poorly, sickly . . .

On the basis of the claim that *un*- attaches only to adjectives that are productively derived, we would expect that the examples in [48] are more apt to serve as a base for *un*- prefixation, which appears to be true. A similar example concerns adjectives that end in -*able*. Here again the prediction would be that only adjectives that are productively derived undergo *un*-prefixation:

[50] unaccountable, unanswerable, unbelievable, undeniable,
unbearable, unknowable, unsearchable, unwarrantable,
unreadable, undrinkable, unthinkable, unbreakable . . .

[51] *unadmissable, *uncapable, *uncomprehensible, *unedible,
*unvulnerable, *uncorrigible, *undefensible, *unlegible,
*undivisible, *undelible[24]

The ungrammaticality of the forms in [51] cannot be explained in terms of blocking since blocking as defined by Aronoff does not apply to productive formations (1976, 43ff.). Invoking a notion such as blocking also leaves unexplained why the following alternations exist:

[52]

inapproachable	unapproachable
incontrollable	uncontrollable
indecomposable	undecomposable
inexcusable	unexcusable
inconsumable	unconsumable
indescribable	undescribable
irredeemable	unredeemable
irreplaceable	unreplaceable
indistinguishable	undistinguishable

These observations suggest that the domain of *un-* is actually not the set of adjectives, but rather the set of functions that yield adjectives. As is expected given the definition in [23] any function into the set of adjectives is equally well suited for composition as long as the function is productive:

[53]

$$\begin{array}{ccc} & & f_{un} \\ & & (A) \rightarrow A \\ f_g & & f_{un} \circ f_g \\ X \rightarrow (A) & \longrightarrow & X \rightarrow A \end{array}$$

The analysis above straightforwardly accounts for Zimmer's and Aronoff's observations concerning the productivity of f_{un}. That function needs to compose with another function just as the functions f_{ity} and f_{ation} need to compose with other functions. This explains why formations with either monomorphemic or unproductively derived bases (*unclean, unsightly,* etc.) seem fossilized.

Note that an analysis in terms of level ordering cannot make sense of the data in that it fails to account for the observation that *un-* does not apply to adjectives that are not productively derived.

4.5. What Is Good about *lengthen?*

The suffix *-en* maps adjectives into verbs:

[54]

dark	darken
wide	widen
sweet	sweeten

The following examples have been adduced as evidence for the claim that in some cases this suffix will also attach to deadjectival nouns:

[55]

long	lengthen
strong	strengthen
high	heighten

However, Marchand informs us that originally the suffix *-en* attached to both adjectives and nouns:

> Semantic elements may have helped to coin some earlier desubstantival verbs, too. *Threaten* had in OE the meaning 'urge, press', and in ME developed the nuance 'try to influence by using menaces'. This may have led to *strengthen* on the basis 'try to influence by giving (moral) strength'. The original meaning of *strengthen* (14th c.) is, indeed, 'give courage'. Into this group, *hearten* 1526 and its opposite *frighten* fitted easily. On the other hand, the sense 'give strength' made possible the verb *lengthen*, orig. 'give length', i.e. 'eke out' and *lengthen* was followed by *heighten* 1523. [1966, 214]

I conclude that at the time when *-en* was a productive suffix it did not refer to word-internal structure.

Analyses of morphological data requiring an affix to "peek" inside its base in order to "find out" whether or not to attach are in fact quite rare. In this section I have discussed all relevant cases from English that I am aware of.[25] Once the representation of words in terms of hierarchical arrangements of morphemes is called into question one is led to look for alternative explanations to account for restrictions on affixation. Apart from the cases where in fact there is nothing to be explained (cases 4.3. and 4.5.), analyses in terms of functional composition or reference to phonological structure give rise to more straightforward and more general accounts.[26]

5. THE EVIDENCE FROM INFLECTIONAL MORPHOLOGY

In closing, I would like to point out that also with regard to inflectional morphology a categorial analysis offers explanation where an Item-and-Arrangement analysis does not go beyond restating the facts. Consider Selkirk's rules for generating inflected forms:

[56] **a.** $N \rightarrow N \quad \underset{\begin{bmatrix}\text{m case}\\ \text{m plur}\\ \text{m gend}\end{bmatrix}}{\text{Af}}$

b. $N \rightarrow N \quad \underset{\begin{bmatrix}\text{m gend}\\ \text{m plur}\end{bmatrix}}{\text{Af}} \quad \underset{[\text{m case}]}{\text{Af}}$

c. $N \rightarrow N \quad \underset{[\text{m gend}]}{\text{Af}} \quad \underset{\begin{bmatrix}\text{m case}\\ \text{m plur}\end{bmatrix}}{\text{Af}}$

d. $N \rightarrow N \quad \underset{[\text{m gend}]}{\text{Af}} \quad \underset{[\text{m plur}]}{\text{Af}} \quad \underset{[\text{m case}]}{\text{Af}}$

This enumeration of rules is hardly satisfactory. In particular this approach fails to explain why case is always in peripheral position. However, this ordering of affixes could not be otherwise within the present framework because of the syntactic function of case-marked nouns. They constitute the domain of verbs and prepositions. Assuming that case is precisely the function that maps nouns into this set, the case suffix must necessarily be in peripheral position. If gender or number would apply after case, the case information would get canceled and the items in question would simply not be in the domain of verbs and preposition. This raises the question of whether gender and number can be canceled without any ill consequences. The specification of verbs and prepositions answers this question: these functions require the items in their domain to have a specific case (for example German *helfen* 'to help' and *mit* 'with' apply to items in the dative set, *unterstützen* 'to support' and *ohne* 'without' apply to items in the accusative set) but have no concern for number or gender.

In the rules listed above the order of affixes seems accidental; this is why they have to be listed. It comes as no surprise that they are incomplete; the German form *Kindern,* for example, requires the following rule in Selkirk's scheme:

[57]	**e.** N →	N	Af	Af
		[m gend]	[m plur]	[m plur]
				[m case]

Worse than being incomplete, these rules offer no concept of 'possible arrangement of inflectional affixes'.

6. CONCLUDING REMARKS

The Item-and-Arrangement approach is so well established in modern generative linguistics that most linguists will find outlandish the objective of this paper: to argue against the representation of words in terms of their configurational structure. This preconception is illustrated by the following quote from an early paper by Chomsky, Halle, and Lukoff where they claim that constituent structure should also be introduced into the phonological level:

> A constituent hierarchy has always been considered a characteristic feature of the higher levels of morphology and syntax. . . . Every linguistic level, then, has the basic form of a linear system of symbols, organized into a hierarchical arrangement. [1956, 79]

By contrast, Sapir, who believed in processes, would no doubt eschew such a view; so Chomsky, Halle, and Lukoff are wrong in their historical assessment. Although generativists subsequently rejected the Item-and-Arrangement approach and adopted a very process-oriented terminology, there is a clear sense in which they remained Item-and-Arrangement grammarians—certainly in the configurational sense. That is, all of the composed *items* are *arranged* at some level of structure; X-bar theory is the epitome of such items so arranged. Hockett noted that Item-and-Arrangement ended up being taken for granted because of historical accident and not because it has been shown to be superior.

THE ROLE OF INTERNAL SYNTAX IN THE HISTORICAL MORPHOLOGY OF ESKIMO

Willem J. de Reuse

INTRODUCTION

In this paper, I will argue that the rich affixal morphology of Eskimo can be divided into three types: derivational morphology, a type I will call internal syntax, and inflectional morphology. Then, I will show that there is a historical tendency for affixes of the internal syntax to evolve into either derivational or inflectional affixes, and I will provide a possible explanation for these tendencies. The examples given are from the literature and my own fieldwork on the Central Siberian Yupik Eskimo language (CSY), spoken on Chukotka peninsula, in the Soviet Far East, and on St. Lawrence Island, Alaska, but the facts discussed here are valid for all Eskimo languages.

Before focusing on the main arguments of this paper, it will be helpful to give a brief overview of Eskimo morphology. As seen in the formula in [1], the Eskimo word contains: (*a*) one base (or stem); (*b*) zero, one, or several derivational suffixes called postbases in the literature on Eskimo; and (*c*) an obligatory inflectional ending that marks, for nouns, case, number, and sometimes person and number of the possessor, and for verbs, mood and person and number of the subject, as well as person and number of the direct object, if the verb is transitive. The inflectional ending may be followed by zero, one, or several enclitics, which are suffixes phonologically bound to the preceding word, but that function as independent discourse-marking or conjunctional particles.

[1] base + postbases_0^n + ending + enclitics_0^m

The ordering of the postbases is based on the semantic principle that a postbase occurring on the right has scope over everything to the left of it; there are exceptions to this principle. In example [2], the base is the verb *yughagh-* 'to pray', which is followed by the postbase deriving a noun from the verb 'to pray', *-vig-* 'place to V', resulting in *yughaghvig-* 'church'. This is followed by the postbase *-ghllag-* 'big N', deriving a noun from another noun; *yughaghvigllag-* is thus 'big church'. This is followed by the postbase deriving a verb from a noun, *-nge-* 'to acquire N', resulting in *yughaghvigllange-* 'to acquire a big church'. Then the verbal postbase *-yug-* 'to want to V' follows, resulting in *yughaghvigllangyug-* 'to want to acquire a big church'. Then follows a verb inflectional ending, which can be segmented into *-tugh-*, marking Indicative mood, and *-t,* marking third person plural subject. The word ends with the enclitic particle *=llu* 'also, and, too'.

[2] yughaghvigllangyugtutlu
yughagh-vig-ghllag-nge-yug-tugh-t=llu
pray-place.to.V-big.N-acquire.N-want.to.V-IND-3p-also[1]
'also, they want to acquire a big church'

This paper will concentrate on the postbases, which constitute by far the richest and most complicated area of Eskimo morphology. There are about four hundred postbases in Eskimo, and these can occur in strings of five or more after the same stem. Eskimo is thus considered to be an extremely polysynthetic language. Postbases can be classified into four types: those that derive nouns from nouns, (such as *-ghllag-* in example [2]—called NN postbases), those that derive verbs from verbs (such as *-yug-* in [2]—VV postbases), those that derive verbs from nouns (such as *-nge-* in [2]—NV postbases), and those that derive nouns from verbs (such as *-vig-* in [2]—VN postbases).

1. INTERNAL SYNTAX AND "REAL" DERIVATIONAL MORPHOLOGY

In the literature on Eskimo, the postbases have generally been called derivational suffixes, and indeed they appear to have at least the positional characteristics of derivational suffixes, since they occur between the base and the inflectional ending (Muysken 1986). However, I will suggest that the large majority of these postbases actually have syntactic, semantic, and morphological ordering properties more reminiscent of full words in less synthetic languages, than of the derivational morphology of such languages, and that this morphology forms a system more appropriately called internal syntax (Swadesh 1939; 1946). For Eskimo, it might thus be necessary to distinguish between what I would like to call real derivational morphology, (RD), and this internal syntax (IS).

I should emphasize at this point that the exposition of the differences between IS and RD that follows is tentative, and should be a lot more detailed in order to be fully convincing. I have not yet worked out refined syntactic tests that would be diagnostic in a large number of cases. The point I wish to make is that, once the possibility of such a distinction is recognized, certain historical tendencies of Eskimo morphology can be accounted for. I will turn to these historical tendencies in section 2. In this section, I will describe some of the properties differentiating "real" derivational morphology and internal syntax, in Eskimo, and then I will discuss the differences between IS and RD from a theoretical point of view, and from the point of view of other languages. The following chart outlines some properties differentiating "real" derivational morphology and internal syntax:

[3]	Internal Syntax	Real Derivation
1. Fully productive?	yes	no
2. Recursive?	yes	no
3. Affixal only?	yes	no
4. Branching?	no	yes

Property 1, productivity, means that elements of IS are completely productive and that their presence is conditioned by semantic plausibility only, and not by selectional restrictions. Actually, the number of sequences an element of IS can occur in is so high that it is very unlikely that native speakers would have the ability to memorize the resulting sequences, or to store them in the lexicon (Smith 1978; Fortescue 1980; de Reuse 1988). On the other hand, an element of RD is not productive in this manner, and combinations involving one must be stored in the native speaker's lexicon. The forms in [4] demonstrate the productivity of IS postbases. All contain the verb base *negh-* 'to eat', and one or more of five VV postbases that belong to the IS: *-yaghtugh-* 'to go and V', *-yug-* 'to want to V', *-uma-* 'past tense', *-yagh-* 'to V in vain; to V but . . . ', and *-pete-* (with the allomorph *-fte-* after vowels) 'to apparently V; it turns out that V'. The inflectional ending *-aa* is segmentable into *-agh-,* marking the transitive indicative mood, and *-a*, marking third person singular subject and third person singular object. The forms have to be translated in the past tense, even when the past tense marking postbase *-uma-* does not occur, because agentive verbs in the indicative mood automatically have a recent past tense implication—unless a tense-marking postbase or another mood cancels that implication. Thus *neghaa,* without any postbases, is 'he ate it', rather than 'he eats it'. In order to distinguish between the forms with an unmarked past implication and forms with the past-marking postbase *-uma-,* I have somewhat arbitrarily translated the latter with the English present perfect, even though *-uma-* cannot always be accurately translated in this way.

[**4**]

Postbases		Gloss
1	neghyaghtughaa	's/he went to eat it'
2	neghyugaa	's/he wanted to eat it'
3	neghumaa	's/he has eaten it'
4	neghyaghaa	's/he ate it, but . . .'
5	negheftaa	'it turns out s/he ate it'
1+2	neghyaghtughyugaa	's/he wanted to go eat it'
1+3	neghyaghtuumaa	's/he has gone to eat it'
1+4	neghyaghtughyaghaa	's/he went to eat it, but . . .'
1+5	neghyaghtughpetaa	'it turns out s/he went to eat it'
2+3	neghyugumaa	's/he has wanted to eat it'
2+4	neghyugyaghaa	's/he wanted to eat it, but . . .'
2+5	neghyugpetaa	'it turns out s/he wanted to eat it'
3+4	neghumayaghaa	's/he has eaten it, but . . .'
4+5	neghyaghpetaa	'it turns out s/he ate it, but . . .'
3+5	neghumaftaa	'it turns out s/he has eaten it'
1+2+3	neghyaghtughyugumaa	's/he has wanted to go eat it'
1+2+4	neghyaghtughyugyaghaa	's/he wanted to go eat it, but . . .'
1+2+5	neghyaghtughyugpetaa	'it turns out s/he wanted to go eat it'
1+3+4	neghyaghtuumayaghaa	's/he has gone to eat it, but . . .'
1+3+5	neghyaghtuumaftaa	'it turns out s/he has gone to eat it'
1+4+5	neghyaghtughyaghpetaa	'it turns out s/he went to eat it, but . . .'
2+3+4	neghyugumayaghaa	's/he has wanted to eat it, but . . .'

(*Continued*)
[**4**]

Postbases		Gloss
2+3+5	neghyugumaftaa	'it turns out s/he has wanted to eat it'
3+4+5	neghumayaghpetaa	'it turns out s/he has eaten it, but . . .'
1+2+3+4	neghyaghtughyugumayaghaa	's/he has wanted to go eat it, but . . .'
1+2+3+5	neghyaghtughyugumaftaa	'it turns out s/he has wanted to go eat it'
1+2+4+5	neghyaghtughyugyaghpetaa	'it turns out s/he wanted to go eat it, but . . .'
1+3+4+5	neghyaghtuumayaghpetaa	'it turns out s/he has gone to eat it, but . . .'
2+3+4+5	neghyugumayaghpetaa	'it turns out s/he has wanted to eat it, but . . .'
1+2+3+4+5	neghyaghtughyugumayaghpetaa	'it turns out s/he has wanted to go eat it, but . . .'

One could conclude from [4] that all combinations of the five IS postbases are possible, but only in the order 1 + 2 + 3 + 4 + 5. Generally, there are semantic restrictions on the orders of pairs of postbases with respect to one another that result in the above pattern. This does not mean, however, that it is possible to set up a number of position classes in Eskimo. Indeed, a few postbases can occur in several possible orders with respect to one another—for example, to indicate differing scopes of negation. In [5] the past postbase has scope over the negative postbase:

[5] angyanghisimalghiit
angyagh-nghite-uma-lghii-t
go.boating-NEG-PST-INP-3p
'they did not go boating' [Jacobson 1983, 21]

In [6] the negative postbase has scope over the past postbase:

[6] puughsimanghitaki?
puughte-uma-nghite-a-ki

fool-PST-NEG-INT-3s>3p
'is it not the case that he fooled them?' [Slwooko 1979, 61]

As will be seen below, some postbases can occur recursively, and this fact also argues against a position class analysis.

Let us now consider example [7], a word containing RD suffixes. By convention, I am using a [+] boundary to indicate that the two elements joined by it form a nonproductive sequence of a base and an RD suffix, or of two RD suffixes. Such combinations must therefore be listed in the lexicon. Expectedly, their meanings are not fully predictable from the sum of their parts, and the resulting combination is more conveniently translatable as a unit.

[7] igamsiqayugviksugapung
igamsiqa+yug+vig+ke-yug-agh-pung
feel.thankful.toward-want.to.V-IND-1d>3p
'we wish to thank them' [fieldnotes, 6–58]

In [7] the form *-yug-* occurs twice, and both forms are etymologically the same. However, from a synchronic point of view, they are only formally identical. The first *-yug-* is an RD suffix that is not readily translatable, and whose function is to convert a class of roots expressing emotion, such as *igamsiqa-* 'thankful', into intransitive verbs, in this case *igamsiqayug-* 'to feel thankful'. On the other hand, the second *-yug-* is a fully productive element of IS, and means, as seen in examples [2] and [4], 'to want to V'. Before the second *-yug-*, there are two other RD suffixes: the VN postbase *vig-* 'place to V', and the NV postbase *-ke-* 'to have as one's N'. Their combined effect is that of a transitivizer, but for certain verb bases only. *igamsiqu+yug+vig+ke-* is the commonest way to express 'to thank' (someone)'; it could be translated literally as: 'to have (someone) as a place to feel thankful'.[2]

Property 2, Recursion, means that the same IS postbase can be used several times within the same word; RD postbases can never be used in this way. Recursion is certainly connected to productivity (property 1), since it is hard to imagine recursion without a full productivity of the morphemes involved. In [8], the VV postbase *-ngwaagh-* 'to thoroughly V', is used twice for added emphasis, much as in colloquial English one could say, 'it is really really finished'.

[8] qamagtengngwaaghwaaghluni
qamagte-ngwaagh-ngwaagh-lu-ni
be.finished-thoroughly.V-thoroughly.V-APO-3s
'it is completely finished' [Angi et al. 1975, 20, 27]

In [9] the two occurrences of the VV postbase *-sqe-* 'to ask to V' also show that it can be used recursively. The verb *iitghesqesaghtiisqelluku* literally means 'he (the old man) asked them (the girls) to go and ask him (the White Eagle, a mythical figure) to come in', and the whole sentence is thus more literally: 'The old man sent the girls$_i$, asking them$_i$ to go and ask him$_j$, the White Eagle$_j$ to come in.'

[9] Nanevgam aghnaghaat kayagtii
nanevgagh-m aghnagh+ghagh-t kayagte-agh-i
old.man-RL girl-ABp send-IND-3s>3p

iitghesqesaghtiisqelluku Qawaak
itegh-sqe-yagh+tugh-sqe-lu-ku qawaag-ø
come.in-ask.to.V-go.V-ask.to.V-APO-3s>3s bird-ABs

Qatelghii.
qategh-lghii-ø
be.white-INP-ABs
the elderly eagle sent the girls out to have them tell the White Eagle to come in [Slwooko 1979; 105]

Property 3, affixal only, means that IS postbases cannot be nonconcatenative morphology, such as morpheme internal change or reduplication. This property is actually a corollary of recursion, (property 2), since it is hard to imagine how nonconcatenative morphology could be fully recursive.

Finally, property 4, concerning branching affixes, means that some suffixes in the IS can be built of a lexicalized combination of two or more RD suffixes, whereas IS suffixes cannot form a productive combination functioning as a whole as an IS suffix. The result is that the Eskimo word will not necessarily have a uniform left-branching structure, where each additional suffix necessarily derives a longer base, as is implied by Aronoff's (1976) word formation rules, but some affixes will have their own branching affix node. For example, [10] contains the combination of two suffixes *uma+ nginagh-*. This combination is lexicalized and semantically unproductive—that is, semantic compositionality does not obtain in it. It has the unpredictable meaning 'to continually V', instead of the expected meaning '[only [in the past V]]'. As illustrated in [10a], this lexicalized combination occurs in IS, and will have the morphological structure [10b], where *-uma +nginagh-* is dominated by its own affix node.

[10] **a.** iknaqughsaamanginaghnaaghii
iknaqe+ugh−sagh−uma+nginagh−naagh−agh−i
become.stronger-cause.toV-V.continously-eventually.V-IND-3s>3p
'he will keep them stronger continuously' [fieldnotes, 9–49]

b.

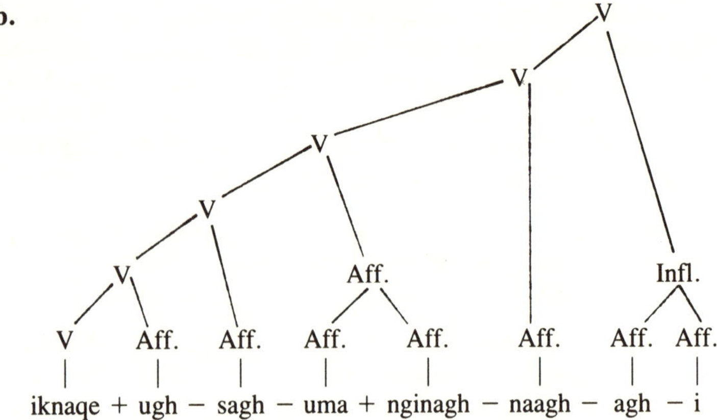

The lexicalized combination *-uma+nginagh-* can be compared to *-nginagh-uma-*, a fully productive sequence, as in [11]. The sequence here has the expected meaning '[in the past [only V]]'; a nonlexicalized semantically productive sequence *-uma-nginagh-* does not appear to exist:

[11] igleghtengnginaamaluteng
igleghte-nginagh-uma-lu-teng
travel-only.V-PST-APO-3p
'they were only traveling' [fieldnotes, 6–46]

It was already pointed out in the discussion of example [7] that the same formal element can occur twice in the same word, once as an RD suffix, and once as an IS suffix. Example [12] illustrates this again with the formal element *-uma-*, which first occurs as a part of the IS VV postbase *-yug+uma-* 'to be easy to V', and then as a past tense marker that is part of the IS.

[12] sugagyugumamaaq
sugag-yug+uma-uma-ugh-ø
feel.offended-be.easy.to.V-PST-IND-3s
'he was easily offended' [Slwooko 1979, 21]

It should be noted that the four properties of IS described above have fairly obvious parallel characteristics in regular "external" syntax: (*a*) 'external' syntactic structures, with the exception of idioms and proverbs, are not listed in the lexicon; (*b*) syntactic structures can be recursive; (*c*) there is no nonconcatenative syntax; and (*d*) elements of syntax such as phrases or clauses, like IS, are not necessarily built with trees that branch only in one direction. This last point of comparison is relevant only for languages with either prefixation only or suffixation only, since a language with both prefixation and suffixation will have branchings in both directions, regardless of the kind of morphology involved.

I now turn to a more theoretical discussion of the differences between IS and RD, in particular regarding the application of the Lexicalist Hypothesis. The claims of the Lexicalist Hypothesis (Chomsky 1970) is that derivational word formation is carried out in the lexicon, and that therefore the syntax cannot have access to and manipulate derived words. It appears that this claim is valid for RD, but not for IS, and that the IS is thus not derivational morphology. The examples in [13] show one way in which IS interacts with the external syntax of Eskimo. Example [13a] contains the IS NV postbase *-leg+u-* 'to have N', an incorporating postbase (it attaches not just to a noun but rather to the head of the noun phrase). In effect, even though morphologically *-leg+u-* is added to the head noun *qikmigh-* 'dog', syntactically it has not been added to the noun 'dog', but actually to the whole noun phrase 'big dog'.

As Sadock (1980; 1985) has demonstrated on the basis of parallel structures in Greenlandic Eskimo, *-leg+u-* acts like a morphologically intransitive verb, and like other intransitive verbs, it can occur with a direct object in an oblique case (here the modalis (MD)). Since postbases cannot attach to inflected words, the MD case marking cannot show up on *qikmigh-*, but it does show up on its morphologically free and stranded adjectival modifier *aangelghiimeng* 'big', and this is expected, since in Eskimo modifiers agree in case with their heads. Compare [13a] to [13b], where a semantically equivalent sentence without incorporating *qikmigh-* is given. Here, *-leg+u-* is affixed to a semantically empty base, *pi-*. In [13b] the unincorporated form *qikmigh-* does show the MD case ending that is present underlyingly only in [13a].

[**13**]	**a.**	Atan	aangelghiimeng	qikmilguuq.
		ata-n	aange-lghii-meng	qikmigh-leg+u-ugh-ø
		father-AB(2s-s)	be.big-INP-MDs	dog-have.N-IND-3s
		'your father has a big dog' [Fieldnotes, 4–6]		

	b.	(. . .) aangelghiimeng	qikmimeng	pilguuq.
		(. . .) aang-lghii-meng	qikmigh-meng	pi-leg+u-ugh-ø
		(. . .) be.big-INP-MDs	dog-MDs	thing-have.N-IND-3s
		'(your father) has a big dog' [ibid.]		

I will now speculate on whether languages other than Eskimo differentiate between IS and RD. One would expect the distinction to exist in the other languages called polysynthetic, such as, for example, the ones belonging to the following families in North America: Algonquian, Athabaskan, Caddoan, Chemakuan, Iroquoian, Kiowa-Tanoan, Salish, Uto-Aztecan, and Wakashan. However, since Eskimo languages have far larger numbers of productive affixes than any of these families, Eskimo might well have by far the most elaborate IS system. The Wakashan languages are a possible exception, since they might have numbers of suffixes comparable to those of Eskimo. According to Sapir and Swadesh (1939), the Wakashan language Nootka has 595 productive suffixes, but some of these might be inflectional or productive combinations, and in any case they certainly do not have the faculty to combine in long strings in the Eskimo fashion.

Other languages in which a distinction might be found are morphologically poorer but agglutinative languages such as Japanese, Quechua and Turkish. These typically have productive affixes such as causative suffixes or suffixes meaning 'to want to' which are likely to be IS. However, these languages appear to have only a handful of affixes with these properties.

It is also necessary to differentiate between IS and the phenomenon called syntactic affixation in recent theoretical literature. Fabb (1984) has argued that a few cases of English derivational affixation (involving nominalizing *-er* and *-ing, -able, -ly,* and *-ness*) are actually instances of syntactic affixation (i.e., affixation that takes place in the syntax, and not in the lexicon). He supports this view with a fairly complex argument (which I will not replicate here) involving the high productivity of these affixes, and crucially their ability to assign case and the fact that their attachment does not violate the Projection Principle. It is clear that the phenomenon of English syntactic affixation as discussed by Fabb only partially overlaps with what I have called IS because his syntactic affixation only occurs at the edge of the word and can only occur once per word. Thus, Fabb's theory will not allow for syntactic affixation in sequences, which is precisely what is typical for Eskimo IS.

Since I have differentiated at the beginning of this paper between derivation and inflection, it is also necessary to point out the differences between IS and inflection. As shown by Anderson (1982; 1988), inflection is fully productive and interacts with the syntax. I have argued that this also true for IS. The difference between the two is that, whereas inflectional morphology is determined by properties assigned to it in the syntax (agreement morphology or case morphology), IS morphology is not determined by syntactic properties. Inflection is also different from IS in that it is not recursive, but rather its forms can be easily listed in a paradigm. Finally, unlike IS, inflection is not necessarily affixal.

3. A CASE OF MORPHOLOGICAL LOSS IN CENTRAL SIBERIAN YUPIK

I will argue that IS is relatively marked, and that it had a tendency to evolve historically into a type of morphology that is less marked, such as inflectional or RD morphology. IS is marked because it is formally morphology, but at the same time it has a number of characteristics of "external" syntax, as seen above. As will become apparent later in this section, I do not mean to imply that Eskimo is on the way to losing its IS morphology, nor that languages generally lose IS morphology and cannot acquire it. Rather, it is the relative instability of IS morphology over time that shows it is marked, as opposed to the relative stability of inflection and derivation. Furthermore, a rich system of IS morphology, as opposed to a poor system involving only a handful of IS affixes, is rare in the languages of the world, and no family appears to have an IS system as elaborate as Eskimo. One might assume that a rich IS system will be less stable and hence more marked, than a poor IS system.

In Central Siberian Yupik (CSY), there is a type of morphological reduction that results in the reanalysis of an element of IS into an element of inflectional morphology.

Almost all Eskimo languages possess two VV IS postbases that can be reconstructed as Proto-Eskimo **-yukə-* 'to think or believe that oneself or another is V-ing', and **-na+yukə-* 'to think that oneself or another might V' (a lexicalized combination of **-na-*, marking irrealis or future, and **-yukə-*) (Fortescue 1985, 217).

Based on data from Fortescue (1983), [14] lists attested cognates of Proto-Eskimo **yukə-* and **-nayukə-* that appear in Eskimo varieties that are part of the Inuit-Inupiaq (or Eastern Eskimo) dialect chain. All dialects appear to have one or two cognate forms. One can derive all those forms from Proto-Eskimo via regular sound changes, but I do not know about the origin and function of the element *-ga-* occurring in several dialects.

[14]	East Greenlandic		-nasii-	68
	West Greenlandic	-(ga)sugi-/-(ga)suri-		38
	Labrador	-gasugi-		70
	Polar Eskimo		-nahugi-	68
	Tarramiut	-juri-		38
	North Baffin–Aivilik	-gasugi-	-nasugi-	69
	South Baffin	-gasugi-	-nasugi-	70
	Copper		-nahugi-	39
	North Slope		-nasugi-	39

In [15], a list of attested cognates in the other branch of Eskimo (Yupik, or Western Eskimo), the correspondences are even more straightforward—the appearance of Proto-Eskimo **-yukə-* and **-nayukə-* is traced from southeast to northwest. I was unable to find cognates in the Naukanski and Sirenikski languages of the Soviet Far East.

[15]	Koniag Alutiiq	-yuke-	-nayuke-	[Leer 1985, 126]
	Central Alaskan Yupik	-yuke-	-nayuke-	[Jacobson 1984, 506, 599]
	Central Siberian Yupik	-yuke-	-nayuke-	

Concentrating now on CSY, the striking fact is that the cognates do not have the expected morphological and semantic properties; indeed, CSY *-yuke-*

and *-na+yuke-* do not to mean 'to think', but have become inflectional mood markers. How did such a morphological change come about? The cognates of *-yuke-* and *-na+yuke-* in other Yupik languages can occur in several positions between a word, one of which is immediately in front of the inflection. Furthermore, when these postbases occur in that preinflectional position, this inflection consists of a combination of indicative mood and person endings that is often homonymous with person endings that would be appropriate after a type of moods, often called subordinate moods, used only in subordinate clauses. What happened in CSY is that the *-yuke-* and *-na+yuke-* that were not in the preinflectional position were lost, but the postbases in preinflectional position were reinterpreted as inflectional mood markers of the subordinate type, and the original mood plus person ending was reinterpreted as being just a person ending. The resulting mood markers have changed semantically, and can be translated as 'for fear that V', 'lest V', and, like the other subordinate verb moods of Eskimo, occur only in subordinate clauses. I have called this new mood, unique to CSY, the volitive of fear (VFO), exemplified in [16] and [17]. In [16] it is still possible to see how the change in meaning from 'to think that V' to 'fearing that V' could have come about, since on the surface, [16] could still be semantically interpreted as 'I was afraid, thinking that I might die' as well as 'I was afraid, fearing that I might die':

[16] alingumaanga tuqunayukama
alinge-uma-agh-nga tuqu-na+yuke-ama
be.afraid-PST-IND-1s die-VFO-1s
'I was afraid that I might die'
[fieldnotes, 6–12]

On the other hand, in [17] the element of fear is conveyed by *-na+yuke-* only, and not by the main verb *simighaqluki*:

[17] simighaqluki naavumanayukata
simigh-aqe-lu-ki naave-uma-na+yuke-ata
replace-PROG-APO-3p>3p get.ruined-PST-VFO-3p
'they would replace them (the cartridges on whaling bomb guns), for fear that they might have gone bad' [Apassingok et al. 1985, 134]

Thus, since every Eskimo verb contains one obligatory mood inflection, occurring immediately before the person endings, CSY *-na+yuke-* will always occupy precisely this slot. Furthermore, the precise form of the person inflection that follows it is determined by what type of mood precedes. Since the VFO mood is a type of subordinate mood, it must be followed by the appropriate person endings, and *-ama* in [16] and *-ata* in [17] are in fact forms of person endings possibly only after a subordinate mood.

I have described above the mechanism by which *-yuke-* and *-na+yuke-* became inflectional mood markers. It is not obvious why the original postbases should have been lost, especially since they form the main productive way of expressing the concept 'to think' in other Eskimo languages. The explanation can be given in terms of language contact. For several centuries, speakers of CSY have been in contact with economically and numerically dominant speakers of Chukchi, a Paleo-Siberian language native to a large area of the Soviet Far East (Vdovin 1961; Menovshchikov 1986). Among the Eskimos there has been widespread Chukchi-Eskimo bilingualism, which apparently resulted in the adoption of many Chukchi loanwords into Eskimo, including more than a hundred sentence adverbial and conjunctional particles. These particles are often synonymous to postbases of IS, and in a few cases seem to have caused the disappearance of these postbases. In particular, it is no coincidence that CSY has borrowed many particles from Chukchi that could be loosely translated as 'I think', 'you think', 's/he thinks', or 'it is thought'. Some of these particles of Chukchi origin are: *agnepa* 'I think', *gaymaangi* 'maybe, come to think of it', *enekiitek* 'maybe', *entaqun* 'I think', *iitegqun* 'perhaps', *langetaq* 'I think', and *luuraq, miiwen, qemall,* and *wiisam* 'maybe' (de Reuse 1988). My thesis, then, is that these borrowed Chukchi particles either caused the loss of the semantically corresponding IS postbases, or caused the semantically corresponding preinflectional IS postbases to be reinterpreted as mood endings.

In fact, there is philological evidence that the forms *-yuke-* and *-na +yuke-* existed at one time in CSY as productive IS postbases, and that their reinterpretation as inflectional endings is a fairly recent phenomenon. In the dialogue lines of several versions of the same CSY *ungipaghaan* (pl. *ungipaghaatet*) or traditional story, I have found examples of *-yuke-* and *-na+yuke-* used as IS postbases. Their survival there is due to the fact that folklore texts (in particular, dialogues by mythical beings or animals) are memorized from generation to generation, and therefore contain forms that are obsolete in the everyday language. The examples below come from several versions of the same *ungipaghaan*—the story of a girl held captive by a giant. The girl asks various animals that happen to pass by to help untie her. But the animals all respond in one stereotyped line: 'I think I will untie you eventually! (and end up not doing it). Example [18a] is a version of this line with *-yuke-*, and [18b] is a version of the line with *-na+yuke-*. This line is not part of a subordinate clause, and indicative mood endings and the personal endings appropriate for the indicative mood are present; therefore, a VFO interpretation is not possible, and *-yuke* and *-na+yuke-* must be postbases of the IS.

[18] a. itemuteqaghhnaaghyukamsi
iteme+ute-qaghte-naagh-yuke-agh-msi
untie.TR-please.V-V.eventually-think.that.V-IND-1s>2p
'I think I will untie you (pl.) eventually'
[Slwooko 1979, 7–13; Seppilu 1985, 3; fieldnotes, 52–59]

b. itemuteqaghhnayukamsi
iteme+ute-qaghte-na+yuke-agh-msi
untie.TR-please.V-think.that.might.V-IND-1s>2p
'I think I might untie you (pl.)' [Rookok n.d., 1]

Later on in the same story, and after a failed escape attempt, the girl tries to pacify the angry giant by saying, again in a rather stereotyped line: 'you think you could use me as a lice picker'. Example [19] is a version of this line in which the IS postbase *-yuke-* is followed by an indicative mood inflection:

[19] kumakightekaghnaaghyukaghpenga
kumakigh-te-kagh-naagh-yuke-agh-penga
pick.lice-Ver-have.as.one's.N-eventually.V-think.that.V-IND-2s>1s
'you think you will have me as your lice picker' [Rookok n.d., 2]

As is to be expected, since this use of the postbase is now obsolete, the storyteller has trouble giving the precise meaning of words containing such forms, and seems to rely on the context to translate them.[3]

4. CONCLUSIONS

In the preceding section, I have reviewed the evidence showing that the IS postbases *-yuke-* and *-na+yuke-* became elements of inflectional morphology, and I assumed that this morphological change was facilitated by the fact that the IS is a marked type of morphology. The same argument can be extended to cases in which there is an etymological connection between an RD affix and an IS affix. An example of a form that can be either an RD affix or an IS affix is *-yug-*, already discussed in example [7]. Presumably, one could historically consider one type of postbase as original and the other as derived. If the assumption is correct that IS morphology is more marked, one can conclude that, parallel to a tendency for IS elements to be reinterpreted as inflectional endings, there is also a tendency for IS elements to be reinterpreted as RD elements. Conversely, there will be no tendency for either inflectional or RD elements to become elements of the IS. Thus, I postulate that there was a morphological split of an original IS element **-yug-* into the present-day IS postbase *-yug-* 'to want to V' and the RD postbase *-yug-* 'to feel (like) V', rather than a morphological split of an original RD element *-yug-*.

If there is such a gradual erosion of the IS to benefit either inflection or derivation, one might ask how the IS system has apparently maintained its complexity and relative stability for centuries. Indeed, all Eskimo languages have retained IS postbase systems of comparable complexity, since they all have approximately the same number (about 300) of IS postbases, and since all use them for marking roughly the same semantic distinctions. Clearly, there is a need for Eskimo to preserve its IS system. However, if the IS system appears to be stable from a purely synchronic perspective, it is not so from a diachronic perspective. Whereas many Proto-Eskimo stems and most elements of the inflectional morphology have cognates in the various Eskimo languages and are thus easy to reconstruct, it appears that of the IS system, only about 120 postbases can be traced back to a Proto-Eskimo form (Fortescue 1985, 217–19).[4] This lack of reconstructable cognates must be due to a high rate of postbase replacement, and the problem that needs to be addressed is the origin of these new IS postbases.

It appears that the erosion of the IS system is constantly undone by the creation of lexicalized combinations of two IS postbases, which then function like new IS postbases, whose original elements of course becoming elements of RD. Examples of such lexicalized combinations are *-yagh+tugh-* in [9], *-uma+nginagh-* in [10a] and [10b], *-yug+uma-* in [12], and *-leg+u-* in [13a] and [13b]. Nothing prevents such combinations to ultimately move out of the IS system, and this is of course what happened to the VFO combination *-na+yuke-* in sentences [16] and [17]. The argument that most of these lexicalized combinations are not old is supported by the fact that very few can be reconstructed for earlier stages of Eskimo. That means that every Eskimo language has been independently creating its own combinations for a long time.

To conclude, there are tendencies of morphological change within the Eskimo word resulting in elements of the IS moving from their central position in the word in two opposite directions: either toward the stem or toward the inflectional system. If they move toward the stem, they tend to become elements of the "real" derivational system, and if they move toward the inflection, they are ultimately integrated into it. Furthermore, IS postbases might become frozen lexical units that are themselves new IS postbases.[5]

From the point of view of comparative Eskimo, one can also conclude that both RD morphology and inflectional morphology are potentially useful in the internal reconstruction of the "internal syntax" of polysynthetic languages. In fact, a lost element of IS might survive either in the inflectional morphology (cf. *-yuke-* and *-na+yuke-* as VFO mood markers) by a process of morphological change that one might call inflectionalization. Alternatively, a lost element of IS might survive in the derivational morphology, by a process of morphological change one might call derivationalization. I have not yet found a clear-cut case of this, but it is easy to conceive of a situation where, for some reason, the IS postbase *-yug-* 'to want to V' is lost and replaced by a semantically equivalent free verb, and where the RD postbase

-yug- 'to feel (like) V' would be retained. If IS is as special and marked as I maintain in this paper, one could even claim that the processes of morphological change I have called inflectionalization and derivationalization are nothing but types of morphologization, in that the internal syntax has evolved into the two more conventional and unmarked types of morphology, without ever leaving the bounds of the word.

NOTES AND REFERENCES

INTRODUCTION

Note

1. I except here such pioneering works as Zimmer's 1964 monograph on affixal negation and Matthews's 1972 book on Latin morphology.

CHAPTER 1

Notes

Thanks to the many people who helped me with this work. Larry Stephens helped with sources. Frank Anshen, Steve Anderson, Robert Beard, Morris Halle, Martin Haspelmath, Robert Hoberman, Richard Larson, Alec Marantz, Igor Mel'cuk, Richard Sproat, and Arnold Zwicky provided helpful comments on an earlier draft. I also benefited from the comments of those who heard presentations of some of this work at the University of Delaware and at the 1989 LSA Institute in Tucson. Finally, I am indebted to the University at Stony Brook for the leave during which most of this article was written.

1. Monteil (1970), for example, defines the theme (p. 35) as "le mot complet amputé de sa désinence" (the whole word with its desinence cut off).

2. For the moment, I will be using terms like *root* and *lexical* in a pretheoretical sense. Later, I will clarify more precisely what I mean by these terms.

3. In the system of the Classical Latin grammarians—Donatus (Fourth Century) or Priscian (Sixth Century), for example—and in subsequent traditional Western school grammars based on the Latin model, one member of an inflectional paradigm was formed from another, rather than both being formed from a third more abstract form, as in the Sanskrit and modern formal traditions. Hence the name Priscianic for such a formation when it is called for in modern treatments.

4. The future participle, because it is an adjective, always carries an agreement suffix after the *-uur-* suffix. However, in this paper, *future participle* will designate the "abstract" form that ends in *-uur-*, without any agreement suffix.

5. In addition to the standard abbreviations, I will use the following in the Latin glosses: Th - theme vowel; T - 3 stem marker (the notion of the 3 stem will be explicated in section 3.3.); FP - future (active) participle. I use doubled vowels in place of the macron, following recent phonological theory.

6. In the tables, I note only the morphs that are relevant to the discussion. Irrelevant morph boundaries are not indicated.

7. In this paper, the term *Perfect Participle* and its abbreviation (*PP*) will be used to refer to the Perfect Participle minus any adjectival agreement suffix—that is, the form that ends with the *-t-* (or *-s-*) suffix. This form never actually occurs "on the surface," since an agreement suffix is obligatory.

8. Whether it is *s* is not always predictable on phonological grounds.

9. The best-known exception is the verb *mor-i-* 'die', whose perfect participle is *mortu-*, but whose future participle is *morituur-*. Most of the other exceptions are first conjugation verbs with a theme-vowelless perfect participle but a thematic future participle. An example is *sec-aa* 'cut', with PP *sect* but FP *sec-aa-t*. There are perhaps a half dozen such verbs.

10. With the verbs *posse* and *velle* in table 2, the absence of both the perfect and future participles can be attributed to the absence of the former. With *esse*, one might wish to claim that the perfect participle is not used for semantic or syntactic reasons, although it "exists" in some potential sense.

11. There is one fairly widespread circumstance under which the perfect participle is not passive: with the so-called deponent verbs, which are passive in form throughout the paradigm, but active in meaning. They will be discussed below.

12. The careful reader will realize that this is not Matthews's sense of *lexeme*, but rather an American Structuralist version of it.

13. The distinction that Bloomfield makes may be important. I will not, however, discuss it in this work.

14. One might invoke various solutions involving existing but nonoccurring forms, but these are all too dangerous for my blood.

15. The Latin word means literally 'lying on the back' and is intended to convey that the verb here is inert, neither active nor passive in force. It is derived from the Greek grammatical term *hyption*, originally a wrestling term. The etymology of *supinum* is discussed in Benveniste (1932).

16. The supine appears to be defective, having only two of the expected five case forms. However, this may be due to its syntax rather than to its morphology.

17. Unlike nouns, whose declension is fixed, first and second declension adjectives have their declension (first or second) determined by the gender (not declension) of their head noun. Feminine nouns trigger the first declension, while masculine and neuter nouns trigger the second declension. Third declension adjectives do not vary in this way.

18. The final brackets hold the case, number, and gender suffix. Within each pair of brackets, the left column represents the constant properties of the form in question, while the right column holds the variable properties, fixed in any given case by agreement or government. All the (morphosyntactic) properties within this pair of brackets are abstract, with a given combination triggering affixation of a particular unit suffix. For example, in the supine, because it is always 4 decl. masc. sg., in the accusative case we will find the suffix *-um*, which is triggered by 4 decl. masc. sg. acc. Note that this suffix is also triggered by other combinations of morphosyntactic features.

19. Historically, the past participle is an *-o-* stem, while the supine is a *-u* stem. However, a sound change in Old Latin changed *o* to *u* under certain circumstances, resulting in the homophony of the accusative singular case forms. It is also worth noting here that there is another type of nominal, identical to the supine in form, that is found in such words as *fructus* 'enjoyment, profit', *sensus* 'perception', and *actus* 'movement'. This nominal is related historically to the supine in the same way that English *-ing* developed a nominal as well as a gerund use (Wasow and Roeper 1972). For an illuminating discussion of the relation between the two, see Panagl (1987). The classic discussion of Latin *t-* nominals of all sorts is Benveniste (1948).

20. One might counter on the side of the supine that its neutrality with respect to voice makes it a better candidate semantically for the base of the future participle than the usually passive past participle. But this argument is not much more forceful than the last.

21. Underlyingly, the suffix is *-oor*, but the vowel shortens by a regular rule in the nominative citation form.

22. In general, a *-trix* feminine can be found corresponding to a *-tor* masculine form, but for *-sor* masculines *-rix* feminines are systematically lacking, except for *expultrix* 'she who drives away' (cf. *expulsor*) and *tonstrix* 'hairdresser' (cf. *tonsor*). The form *expultrix* is irregular, the expected form being **expulstrix*, and in both cases we see that the *-t* has been reanalyzed as part of the suffix rather than part of the stem.

23. With verbs whose theme vowel is *-aa*, the iterative form is regularly built on the bare stem, rather than on the 3 stem. So, we find forms like *roogitoo*, from *rogoo, rogaare* 'ask', rather than the expected **roogaatitoo*. This is probably due to some sort of haplology (Menn and MacWhinney 1984), although it might have to be formulated as a truncation rule.

24. These form types are systematically built on the 3 stem. Other types are sometimes built on this stem, but I will not consider them here.

25. For nouns, this is the nominative singular and for verbs, the first person singular present indicative active.

26. A similar solution is proposed by Kuhner and Holzweissig.

27. I assume that there is a valid distinction between morphological realization, which is the concern of this work, and phonology. Lexical Phonology (Kiparsky 1982; Mohanan 1986) is one attempt to work out the interaction between the two.

28. I assume without argument that adverbs are adjectives and that adposition is not a lexical category. I also assume that all languages have the three categories of noun, adjective, and verb as syntactic categories, although morphology does not usually reliably distinguish all three.

29. I discuss this sense of *lexical* in Aronoff (1988), where I distinguish it from the sense meaning 'having to do with members of major lexical categories' and trace the history of the two senses.

30. I assume that whether a given lexeme is actual or not is a question about the mental lexicon. Stemberger and MacWhinney (1988) have shown that a word can be used without its being stored in the mental lexicon. For other recent discussion of morphology in the mental lexicon, see Henderson et al. (1988).

31. I am not claiming here that every lexeme must be representable by a single decontextualized form from which all contextual forms are generated (a form that is usually called the lexical representation). This claim, which may be sustained in the vast majority of cases, runs up in some instances against the conflicting demands of the (permanent) lexicon: there are many lexemes for which, because of morphophonological irregularities of varying degrees, some contextualized forms must be listed in the lexicon. Some linguists assume that each lexeme is a set of fully inflected forms. Saussure says that "Latin *dominus, domini:, domino:,* etc. is obviously an associative group formed around a common element, the noun theme *domin-*. . . " (1959, 126). Bybee (1985, 1988) and others have proposed network models that dispense with the lexical representation in all cases. I mention all this only to underscore that for the moment it is irrelevant to me exactly what the internal organization of a lexeme is. I care only that each lexeme be given some independent status.

32. Remember again that this definition of *stem* is very different from Bloomfield's. For Bloomfield, a stem is a bound form, and he has no term that expresses the notion that I am getting at. Mel'cuk seems to have a similar concept in mind to mine, but he says that "the notion of stem is quite important for morphological description, but at present I am not able to suggest a rigorous definition for it. . . " 1982, 131).

33. It may be noted that the grammatical term *root* comes from Semitic grammar, where the root is an abstract unpronounceable sequence of consonants.

34. As Robert Hoberman has reminded me, in the Semitic tradition, the citation form is not the address, for which the root is normally used, dictionaries being alphabetized according to roots.

35. This is essentially equivalent to Halle's (1973) list of morphemes.

36. Lieber does not broach the question of the semantic relation between the terminal elements related by her morpholexical rules. The question is not trivial, since these terminal elements, being listed in the permanent lexicon, must have semantic representations, unless we distinguish the morphological lexicon from another syntactic lexicon.

37. Incidentally, for productively derived lexemes (what I call potential lexemes) whose stems are predictable, as in this case, it is impossible to talk about these nonexistent stems of nonexistent lexemes being listed in a permanent lexicon. Thus, even if we were to allow the more than 96 percent of first conjugation verbs whose stems are all predictable from the theme vowel to have all these stems listed (following, say, Bybee), we would still not be able to claim that the rules for regularly derived stems are not productive.

38. There is no special connection between a theory's being lexeme-based and its permitting a complex mapping between form and meaning. For instance, Marantz (1984), while not explicitly lexeme-based, certainly argues for nonisomorphism.

39. In general, when a morph occurs with a particular possible meaning only in a morphologically restricted environment, it is difficult to decide whether that morph has significance or whether its presence simply as a form is conditioned by the environment or construction, which as a whole bears the significance that is in question. Thus, one might wish to claim for Greek compounds that the linking vowel signals that the stem preceding it is a bound member of a compound or that it links the members of a compound, but since the linking vowel occurs only between members of compounds, then the traditional analysis—that the linking vowel is semantically empty—is equally reasonable and more parsimonious, especially since some compounds show no linking vowel and would have to contain a zero if the linking vowel were semantically significant.

Troubetskoy calls junctural phonological phenomena like word-final devoicing boundary signals, even though they are automatically conditioned phonological alternations. At a superficial level, they do serve to mark the juncture even though they are, strictly speaking, predictable from it. We are dealing here with a similar phenomenon.

40. The theme vowel usually shows up in the present active infinitive. This is not true of *i*, which is neutralized to *e*.

41. Note that the theme vowel *aa* appears "after" the null suffix for intensives. If we do not allow zero morphs, as seems reasonable within a process framework, and if we insist that morphs (forms) rather than lexemes condition the quality and quantity of the theme vowel, then we must say that the *aa* theme vowel is the default. This conclusion is reasonable, on grounds of frequency and further historical development (it is the default theme vowel in all Romance languages).

42. There is, as I have already mentioned, a small number of very high frequency irregular verbs that lack a theme vowel. These verbs, to the extent that they are regular, take the same endings as *e* theme verbs.

43. As noted above, about two-thirds of the verbs in this conjugation are regular.

44. Of the five, three occur independently as verbs. One, *-lee,* occurs only in the verb *deelee,* which quite transparently contains the privative prefix *dee-*. The other (*-plee*) occurs with a number of prefixes (e.g., *ex-*, *con-*) and has the general meaning 'fill'.

45. Assuming that the *i* of *viee* is a glide.

46. Note that there are no other second conjugation verbs with "vowelless" roots, all other verbs of this conjugation being disyllabic when the *ee* is included.

47. The fact that a stem and not a lexeme has a theme vowel is consonant with my claim above that morphs determine the quality of theme vowels. Most interesting in this regard are the third conjugation verbs that show mixed conjugation. This class includes all verbs with the intensive suffix *-ess,* which have the theme vowel *e* in the present stem, but *ii* in the perfect and *t* stem. The suffix thus determines the form of the resulting verb in a complex manner, selecting different theme vowels for different stems. Sometimes included with *-ess* are verbs with the inceptive suffix *-sce,* whose perfects lack the suffix (e.g., *quieescoo, quieevii* 'become quiet'). Here, however, the derived verb is lacking the perfect stem altogether and the perfect stem of the base is used instead.

48. Where the nasal is retained throughout, we know from etymology that the root has no nasal. For example, *iunge* is transparently derived from the root *iug* 'yoke'. In this case, a less frequent verb, *iugaa* 'tie together', is also formed from the same root without a nasal infix.

49. Traditional grammars say that nonpresent stems of these verbs are formed on the root. For morphologically simple verbs, the lexical representation will indeed be the root.

50. Note that this type of idiosyncratic stem selection would be much more difficult to state in a simple morpheme-based treatment, since it is not clear that the different forms of a single lexeme that may be selected as stems can always be treated as allomorphs, without doing severe damage to the notion of allomorph. That is because some stems are morphologically complex, while others are not, for the same operation. Semantically, the two stem types must be treated identically, which leads to difficulties in grouping forms into traditional morphemes.

51. I have not included any verb without a theme vowel, since they are all idiosyncratic, but it should be noted that these verbs by and large take the same endings as *e* verbs and that they are perfectly regular in the nonpresent forms.

52. *ii* and *i* conjugations, for example, are identical in all but a few cases, and in just those cases where they differ, the *i* and *e* conjugations are identical.

53. This analysis of the function of theme vowels can be traced to the Latin grammarians. Monteil (1970) restates it within a Benvenistian framework.

54. The term *stem type* is used to refer to general notions on the level of *t* stem, present stem, perfect stem, and so forth, as opposed to individual stem tokens like *portaat-* or *portaa-*.

55. This generalization holds only for inflection. In derivational word formation we do find exceptions, so that a given suffix that usually selects a given stem type may exceptionally be formed on another stem type in a particular instance. Derivational suffixes also vary in regularity in this respect. But such variation is the hallmark of derivation.

56. All deponents have the following active forms: present and future participles, future infinitive, gerund, and supine.

57. There are a few verbs (all of them very frequent) that occur only in one or two individual verb forms. Some common ones are *aioo* 'affirm', which occurs only in the present and imperfect indicative, and *inquam* 'say', which occurs in a few scattered forms.

58. Note also that I am looking at stem types, not morphs. It should be very clear already that each stem type is a phonologically abstract entity that is realized in a great variety of ways rather than a phonologically specified (albeit abstract) entity on the level of, say, English /z/, the plural noun/third person present verb/genitive marker.

59. Modern syntacticians regard infinitives and participles as being tenseless, tense being associated only with finite forms of the verb. In keeping with traditional Latin grammar, I depart from that view in this table, although it may be that a proper understanding of Latin syntax will allow us to treat infinitives as untensed.

60. I assume that this suffix is followed by a theme vowel: *aa* in the imperfect and *e* in the future. This will ensure that the person and number suffixes have the proper forms.

61. The 1 sg. suffix *am* deletes the preceding vowel in all instances. Similarly, the 3 sg. suffix *t* shortens the preceding vowel in all instances.

62. Note that the *b* stem is not basic, but derived in all cases, so that it does not ever have to be listed in the permanent lexicon (a point to which I will return shortly).

63. We also see from this particular example that the former type can sometimes be constructed on the latter, the *b* stem being built on the present stem.

64. The major evidence for the listing of stems in Latin verb morphology is the existence of irregular and suppletive stems. One might look for similar evidence for *b* stems. If, for example, we could show that an irregular verb was irregular precisely at this level, then that would constitute evidence for listing some *b* stems. I have not been able to find such evidence. The only possible cases is the verb *sum* 'be', which is peculiar in that it forms the future and imperfect tenses with the same desinences that are found with *aa* and *ee* verbs, but on a peculiar stem (*es*/*er-*, the alternation being governed by rhotacism) that lacks the suffix *VVb* that normally precedes these desi-

nences in these tenses. One might wish to conclude from this pattern that the peculiar *b*-less stem is an irregular *b* stem. On closer inspection, however, it becomes clear that the putative irregular *b* stem is in fact an irregular present stem and that what is peculiar about this one verb is that the desinences of the imperfect and future tenses are added directly to the present stem. There is therefore no necessity to refer to an irregular *b* stem for this verb, since it lacks the *b* form entirely. The evidence for this last conclusion comes from the present (active) infinitive, which is always formed on the present stem of a verb. For this irregular verb, this infinitive and the future and imperfect tenses are all formed on what was thought to be the irregular *b* stem, which is in fact the present stem.

The relevant forms are found in [i]:

[i]	*conjugation*	*present*	*future*	*imperfect*	*infinitive*
	aa	amaatis	amaaboo	amabam	amaare
	ee	habeetis	habeeboo	habeebam	habeere
	e	ducitis	ducam	duceebam	ducere
	sum	estis	eroo	eram	esse

Note that the alternation between *s* and *r* is regular, due originally to rhotacism.

References

Allen, J. H., and H. B. Greenough. 1894. *New Latin Grammar*. Boston: Ginn.

Allen, Margaret. 1978. *Morphological Investigations*. Ph.D. diss., University of Connecticut, Storrs.

Anderson, Stephen R. Ms. *A-Morphous Morphology*. Unpublished ms., The Johns Hopkins University.

Aronoff, Mark. 1976. *Word Formation in Generative Grammar*. Cambridge, Mass.: M.I.T. Press.

———. 1978. Lexical Representations. In *Proceedings of the Parasession on the Lexicon*, pp. 12–25. Chicago Linguistic Society, Chicago.

———. 1983. Actual Words, Potential Words, Frequency and Productivity. In *Proceedings of the Thirteenth International Congress of Linguists*, ed. S. Hattori and K. Inoue. pp. 163–71, Comitè International Permanent de Linguistes, Tokyo.

———. 1988. Two Senses of 'lexical'. Proceedings of the Eastern States Conference on Linguistics, 1988: 1–11.

Beard, Robert. 1981. *The Indo-European Lexicon*. Amsterdam: North-Holland.

———. 1987. Morpheme Order in a Lexeme/Morpheme-Based Morphology. *Lingua* 72:1–44.

Benveniste, Emile. 1932. Supinum. *Revue de philologie* 58:136–37.

———. 1948. *Noms d'agent et noms d'action en Indo-Europeen.* Paris: Adrien-Maisonneuve.

Bloomfield, Leonard. 1933. *Language.* New York: Henry Holt.

Botha, Rudolf P. 1968. *The Function of the Lexicon in Transformational Generative Grammar.* The Hague: Mouton.

Bybee, Joan. 1985. *Morphology: A Study of the Relation between Meaning and Form.* Typological Studies in Language, no. 9. Amsterdam: John Benjamins.

———. 1988. Morphology as Lexical Organization. In *Theoretical Morphology,* ed. M. Hammond and M. Noonan. pp. 119–41. San Diego: Academic Press.

Carstairs, Andrew. 1987. *Allomorphy in Inflexion.* London: Croom Helm.

Halle, Morris. 1973. Prolegomena to a Theory of Word Formation. Linguistic Inquiry 4:3–16.

Henderson, Leslie, Max Coltheart, Anne Cutler, and Nigel Vincent, eds. 1988. *Linguistic and Psychological Approaches to Morphology. Linguistics* 26–4.

Hoberman, Robert. 1989. *The Syntax and Semantics of Verb Morphology in Modern Aramaic.* New Haven: American Oriental Society.

Hockett, Charles. 1947. Problems of Morphemic Analysis. *Language* 23:321–43.

Hoeksema, Jack. 1985. *Categorial Morphology.* New York: Garland.

Kuhner, Raphael, and Friedrich Holzweissig. 1912. *Lateinische grammatik.* 2d ed., repr. 1974), Hannover: Hahnsche Buchhandlung.

Lieber, Rochelle. 1980. *On the Organization of the Lexicon.* Ph.D. diss., M.I.T.

Lyons, John. 1977. *Semantics.* Cambridge: Cambridge University Press.

Marantz, Alec. 1984. *On the Nature of Grammatical Relations.* Cambridge, Mass.: M.I.T. Press.

Matthews, P. H. 1972. *Inflectional Morphology.* Cambridge: Cambridge University Press.

———. 1974. *Morphology.* Cambridge: Cambridge University Press.

Mel'cuk, Igor. 1982. *Towards a Language of Linguistics.* Munich: Wilhelm Fink.

———. 1989. Subtraction in Natural Language. Unpublished ms., Université de Montreal.

Menn, Lise, and Brian MacWhinney. 1984. The Repeated Morph Constraint: Toward an Explanation. *Language* 60:519–41.

Mohanan, K. P. 1986. *The Theory of Lexical Phonology.* Dordrecht: Reidel.

Monteil, Pierre. 1970. *Eléments de phonétique et de morphologie du Latin.* Paris: Fernand Nathan.

Panagl, Oswald. 1987. Productivity and Diachronic Change in Morphology. In *Leitmotifs in Natural Morphology*, ed. W. Dressler, W. Mayerthaler, O. Panagl, and W. Wurzel, pp. 127–51. Amsterdam: John Benjamins.

Saussure, Ferdinand de. 1959. *Course in General Linguistics*, tr. W. Baskin. New York: Philosophical Library.

Stemberger, Joseph Paul, and Brian Macwhinney. 1988. Are Inflected Forms Stored in the Lexicon? In *Theoretical Morphology*, ed. M. Hammond and M. Noonan, pp. 101–16. San Diego: Academic Press.

Wasow, Thomas, and Thomas Roeper. 1972. On the Subject of Gerunds. *Foundations of Language* 8:44–61.

Wheelock, Frederick. 1960. *Latin.* 2d ed. New York: Barnes and Noble.

Williams, Edwin. 1981. On the Notions 'lexically related' and 'head of a word'. *Linguistic Inquiry* 12:245–74.

Zwicky, Arnold. 1986. The general Case: Basic Form versus Default Form. *Berkeley Linguistics Society* 12:305–14.

———. 1989. Quicker, more quickly, *quicklier. *Yearbook of Morphology* 2.

CHAPTER 2

Notes

The data in this paper were taken primarily from Bhat and Ningomba (1986) and from my own notes and tapes gathered during fieldwork in New Delhi in 1984, and in Manipur State and New Delhi in 1986 and 1987. Additional data are from the works on Manipuri listed in References. I would like to thank Hyunsook Kang, Willem de Reuse, Curtis Rice, and Anthony Woodbury for helpful comments and discussion on earlier versions of this paper. Responsibility for any shortcomings in the analysis is mine.

The following abbreviations are used in the morphological analyses:

agen	agentive	inf	infinitive
ass	associative	INFL	inflection
att	attributive	nom	nominalizing
casem	case marker	perf	perfective
dat	dative	pres	present tense
dsource	action takes place from a distant source	prog	progressive aspect
		seq	sequential
dur	durative	vinfl	verb inflection
ex	experiential	3PP	third person possessive
gen	genitive		

1. Manipuri is a Tibeto-Burman language of the Kuki-Chin Group spoken in the central valley of Manipur state in northeastern India.

2. There are two tones in Manipuri: a default high-level tone (unmarked in the examples) and a lexical falling tone (indicated in the examples by a grave accent mark (ˋ) over the vowel of the word or syllable).

3. Additionally, for VAR to apply in compounds, the initial stem must not be an open syllable of the shape (C)V, where the second stem of the compound ends in a nasal. As of yet, I have no explanation for this restriction.

4. In these cases note that the final *k* of *yok, lak,* and *-lə̀k* does not undergo VAR, as that rule applies only on syllable initial voiceless stops.

5. Here, for the sake of space, I limit myself to the discussion of three phonological rules. A more exhaustive analysis of the lexical phonology and morphology of Manipuri can be found in Chelliah (forthcoming), where I discuss the level ordering of eleven phonological rules in Manipuri.

6. These suffixes are derived from etymologically related stems still present in the language and used as stems as well; (e.g., the L1 suffix *-lək* 'action comes from a distant source' and *lak* 'to go'; the L1 suffix *-t^hok* 'do something to completion', and *t^hok* 'out'; the L1 suffix *-k^hət* 'begin to V' and *k^hət* 'out'.) This might explain the unique phonology of these suffixes.

References

Aronoff, M. 1976. *Word Formation in Generative Grammar.* Cambridge, Mass.: M.I.T. Press.

———. 1988. Head Operations and Strata in Reduplication: A Linear Treatment. In *Yearbook of Morphology,* ed. G. Booij and J. van Marle. Dordrecht: Foris.

———, and S. N. Sridhar. 1987. Morphological Levels in English and Kannada. In *Rules and the Lexicon,* ed. E. Gussmann. Lublin: Katolicki Uniwersytet Lubelski.

Bhat, D. N. S., and M. S. Ningomba. 1986. A Manual of Manipuri Grammar. Unpublished ms., Manipur University, Canchipur, Imphal.

Booij, G., and J. Rubach. 1984. Morphological and Prosodic Domains in Lexical Phonology. *Phonology Yearbook* 1:1–27.

———. 1987. Postcyclic versus Postlexical Rules in Lexical Phonology. *Linguistic Inquiry* 18:1–44.

Chelliah, S. Forthcoming. Lexical Phonology and Morphology in Manipuri. *Linguistics of the Tibeto-Burman Area.*

Chen, M. 1985. The Syntax of Phonology: Xiamen Tone Sandhi. Ms. University of California, San Diego.

Cohn, A. 1989. Stress in Indonesian and Bracketing Paradoxes. *Natural Language and Linguistic Theory* 7:167–216.

Devi, P. M. 1979. *Manipuri Grammar*, Ph.D. diss., Deccan College, Poona.

Devi, Phazabi. 1979. *Tone and Tonology in Meteiron*. Master's thesis, Manipur University, Canchipur.

Hoeksema, J. 1985. *Categorial Morphology*. New York: Garland.

Kiparsky, P. 1982. Lexical Phonology and Morphology. In *Linguistics in the Morning Calm*, ed. Linguistic Society of Korea. Seoul: Hanshin.

———. 1983. Word-formation and the Lexicon. In *Proceedings of the 1982 Mid-America Linguistics Conference*, ed. F. Ingemann. Lawrence: University of Kansas.

Laishram, J. 1975. *The Manipuri Verb*. Master's thesis, Manipur University, Imphal.

Marantz, A. 1988. Clitics, Morphological Merger, and the Mapping to Phonological Structure. In *Theoretical Morphology*, ed. M. Hammond and M. Noonan. New York: Academic Press.

Mohanan, K. P. 1986. *The Theory of Lexical Phonology*. Dordrecht: Reidel.

Nespor, M., and I. Vogel. 1986. *Prosodic Phonology*. Dordrecht: Foris.

Pesetsky, D. 1985. Morphology and Logical Form. *Linguistic Inquiry* 16:193–246.

Pettigrew, W. 1912. *Manipuri (Mitei) Grammar*. Allahabad: Pioneer Press.

Primrose, A. J. 1887. *Manipuri Grammar*. Manipur: Government Press.

Selkirk, E. 1986. On Derived Domains in Sentence Phonology. *Phonology Yearbook* 3:371–405.

Singh, N. K. 1964. *Manipuri to Manipuri and English Dictionary*. Imphal, Manipur: O. K. Store.

Singh, N. Nonigopal. 1987. *A Meitei Grammar of Roots and Affixes*. Ph.D. diss., Manipur University, Canchipur.

Sproat, R. 1985. *On Deriving the Lexicon*. Ph.D. diss., M.I.T.

Thoudam, P. C. 1989. Conditioning Factors for Morphophonemic Alternations of Manner in Meiteiron. *Linguistics of the Tibeto-Burman Area* 12, no. 2:93–100.

CHAPTER 3

Notes

The research reported here has been supported by the Netherlands Organization for Pure Scientific Research (NWO) and by the Research Institute for Language and

Speech (OTS) at the University of Utrecht. This paper was presented at the morphology workshop organized by the Linguistic Society of America, in Tucson (July 1989).

1. Generally speaking, the arguments to be presented below can still be followed without problems if one considers the external argument NP to be in the specifier position of IP at D-structure.

2. My assumptions about the external argument being agent and the internal argument being theme in fact restrict the discussion to the minimum necessary: most of my arguments to be presented below can be based on just three types of verbs—transitive, intransitive, and ergative verbs—and on just these two theta roles. The aspects of theta roles that bear on the difference between syntax and the lexical component need some additional elaboration, which is given at the end of section 2.

3. I avoided the use of the term VP here. The V′ in this minimalized structure has a function comparable to the older VP. Also, I used V^{max} rather than VP—which would strictly speaking be the maximal projection—because V^{max} contains more material than the older VP. An argument bearing on this problem is given in section 3.

4. That is, exempted from this discussion are constructions or languages in which expletives are inserted in [Spec,IP] position (in particular impersonal constructions), or constructions or languages in which nominative case can be assigned VP-internally (in particular, postverbal subjects in Romance).

5. As I am concerned with syntax, the syntactic participle is considered rather than the lexical adjective. One of the differences is that the syntactic passive participle may not be input to further affixation processes as opposed to the lexical variant—for example, * *John has been unkilled* versus *John is uneducated* (cf. Chomsky 1981). The difference between the two participles is discussed more extensively at the end of this section.

6. This type of evidence cannot be found in French, because only a finite list of adjectives may precede the head noun. For English the argument seems to be maintainable, but not without additional provisos. If the Head-Final Filter of Williams (1982) explains [i], it can also be invoked to explain [ii].

[i] * the proud of his children man

[ii] * the walking on the street man

As English complements follow V and A, the filter will always apply to this type of examples, as opposed to Dutch, where complements generally precede verbs. The filter would entail that only intransitive and ergative verbs can occur prenominally in English, as illustrated in [iii].

[iii] the [PRO sleeping] man
the [PRO dying] man

A complication may stem from the fact that the examples in [10c] are not necessarily derived in syntax.

7. The passive morpheme (PASS) is then called an implicit argument. If one considers arguments to be nominal by definition, the passive morpheme would be nominal itself. One might then perhaps consider the possibility to discuss them in the section on nominalizations. However, as shown there, nominalizing a verb has quite different effects than passivizing a verb—effects so different that it is at present inconceivable that the passive morpheme nominalizes the verb. Also, it is not necessarily true that arguments of a verb can only be nominal in nature.

8. I agree with Jaeggli (1986) that only the passive morpheme gets assigned the external theta role, such that the projection principle is not violated in the case of passive. Other theories (e.g., Hoekstra 1986) let the perfective morpheme also absorb the external theta role, such that the projection principle is not violated in this case too. In this type of theory the explanatory power is given to the auxiliaries, which are given a mending power comparable to the one illustrated in the main text. Although Hoekstra's view generally seems to be an alternative on the matter, I fail to see how it could work out in small clauses, where there are no auxiliaries. Moreover, the passive morpheme and the perfective morpheme (PERF) can co-occur in one sentence, and it seems to me that they would both like to get assigned the one external theta role if both are implicit arguments.

9. In English the same argument can in fact be given, but the example needs more comments in view of the possibility of the progressive. Hence, the argument holds for English [iv], but not for [v].

[iv] he is [PRO running]

[v] he is running

10. Note that for the specific case illustrated in [24] some additional qualifications have to be made for passive and perfective participles as they may follow the verb *be*. However, I postulate a difference between the main verb *be* and auxiliary *be* (see section 5). The main verb *be* selects A[max,+lex].

11. Here I follow Muysken (1982) with respect to the definition of minimal, maximal, and intermediate projections.

12. More concretely, *keep* subcategorizes for a Nominal constituent, whether lexical or syntactic (*I kept something, I kept [Bill running]*). An alternative would be *I keep Bill [PRO running]*, in which case the construction would be an adjectivalization along the lines of the preceding section. Both analyses avoid the postulation of a prepositional *-ing*.

13. This formulation does not discriminate between an analysis in which the external argument is directly generated in [Spec,NP] position, moved to this position, generated directly in [Spec,DP] position, or moved to this position. The contrast explained here concerns accusative subjects versus genitive subjects.

14. In other words, *-ing* cannot be analyzed as an implicit argument.

15. According to the analysis, [34] is fully ungrammatical, comparable to [33a]. On the other hand, *-ing* could just be an alternative to *-ion*. Under the latter option [34]

could be grammatical as LEX-NOM. The marginal availability of this option accounts for the status of [34] given in the main text.

16. One could probably allow for [+V] in the subcategorization frame of the passive morpheme, but not without an appeal to something like vacuous affixation. This subcategorization frame would in principle allow for passivizing adjectival heads. As adjectives do not have external theta roles in the sense defined in the text, and as the passive morpheme absorbs an external role, passivizing adjectives would result in vacuous absorption. Note that the subcategorization frames in the main text predict that both PERF and PRES-PART may be added to adjectival phrases, a prediction that can be borne out under an analysis in which auxiliaries are superficial elements. (On some abstract level one would, for example, have INFL and PERF adjoined to AP, and insertion of verbal bases would derive *NP has been AP*.) See also section 5 and Drijkoningen (1989).

17. On more details for auxiliary insertion, see Drijkoningen (1989).

References

Anderson, S. 1977. Comments on the Paper by Wasow. In *Formal Syntax,* ed. P. Culicover, T. Wasow, and A. Akmajian. New York: Academic Press.

———. 1982. Where's Morphology? *Linguistic Inquiry* 13:571–612.

Aronoff, M. 1989. Passive *-en*. Unpublished ms., State University of New York, Stony Brook.

Brekke, M. 1988. The Experiencer Constraint. *Linguistic Inquiry* 19:169–80.

Burzio, L. 1986. *Italian Syntax*. Dordrecht: Reidel.

Chomsky, N. 1970. Remarks on Nominalization. In *Readings in English Transformational Grammar,* ed. R. Jacobs and P. Rosenbaum. Waltham, Mass.: Ginn.

———. 1981. *Lectures on Government and Binding*. Dordrecht: Foris.

———. 1986. *Barriers*. Cambridge, Mass.: M.I.T. Press.

Drijkoningen, F. 1989. *The Syntax of Verbal Affixation*. Tübingen: Niemeyer.

Emonds, J. 1978. The Verbal Complex V′–V in French. *Linguistic Inquiry* 9:151–75.

Fabb, N. 1984. *Syntactic Affixation*. Ph.D. diss., M.I.T.

Hoekstra, T. 1986. Passive and Participles. In *Linguistics in the Netherlands 1986,* ed. F. Beukema and A. Hulk. Dordrecht: Foris.

Jackendoff, R. 1977. *X-bar Syntax: A Study of Phrase Structure*. Cambridge, Mass.: M.I.T. Press.

Jaeggli, O. 1986. Passive. *Linguistic Inquiry* 17:587–622.

Levin, B., and Rappaport, M. 1986. The Formation of Adjectival Passives. *Linguistic Inquiry* 17:623–61.

Muysken, P. 1982. Parametrizing the Notion 'Head'. *Journal of Linguistic Research* 2:57–75.

Reuland, E. 1983. Governing *-ing*. *Linguistic Inquiry* 14:101–36.

Riemsdijk, H. van. 1983. The Case of German Adjectives. In *Linguistic Categories: Auxiliaries and Related Puzzles,* ed. F. Heny and B. Richards. Dordrecht: Reidel.

Rizzi, L. 1982. *Issues in Italian Syntax.* Dordrecht: Foris.

Selkirk, E. 1982. *The Syntax of Words.* Cambridge, Mass.: M.I.T. Press.

Wilkins, W. 1986. El sintagma nominal de infinitivo. *Revista Argentina de lingüística* 2:210–29.

Williams, E. 1981. Argument Structure and Morphology. *Linguistic Review* 1:81–114.

———. 1982. Another Argument That Passive is Transformational. *Linguistic Inquiry* 13:160–63.

CHAPTER 4

Notes

I am grateful to Mark Aronoff, Joan Bybee, and two anonymous reviewers for helpful comments on an earlier version of this paper.

1. Cf. Bally (where *déterminé* is equivalent to 'head'): "Signalons enfin que les rapports d'accord et de rection n'existent pas seulement entre les mots, mais se retrouvent à l'intérieur des mots eux-mêmes (composés, . . . préfixaux et suffixaux). . . . Les suffixaux sont en général de rection et le suffixe est le déterminé: *encrier* = «chose pour l'encre», *règlement* = «action de régler», *potier* = «celui qui (fait) des pots»" (1932, 112–13).

2. But see Bauer (1990) for a skeptical assessment.

3. Cf. Vincent (1989) for a similar recent attempt to draw together ideas from Grammaticization Theory and Government-Binding Theory.

4. Except in the sense of gradual diffusion through the speech community, or in the sense that speakers for some time had both representations, *pease* and *pea-s,* and gradually came to prefer using the latter.

5. Bally: "Seuls les suffixaux appréciatifs (diminutifs, péjoratifs, etc.) . . . sont régis par l'accord, et le suffixe est le déterminant: *jardinet* = «petit jardin», *criailler* = «crier désagréablement», *vieillot* = «un peu vieux»" (1932, 113).

6. As an anonymous reviewer reminds me, in some languages (e.g., Ancient Greek and German) diminutive affixes do determine the gender of the resulting noun. This is not a counterexample to Grammaticization Theory (which would have to be a case where a previous syntactic head is grammaticized to an affix but does not retain any headlike properties at all), it just shows that Grammaticization Theory does not predict everything.

7. Di Sciullo and Williams (1987, 25–28) accept Selkirk's criticism and come up with a similar solution that is somewhat different conceptually. As before, only head features can percolate, but words can have several different heads: The head_F of a word is defined as the rightmost element of the word marked for the feature F.

8. She points out that the assumption that inflectional affixes cannot be heads is consistent with the fact that they tend not to be "category-changing." But this statement seems circular, because changing of syntactic category is often used as a criterion for the inflection/derivation distinction. Otherwise it is not too difficult to find counterexamples of category-changing inflections (e.g., participles and nominalizations of various kinds).

9. The claim that compositionality rather than percolation determines the meaning of complex words like the one in [8] does not imply that percolation is not needed at all. Something like percolation seems to play a role in the specification of features with little semantic content like syntactic category, gender, conjugation class, [+Latinate], and so forth. A word cannot be specified twice for gender or syntactic category in the same way as it can be specified twice for tense or voice. It is not clear to me exactly what the basis for this distinction between percolating and composing features is, but it is not the inflection versus derivation distinction, because affixes determining gender and syntactic category can be either inflectional or derivational.

10. A particularly striking example of this bias is the Righthand Head Rule, which is presented as if it were universal in Williams (1981) and Di Sciullo and Williams (1987), although it does not even hold in Italian (Scalise 1984, 96).

11. An example of morphological government can also be found closer to home, in the Romance adverb: *-mente* governs the feminine form of the adjective (e.g., Portuguese *exat-a-mente* 'exactly'). As in the Georgian case, it is not possible to analyze the suffix as *-amente* because of consonantal adjective stems like *mental-mente* 'mentally' and coordination reductions like *temporária ou definitivamente* 'temporarily or definitively'. The suffix *-mente,* of course, arose through the grammaticization of the feminine Latin noun *mente* 'with a . . . mind', used in an NP together with an adjective governed by its head noun.

12. Abbreviations used in morphemic glosses of Abkhaz: abs = absolutive, dyn = dynamic, erg = ergative, fin = finite, obl = oblique.

13. Some linguists seem to show little interest in historical explanations, preferring instead explanations that make reference to innate principles because these tell us something about the nature of the human mind. However, there is no contradiction between historical explanations of the type proposed by Grammaticization Theory and

innate principles. It is very plausible that the fact that human languages change in particular ways but not in others (constrained by theories of language change like Grammaticization Theory) is ultimately due to innate properties of the human mind (see, for example, Claudi and Heine 1986).

14. Gradient syntactic category membership is also assumed in the GB-based syntactic theory of Mayerthaler and Fliedl (forthcoming).

References

Anderson, J. 1980. Towards dependency morphology. In *Studies in Dependency Phonology,* ed. J. Anderson and C. J. Ewan. Ludwigsburg.

Baker, M. 1988. Morphological and Syntactic Objects: A Review of A. M. di Sciullo and E. Williams, On the Definition of Word. In *Yearbook of Morphology,* ed. G. Booij and J. van Marle, pp. 259–83. Dordrecht: Foris.

Bally, C. 1932. *Linguistique générale et linguistique française.* 2d ed. (1944). Berne: A. Francke.

Bauer, L. 1990. Be-heading the Word. *Journal of Linguistics* 26:1–31.

Booij, G., and J. van Marle, eds. 1988. *Yearbook of Morphology.* Dordrecht: Foris.

Bybee, J. L. 1985. *Morphology: The Relation between Meaning and Form.* Amsterdam: Benjamins.

———, W. Pagliuca, and R. D. Perkins. In preparation. *The Grammaticization of Aspect, Tense, and Modality in the Languages of the World.*

Claudi, U., and B. Heine. 1986. On the Metaphorical Base of Grammar. *Studies in Language* 10:297–335.

Dik, S. C. 1978. *Functional Grammar.* Amsterdam: North Holland.

Di Sciullo, A.-M., and Williams, E. 1987. *On the Definition of Word.* Cambridge, Mass.: M.I.T. Press.

Dressler, W. U., W. Mayerthaler, O. Panagl, and W. U. Wurzel. 1987. *Leitmotifs in Natural Morphology.* Amsterdam: Benjamins.

Fleischer, W. 1975. *Wortbildung der deutschen Gegenwartssprache.* 4th rev. ed. Enzyklopädie, Leipzig/Tübingen: Niemeyer.

Heine, B., and M. Reh. 1984. *Grammaticalization and Reanalysis in African Languages.* Hamburg: Helmut Buske.

Heine, B. and E. Traugott, eds. Forthcoming. *Approaches to Grammaticalization.* Amsterdam: Benjamins.

Hewitt, B. G. 1979. *Abkhaz.* Amsterdam: North Holland.

Hoeksema, J. 1988. Head-types in Morpho-syntax. In *Yearbook of Morphology*, ed. G. Booij and J. van Marle, pp. 123–37. Dordrecht: Foris.

Höhle, T. 1982. Über Komposition und Derivation: zur Konstituentenstruktur von Wortbildungsprodukten im Deutschen. *Zeitschrift für Sprachwissenschaft* 1:76–112.

Hudson, R. A. 1987. Zwicky on Heads. *Journal of Linguistics* 23: 109–32.

Jelinek, E. 1984. Empty Categories, Case, and Configurationality. *Natural Language and Linguistic Theory* 2:39–76.

Kahr, J. C. 1976. The Renewal of Case Morphology: Sources and Constraints. *Working Papers on Language Universals* (Stanford) 20:107–51.

Lehmann, C. 1982. *Thoughts on Grammaticalization: A Programmatic Sketch*. Cologne: Institut für Sprachwissenschaft der Universität zu Köln.

———. 1985a. Grammaticalization: Synchronic Variation and Diachronic Change. *Lingua e stile* 20:308–18.

———. 1985b. On Grammatical Relationality. *Folia linguistica* 19:67–109.

Lüdtke, H. 1980. Auf dem Wege zu einer Theorie des Sprachwandels. In *Kommunikationstheoretische Grundlagen des Sprachwandels*, ed. H. Lüdtke. Berlin: de Gruyter.

Marchand, H. 1969. *The Categories and Types of Present-Day English Word-Formation: A Synchronic-Diachronic Approach*. 2d ed. rev. and enl. Munich: C. H. Beck.

Matthews, P. H. 1972. *Inflectional Morphology*. Cambridge: Cambridge University Press.

Mayerthaler, W. 1981. *Morphologische Natürlichkeit*. Wiesbaden: Athenaion.

———, and G. Fliedl. Forthcoming. Natürlichkeitstheoretische Syntax. In *Syntax: An International Handbook of Contemporary Research*, ed. J. Jacobs, A. von Stechow, W. Sternefeld, and T. Vennemann. Berlin: de Gruyter.

Muysken, P. 1981. Quechua Causatives and Logical Form. In *Proceedings of the GLOW Conference on Markedness*, ed. A. Belleti et al. Pisa: Scuola Normale Superiore.

Nichols, J. 1986. Head-marking and Dependent-marking Grammar. *Language* 62:56–119.

Plank, F. 1981. *Morphologische (Ir-)regularitäten: Aspekte der Wortstrukturtheorie*. Tübingen: Gunter Narr.

Scalise, S. 1984. *Generative Morphology*. Dordrecht: Foris.

———. 1988. The Notion of 'Head' in Morphology. In *Yearbook of Morphology*, ed. G. Booij and J. van Marle, pp. 229–45. Dordrecht: Foris.

Selkirk, E. O. 1982. *The Syntax of Words*. Cambridge, Mass.: M.I.T. Press.

Svorou, S. 1988. *The Experiential Basis of the Grammar of Space: Evidence from the Languages of the World*. Ph.D. diss., State University of New York, Buffalo. (Revised version to appear in *Typological Studies in Language*. Amsterdam: Benjamins.)

Toman, J. 1983. *Wortsyntax: Eine Diskussion ausgewählter Probleme deutscher Wortbildung*. Tübingen: Niemeyer.

Vincent, N. 1989. Constituentization. Paper presented at the 9th International Conference on Historical Linguistics, Rutgers University, August 1989.

Vogt, H. 1971. *Grammaire de la langue géorgienne*. Oslo: Universitetsforlaget.

Walinska de Hackbeil, H. 1985. *en*-Prefixation and the Syntactic Domain of Zero Derivation. *Berkeley Linguistics Society* 11:337–57.

Williams, E. 1981. On the Notions 'Lexically Related' and 'Head of a Word'." *Linguistic Inquiry* 12:245–74.

Wunderlich, D. 1986. Probleme der Wortstruktur. *Zeitschrift für Sprachwissenschaft* 5:209–52.

Zwicky, A. M. 1985. Heads. *Journal of Linguistics* 21:1–30.

CHAPTER 5

Notes

I thank Mark Aronoff, Renate Raffelsiefen, and the anonymous reviewers for their useful comments and the University of Pennsylvania and the Netherlands Organization for Scientific Research (NWO) for making it possible for me to spend a sabbatical year at the University of Groningen, during which this paper was written.

1. A number of important issues have been left out of the discussion, including the (non)inheritance of predicative phrases. See Hoekstra (1986) for discussion.

2. The term *subject name* refers to the fact that *-er* derivations are used to characterize individuals or objects which play the role of subjects of the base verbs. Thus, a killer is someone who kills, not someone who gets killed. Likewise, a painkiller is something that (metaphorically) kills pain, not something killed by pain.

3. And they vary somewhat from language to language. Dutch, for example, seems to have many more *-er* nominalizations that refer to events than English. Typical examples are *tegenvaller* 'disappointer = disappointing event, disappointment' and *uitglijder* 'out-glider = slip, error'. See Booij (1986) for more examples.

4. One might expect that lexical word order properties could also be inherited in this way. To test this prediction of the system, it would be necessary to look at a language where some verbs idiosyncratically permit their arguments to occur on a different side than the other verbs. If, furthermore, the direction in which nouns take their arguments is the same as the standard direction for verbs, nominalizations of the exceptional verbs might be expected to take their arguments on the "wrong" side. I am not aware of any evidence that might shed some light on this matter.

5. Puzzling are cases where the nominalization does not seem to correspond directly to the base verb, but rather to some associated passive form (Wasow 1977). Some cases in point are *disgust* and *acquaintance:*

> Janet's acquaintance with statistics (cf. Janet is acquainted with statistics)
> *Janet's acquaintance of Jim with statistics (cf. Janet acquainted Jim with statistics)

and similarly:

> John's disgust at/with the game (cf. John is disgusted at/with the game)
> *John's disgust of us (cf. John disgusted us)

6. *-aar* is a phonologically conditioned allomorph of *-er*.

7. Note, however, *waiter* from *wait on*.

8. In Hoeksema (1985), the category assignment

-er: $\frac{\frac{S}{NP}}{\$} \backslash \frac{N}{\$}$

is proposed, which has the advantage of generalizing to the cases with PP inheritance, since it specified that *-er* maps verbs into nouns that have all the arguments of the underlying verb, except for the subject argument. This more general category, however, needs to be supplemented with information about the domains where the rule is productive, semiproductive, and nonproductive.

9. These examples were provided by Renate Raffelsiefen.

10. Another problem appears to be posed by the existence of languages with relational nouns that have an obligatory possessor (e.g., Vai).

11. Except in sentences such as [i], pointed out to me by Mark Aronoff:

[i] he did not think to leave a message

However, its use in sentences like [ii] is ruled out, whereas the Dutch translation of [ii] in [iii] is fine.

[ii] *he thinks to be sick
[iii] hij denkt ziek te zijn
he thinks sick to be
'he thinks he's sick'

12. This example was taken from Jespersen (1940, 71).

13. Zucchi (1989) cites a paper by Edwin Williams, which I have not seen, entitled "English as an Ergative Language: The Theta Structure of Derived Nouns," in which nominalizations are treated as ergative systems, with *of*-marking for subjects of intransitives and objects of transitives. Such an account only partly fits the data, though, given the possibility of nominalizations with *by* phrases but without overt *of* phrases. This possibility, denied by Zucchi, for instance, was noted in Hoeksema (1985) for cases such as the following in Dutch:

bescherming door de politie
'protection by the police'

vernielingen door voetbalsupporters
'destructions by soccer supporters'

and much earlier in Jespersen (1940, 79–80) for English:

a translation by Hobbes
discovery by the police
for use by the Soviet government

As observed in Hoeksema (1985), the case assignment rules given there, in conjunction with the argument reduction rule, predict that in such cases *by* (*door*) phrases are in direct competition with *of* (*van*) phrases, and indeed, the following examples are also possible with the same subject interpretations for the PP (as well as an object interpretation).

bescherming van de politie
'protection of the police'

vernielingen van voetbalsupporters
'destructions of soccer supporters'

As is common in situations where two constructions are in direct competition, there is often a preference for one over the other, and usually, it seems to me, the *of* phrase is preferred over the *by* phrase for the expression of the subject argument of a transitive nominalization in case the object argument is nonovert. However, it is not correct to state that *by* phrases are always ruled out in such situations.

14. The *by* phrase in this example is not inherited from the verbal base, but is likewise predicted to be impossible, since the agent role is subordinated to the (suppressed) theme role.

15. Note that *attempt* only takes *on* when the meaning entails harmful intentions, as with the other examples. In its more common use, it take *at,* as in *another attempt at the world record.*

16. The observations are attributed to G. Helbig.

References

Ades, Anthony, and Mark Steedman. 1982. On the Order of Words. *Linguistics and Philosophy* 4:517–58.

Amritavalli, R. 1980. Expressing Cross-categorial Selectional Correspondences: An Alternative to the X'-syntax Approach. *Linguistic Analysis* 6:305–43.

Anderson, Mona. 1979. *Noun Phrase Structure*. Ph.D. diss., University of Connecticut.

Booij, Geert. 1986. Form and Meaning in Morphology: The Case of Dutch 'Agent Nouns', *Linguistics* 24:503–17.

———. 1988. The Relation between Inheritance and Argument Linking: Deverbal Nouns in Dutch. In *Morphology and Modularity,* ed. M. Everaert, A. Evers, R. Huybregts, and M. Trommelen, pp. 57–73. Dordrecht: Foris.

———, and Ton van Haaften. 1988. The External Syntax of Derived Words: Evidence from Dutch. *Yearbook of Morphology* 1:29–44.

Bresnan, Joan. 1982. The Passive in Lexical Theory. In *The Mental Representation of Grammatical Relations,* ed. J. Bresnan, pp. 3–86. Cambridge, Mass.: M.I.T. Press.

Di Sciullo, Anna-Maria, and Edwin Williams. 1988. *On the Definition of Word.* Cambridge, Mass.: M.I.T. Press.

Dowty, David. 1982. Grammatical Relations and Montague Grammar. In *The Nature of Syntactic Representation,* ed. P. Jacobson and G. K. Pullum, pp. 79–130. Dordrecht: Reidel.

———. 1988. On the Semantic Content of the Notion of 'Thematic Role'. In *Properties, Types and Meaning,* ed. G. Chierchia, B. H. Partee, and R. Turner, Vol. 2, *Semantic Issues,* pp. 69–129. Dordrecht: Kluwer Academic Press.

Droop, Helmut Günter. 1977. *Das präpositionale Attribut.* Tübingen: Narr.

Fanselow, Gisbert. 1988. 'Word Syntax' and Semantic Principles. *Yearbook of Morphology* 1:95–122.

Fillmore, Charles. 1977. The Case for Case Reopened. In *Syntax and Semantics 8: Grammatical Relations,* ed. P. Cole and J. Sadock, pp. 59–82. New York: Academic Press.

Flynn, Michael. 1983. A Categorial Theory of Structure Building. In *Order, Concord, and Constituency,* ed. G. Gazdar, E. Klein, and G. Pullum, pp. 139–74. Dordrecht: Foris.

Grimm, Jakob. 1837. *Deutsche Grammatik.* Vol. 4. Göttingen.

Gruber, Jeffrey. 1965. *Studies in Lexical Relations.* Ph.D. diss., M.I.T.

Hoeksema, Jack. 1981. Twee theorieën omtrent samenstellende afleidingen. *GLOT* 4½:169–78.

———. 1985. *Categorial Morphology.* New York: Garland Press.

———. 1989. *A Categorial Theory of Reanalysis Phenomena.* Unpublished ms., University of Pennsylvania.

Hoekstra, Teun. 1986. Deverbalization and Inheritance. *Linguistics* 24:549–84.

———, and Frans van der Putten. 1988. Inheritance Phenomena. In *Morphology and Modularity,* ed. M. Everaert, A. Evers, R. Huybregts, and M. Trommelen, pp. 163–86. Dordrecht: Foris.

Jackendoff, Ray. 1983. *Semantics and Cognition.* Cambridge, Mass.: M.I.T. Press.

———. 1987. The Status of Thematic Relations in Linguistic Theory. *Linguistic Inquiry* 18:369–411.

Jespersen, Otto. 1940. *A Modern English Grammar on Historical Principles.* Part 5: *Syntax,* Vol. 4. Copenhagen: Munksgaard.

Kang, Beom-mo. 1988. *Functional Inheritance, Anaphora, and Semantic Interpretation in a Generalized Categorial Grammar.* Ph.D. diss., Brown University.

Lambek, Joachim. 1958. The Mathematics of Sentence Structure. *American Mathematical Monthly* 65:154–69.

Levin, Beth, and Malka Rappaport. 1986. The Formation of Adjectival Passives. *Linguistic Inquiry* 17:623–62.

Lieber, Rochelle. 1983. Argument Linking and Compounds in English. *Linguistic Inquiry* 14:251–86.

Moortgat, Michael. 1985. Function Composition and Complement Inheritance. In *Meaning and the Lexicon,* ed. G. Hoppenbrouwers, P. Seuren, and T. Weyters. Dordrecht: Foris.

———. 1988. *Categorial Investigations: Logical and Linguistic Aspects of the Lambek Calculus.* Ph.D. diss., University of Amsterdam.

Quirk, Randolph, Sidney Greenbaum, Geoffrey Leech, and Jan Svartvik. 1972. *A Grammar of Contemporary English.* London: Longmans.

Randall, Janet. 1982. *Morphological Structure and Language Acquisition.* Ph.D. diss., University of Massachusetts, Amherst.

———. 1988. Inheritance. In *Thematic Relations* ed. W. Wilkins. Vol. 21: *Syntax and Semantics,* pp. 129–46. San Diego: Academic Press.

Rappaport, Malka. 1983. On the Nature of Derived Nominals. In *Papers in Lexical Functional Grammar,* ed. L. Levin, M. Rappaport, and A. Zaenen, pp. 113–42. Bloomington: Indiana University Linguistics Club.

Rozwadowska, Bozena. 1988. Thematic Restrictions on Derived Nominals. In *Thematic Relations,* ed. W. Wilkins. Vol. 21: *Syntax and Semantics,* pp. 147–65. San Diego: Academic Press.

Sassen, Albert. 1980. Kwesties van morfologie. In *Grenzen en domeinen in de grammatica van het Nederlands,* ed. Th. Janssen and N. F. Streekstra, pp. 138–56. Groningen.

Sommerfeldt, Karl-Ernst, and Herbert Schreiber. 1980. *Wörterbuch zur Valenz und Distribution der Substantive.* Leipzig: VEB Bibliographisches Institut.

Stowell, Timothy. 1981. *Origins of Phrase Structure.* Ph.D. diss., M.I.T.

Wasow, Thomas. 1977. Transformations and the Lexicon. In *Formal Syntax,* ed. P. Culicover, T. Wasow, and A. Akmajian. New York: Academic Press.

———. 1980. Major and Minor Rules in Lexical Grammar. In *Lexical Grammar,* ed. T. Hoekstra, H. van der Hulst, and M. Moortgat, pp. 285–312. Dordrecht: Foris.

Williams, Edwin. 1981. Argument Structure and Morphology. *Linguistic Review* 13.1:81–114.

Zaenen, Annie, Joan Maling, and Hoskuldur Thrainsson. 1985. Case and Grammatical Functions: The Icelandic Passive. *Natural Language and Linguistic Theory* 3:441–83.

Zucchi, Alessandro. 1989. The Syntactic and Semantic Status of the *By*-Phrase and the *Of*-Phrase. *NELS* 19:467–84.

CHAPTER 6

Notes

I would like to thank Mark Aronoff, Mike Fortescue, and Sharon Hargus for comments on an earlier draft of this paper.

1. I have found no published Sapir reference to this remarkable term, but it is mentioned in these two Whorf references and in the notes of Newman and Swadesh from the 1932 Primitive Linguistics class at Yale. Sapir apparently coined the term in 1931–32 and was using it in contradistinction to *polysynthesis.*

2. Ahtna forms are cited in the practical orthography with the substitution of *k, k', g::q, q', gg* for the front and back velar series. (The symbols *c, c', g::k, k', gg* are used in the practical orthography.)

3. The distinctions between levels 1 and 2 in this model assume that the them simplest in structure and most general in meaning is at level 1. Alternatively, one might want to have only a bare root at level 1 and have all verb themes formed at level 2. Another possibility is that there is a single recursive level of theme formation and no level 2.

4. In Ahtna some of these suffixation patterns for aspect are rare and/or hyphenated.

5. Fortescue (personal communication, August 1990) has made several observations on this model. He would treat gender as an agreement process and order it later along with inflectional assignment. Other nonasppectual derivations such as benefactive and passive, he would order earlier (say, after level two in figure 1) to place all valence changing derivations before the first aspectual derivation.

6. Especially relevant for comparison is Young and Morgan's (1987, 164–99) presentation of aspects and what they term subaspects. Using my criteria, I treat YM's subaspectual derivations in the following way:

postaspectual derivations: inceptive, seriative, inchoative, prolongative (= errative)

nonaspectual derivations: reversionary, semeliterative

aspectual derivation: terminal (this is simply one specific ads and does not compound with other strings)

not formally distinct: completive, terminative, stative (these are actually suggested glosses for *yi-*, *ni-* and *si-* conjugation prefixes and as such do not have the same status as other strings of affixes)

References

Axelrod, Melissa. 1990. The Organization and Function of Aspect: The Aspectual System of Koyukon Athabaskan. Ph.D. diss., University of Colorado.

Bauer, Laurie. 1988. A Descriptive Gap in Morphology. *Yearbook of Morphology* 1:17–29.

Cook, Eung-Do. 1984. *A Sarcee Grammar.* Vancouver: University of British Columbia Press.

Fortescue, Michael. 1990. Aspect and Superaspect in Koyukon: An Application of the Functional Grammar Model to a Polysynthetic Language. Forthcoming. *Proceedings of the 4th Functional Grammar Conference,* Copenhagen.

Hale, Ken. 1989. The Syntax of Lexical Word Formation. Paper presented at the 4th Pacific Linguistics Conference, University of Oregon.

Hardy, Franklin W. 1979. Navajo Aspectual Verb Stem Variation. Ph.D. diss., University of New Mexico.

Hargus, Sharon. 1986. Phonological Evidence for Prefixation in Navajo Verbal Morphology. *Proceedings of West Coast Conference on Formal Linguistics* 5:53–67.

———. 1988. *The Lexical Phonology of Sekani.* New York: Garland Publishing Co.

Hoijer, Harry. 1945. The Apachean Verb. Part I: Verb Structure and Pronominal Prefixes. *International Journal of American Linguistics* 11:193–203.

———. 1974. *A Navajo Lexicon.* University of California Publications in Linguistics, no. 78.

Jones, Eliza, Melissa Axelrod, and Jules Jetté. Forthcoming. *Koyukon Athabaskan Dictionary*. Fairbanks: Alaska Native Language Center.

Kari, James. 1979. *Athabaskan Verb Theme Categories: Ahtna*. Alaska Native Language Center Research Papers, no. 2.

———. 1989. Affix Positions and Zones in the Athapaskan Verb Complex: Ahtna and Navajo. *International Journal of American Linguistics* 55(4):424–55.

———. 1990. *Ahtna Athabaskan Dictionary*. Fairbanks: Alaska Native Language Center.

Krauss, Michael E. 1973. Na-Dene. *Current Trends in Linguistics* 10:903–78.

———. 1986. Edward Sapir and Athapaskan Linguistics. In *New Perspectives in Language, Culture and Personality*, ed. W. Cowan, M. Foster, and K. Koerner, pp. 147–90.

Leer, Jeff. 1979. *Proto-Athabaskan Verb Stem Variation, Part One: Phonology*. Alaska Native Language Center Research Papers, no. 1.

———. 1989a. Comparison of Noun and Verb Templates. Paper presented at Athabaskan Languages Conference, Tucson.

———. 1989b. Directional Systems in Athapaskan and Na-Dene. In *Athapaskan Linguistics*, ed. E. Cook and K. Rice. Berlin: Mouton de Gruyter.

Randoja, Tiina. 1989. The Phonology and Morphology of Halfway River Beaver. Ph.D. diss., University of Ottawa.

Rice, Keren D. 1985. On the Placement of Inflection. *Linguistic Inquiry* 16:155–61.

———. 1989. *A Grammar of Slave*. Berlin: Mouton de Gruyter.

Sapir, Edward, and Harry Hoijer. 1967. *The Phonology and Morphology of the Navaho Verb*. University of California Publications in Linguistics, no. 50.

Speas, Margaret. 1984. Navajo Prefixes and Word Structure Typology. *M.I.T. Working Papers in Linguistics* 7:86–109.

———. 1986. Adjunctions and Projections in Syntax. Ph.D. diss., M.I.T.

———. 1987. Position Classes and Morphological Universals. In *Native Languages and Grammatical Typology*, ed. P. Kroeber and R. Moore. Bloomington: Indiana University Linguistics Club.

Whorf, Benjamin Lee. 1932. The Structure of the Athabascan Languages. Unpublished ms., Sterling Memorial Library, Yale University, Whorf Coll., 19 pp.

———. 1956. *Language, Thought, and Reality, Selected Writings of Benjamin Lee Whorf*, ed. J. Carroll. Cambridge, Mass.: M.I.T. Press.

Wright, Martha. 1984. The CV Skeleton and Mapping in Navajo Verb Phonology. *Proceedings of NELS* 14:461–77.

———. 1987. Mapping and Movement of Partial Matrices in Navajo. *Proceedings of NELS* 16:27–41.

Young, Robert W., and William Morgan. 1980. *The Navajo Language: A Grammar and Colloquial Dictionary*. Rev. ed., 1987. Albuquerque: University of New Mexico Press.

CHAPTER 7

Notes

Earlier versions of this paper were presented in two talks at the 1989 LSA Summer Institute in Tucson. There I had many stimulating discussions, in particular with Sue Schmerling, Jack Hoeksema, and Michael Moortgat. Also I am indebted to my teacher Mike Brame, who has helped substantially with this paper.

Special thanks to my friends Eric Juvet and Greg Reeves, who spent many hours converting the 1985 edition of the American Heritage Dictionary into a useful data base for statistical analysis.

1. The relevance of Sapir's work as well as the article by Hockett (1954) was brought to my attention by Schmerling (1983).

2. For convenience I will from now on omit square brackets and category labels when stating ordered pairs.

3. The term *Categorial Grammar* subsumes various theories focusing on the question of how language can be a system of reference. Some classic references are Frege (1879), Husserl (1913), and Ajdukiewicz (1935). Montague's work (1974) was very influential and has strongly contributed to the remarkable revival of interest in recent ears. See, for example, Hoeksema (1985), Buszkowski et al. (1988), Oehrle et al. (1988), and references therein. Closely related frameworks include Dependency Grammar and Saumjan's Applicational Grammar (1977).

4. Strictly speaking the function should not be identified with the remaining expression as there are also morphological functions such as umlaut and metathesis that cannot be associated with any "remaining expression." What is meant in general is some sort of abstraction of the phonological operation associated with the function.

5. I will use the category specification A simply for convenience here. Adjectives are also to be categorized in terms of their combinatory properties.

6. It is usually left unmentioned in configurational frameworks that the suffix *-able* attaches to transitive verbs. Maybe this is due to the awkwardness of accounting for this fact in a tree representation.

7. One could also mention arguments related to agreement phenomena. However, given the proliferation of different theories of agreement, it is somewhat difficult to evaluate the significance of the data in question.

8. As a consequence the denotation of an expression such as *friendly* is similar to the denotation of an expression such as *nice*. The intuition behind the meaning-as-reference approach to semantics is reflected in the following quote by Sapir:

> When a word (or unified group of words) contains a derivational element (or word) the concrete significance of the radical element (*farm-*, *duck-*) tends to fade from consciousness and to yield to a new concreteness (*farmer, duckling*) that is synthetic in expression rather than in thought. In our sentence [*The farmer kills the duckling.*] the concepts of *farm* and *duck* are not really involved at all; they are merely latent, for formal reasons, in the linguistic expression.
>
> Returning to this sentence, we feel that the analysis of *farmer* and *duckling* is practically irrelevant to an understanding of its content and entirely irrelevant to a feeling for the structure of the sentence as a whole. From the standpoint of the sentence the derivational elements *-er* and *-ling* are merely details in the local economy of two of its terms (*farmer, duckling*) that it accepts as units of expressions. This indifference of the sentence as such to some part of the analysis of its words is shown by the fact that if we substitute such radical words as *man* or *chick* for *farmer* and *duckling,* we obtain a new material content, it is true, but not in the least a new structural mold [1921, 84–85]

9. Cf. Marchand (1966) and Aronoff (1976).

10. Properly speaking, proper nouns are not nouns. The situation is slightly complicated by the fact that in some German dialects proper nouns do in fact pattern with common nouns and serve as argument for determiners (*Der Hans ist hier.* 'Hans is here.'). A few unlauted alternate forms such as *Hänschen* and *Kläuschen* (from *Klaus* 'masc name') might be due to that fact.

11. I take it that everybody who follows Saussure in regarding a word as an arbitrary but inextricable union of sound and meaning (i.e., a 'sign') shares this concern for compositionality. Let me make two comments:

First, it should be granted that general pragmatic, or commonsense, factors enter into the interpretation of derived forms. Hence *washable* does not simply mean 'can be washed' but rather 'can be washed without damage to texture or color'. Such aspects of meaning need to be filled in on the basis of general knowledge of the world.

Second, even if a word can be productively derived, it is not immune to fossilization. Hence *readable* can mean 'interesting, agreeable and attractive in style' and will be listed. There is a second adjective *readable* with a compositional reading, which will not be listed. The pragmatic factors mentioned above amplify the tendency toward fossilization.

12. Those who suspect that the tenseness of the vowel is the decisive factor distinguishing the cases in [7] from the ones in [8] need to explain the ungrammaticality of the following nouns:

*<precóok, précòok>
*<presóak, présòak>
*<prehéat, préhèat>
*<predáte, prédàte>
*<premíx, prémìx>
*<prepáy, prépày>

13. The expressions *ignore* and *ignorance* are synchronically unrelated.

14. The ungrammaticality of the form *candidity* may also be due to euphony, as there is no noun ending in *-didity*.

15. This has been demonstrated by experimental studies; see Aronoff and Schvaneveldt (1978) and Anshen and Aronoff (1988).

16. An analysis suggesting that *-ability* is a phonological unit was first put forward by Aronoff and Sridhar (1983) and subsequently adopted by Sproat (1985, 466ff.). My analysis differs from theirs in that I claim that *-ability* is also syntactically a unit.

17. My analysis differs from the account given by Anshen and Aronoff, since these authors explain forms such as *compressibility* on a par with analogous formations such as *morphemehood* or *chocoholic* (1988, 648). Although I grant that analogy is a factor in word formation that is to be distinguished from productive processes, the noun *compressibility* is, according to my analysis, to be looked upon as the output resulting from applying the function *-ability* to the verb *compress*.

Also, the line between analogy and productive formations might not always be easy to draw. Why not posit a function *-aholic,* which means 'addicted to' and applies to nouns yielding forms such as *sexaholic, sportsaholic,* and so forth? Is there anything wrong with *pancakeaholic* besides the fact that pancakes generally are not conceived of as being addictive?

18. Interestingly, the phonological restrictions on the function in [24] match the ones applying to the function in [12].

19. This is also confirmed by the studies mentioned in note 15.

20. These formulations make different predictions with respect to cases where brackets still need to be visible within a given level. Since the theory of level ordering does not hold, the difference between these formulations cannot be empirically evaluated.

21. The following eight verbs fulfill only the first, but not the second condition: *interpret, inhibit, exhibit, audit, vomit, transit, contribute, distribute.*

22. Specifying the domain of *-al* is complicated by the fact that there are at least three homophonous functions that need to be distinguished, none of which is fully productive. Apart from the function *-al* under consideration, there is a function *-al* that attaches to adjectives ending in *-ic,* yielding *anarchical, economical.* Another function *-al* attaches to nouns ending in *-ion* (e.g., inspirational).

23. The issue Zimmer addresses here is clearly of vital interest to a generative grammarian but has with a few notable exceptions (e.g., Aronoff 1976; Allen 1978) been ignored in later work on morphology. Some linguists apparently consider it a virtue rather than a shortcoming of their work not to take productivity into consideration:

> In short, productivity is a continuum and belongs to a theory of performance which answers questions about how linguistic knowledge is used, rather than a theory of competence which answers questions about the nature of linguistic knowledge. [Mohanan 1986, 57]

The assumption that the very pervasive correlation between productivity, compositionality, and phonological fossilization is not part of "the nature of linguistic knowledge" is certainly peculiar. This cavalier dismissal of such obviously related phenomena results from a view of grammar as being organized in separate components; on such a view morphologists need not concern themselves with meaning, since this is the semanticist's job. Such an approach certainly does not further our understanding of linguistic phenomena.

24. There are few exceptions to this generalization, such as *unsociable* and *untenable.*

25. Another case where internal structure of morphologically complex words has been referred to is Bruce Hayes's rule of Adjective Extrametricality. For a refutation of this rule see Raffelsiefen (1989).

26. Note that the position of an infix is always defined with regard to prosodic structure. If tree representations are realistic, one would expect infixes to refer to this structure.

References

Ajdukiewicz, K. 1935. Die Syntaktische Konnexität. *Studia philosophica* 1:1–27.

Allen, M. 1978. Morphological Investigations. Ph.D. diss., University of Connecticut.

Anshen, F., and M. Aronoff. 1988. Producing morphologically complex words. *Linguistics* 26:641–55.

Aronoff, M. 1976. *Word Formation in Generative Grammar.* Linguistic Inquiry Momograph no. 1. Cambridge, Mass.: M.I.T. Press.

———, and R. Schvaneveldt. 1978. "Testing morphological productivity," *Annals of the New York Academy of Sciences* 318:106–14.

———, and S. N. Sridhar. 1983. Morphological Levels in English and Kannada, or Atarizing Reagan. In *CLS Papers from the Parasession on the Interplay of Phonology, Morphology and Syntax,* ed. J. F. Richardson et al. Chicago Linguistics Society.

Botha, R. 1981. A Base Rule Theory for Afrikaans Synthetic Compounding. In *The Scope of Lexical Rules,* ed. M. Moortgat, H. van der Hulst, and T. Hoekstra, pp. 1–77. Dordrecht: Foris.

Brame, M. 1986–1989. Lecture notes, University of Washington.

Buszkowski, W. W. Mariczewski, and J. van Benthem. 1988. *Categorial Grammar.* Amsterdam: Benjamins.

Chomsky, N. 1970. Remarks on Nominalization. In *Readings in Transformational Grammar,* ed. R. Jacobs and P. Rosenbaum, pp. 184–221. Waltham, Mass.: Blaisdell.

———, and M. Halle. 1968. *The Sound Pattern of English.* New York: Harper and Row.

———, M. Halle, and F. Lukoff. 1956. On Accent and Juncture in English. In *For Roman Jakobson.* The Hague: Mouton.

Frege, G. 1879. Begriffsschrift. Halle: L. Nebert.

Guerssel, M. 1983. A Lexical Approach to Word Formation in English. *Linguistic Analysis* 12:183–243.

Harris, Z. 1951. *Methods in Structural Linguistics.* Chicago: University of Chicago Press.

Hayes, B. 1980. A Metrical Theory of Stress Rules, Ph.D. diss., M.I.T.

Hockett, C. 1954. Two Models of Grammatical Description. *Word* 10:210–31.

Hoeksema, J. 1985. *Categorial Morphology.* Proefschrift, Rijksuniversiteit te Groningen. Groningen: van Denderen.

Husserl, E. 1913. *Logische Untersuchungen.* 2d ed. Halle: Max Niemeyer.

Kiparsky, P. 1982a. From Cyclic Phonology to Lexical Phonology. In *The Structure of Phonological Representations,* ed. H. van der Hulst and N. Smith, pp. 131–95. Vol. 1. Dordrecht: Foris.

———. 1982b. Lexical Morphology and Phonology. In *Linguistics in the Morning Calm; selected papers from SICOL-1981,* pp. 3–91. The Linguistic Society of Korea. Seoul: Hanshin Publishing Company.

Lapointe, S. 1980. A Theory of Grammatical Agreement. Ph.D. diss., University of Massachusetts.

Lieber, R. 1981. *On the Organization of the Lexicon.* Bloomington: Indiana University Linguistics Club.

Marchand, H. 1966. *The Categories and Types of Present-Day English Word-Formation.* Tuscaloosa: University of Alabama Press.

Mohanan, K. P. 1982. Lexical Phonology. Ph.D. diss., M.I.T. Distributed by Indiana University Linguistics Club, Bloomington.

———. 1986. *The Theory of Lexical Phonology.* Studies in Natural Language and Linguistic Theory. Dordrecht: Reidel.

Montague, R. 1974. *Formal Philosophy: Selected Papers of Richard Montague,* ed. R. H. Thomason. New Haven: Yale University Press.

Muthmann, G. 1988. *Rückläufiges deutsches Wörterbuch.* Tübingen: Niemeyer.

Nida, E. A. 1949. *Morphology: The Descriptive Analysis of Words.* 2d ed. University of Michigan Publications in Linguistics, no. 2 (Ann Arbor).

Oehrle, R., E. Bach, and D. Wheeler, eds. 1988. *Categorial Grammars and Natural Language Structures.* Dordrecht: Reidel.

Pesetsky, D. 1979. *Russian Morphology and Lexical Theory.* Unpublished ms., M.I.T.

———. 1985. Morphology and Logical Form. *Linguistic Inquiry* 16: 193–246.

Raffelsiefen, R. 1989. Refuting 'Adjective Extrametricality'. Unpublished ms. University of Washington, Seattle.

Sapir, E. 1921. *Language: An Introduction to the Study of Speech.* New York: Harcourt, Brace.

Saumjan, S. K. 1977. *Applicational Grammar as a Semantic Theory of Natural Language.* Edinburgh.

Schmerling, S. 1983. Two Theories of Syntactic Categories. *Linguistics and Philosophy* 6:393–421.

Selkirk, E. 1982. *The Syntax of Words.* Linguistic Inquiry Monograph, no. 7. Cambridge, Mass.: M.I.T. Press.

Siegel, D. 1974. Topics in English Morphology. Ph.D. diss., M.I.T.

———. 1978. The Adjacency Condition and the Theory of Morphology. In *Proceedings of the Eighth Annual Meeting of the North Eastern Linguistic Society,* ed. M. J. Stein. University of Massachusetts, Amherst.

Spencer, A. 1988. Bracketing Paradoxes and the English Lexicon. *Language* 64:663–82.

Sproat, R. 1985. *On Deriving the Lexicon.* Ph.D. diss., M.I.T.

Strauss, S. 1982. *Lexicalist Phonology of English and German.* Dordrecht: Foris.

Wellmann, H. 1975. *Deutsche Wortbildung 3: Das Adjektiv.* Düsseldorf: Pädagogischer Verlag Schwann.

Williams, E. 1981. On the Notions 'lexically related' and 'head of a word'. *Linguistic Inquiry* 12:245–74.

Zimmer, K. 1964. Affixal Negation in English and Other Languages: An Investigation of Restricted Productivity. *Word.* Monograph no. 5 (New York).

CHAPTER 8

Notes

I wish to thank Linda Badten, Tim Gologergen, Gordon Irrigoo, Vera Metcalf, Jim Toolie, Mary-Ann Wongittilin, and Nick Wongittilin for providing tape-recorded texts and native-speaker judgments, Mary Alexander, Michael Krauss, Elinor Oozeva, Eva Tungiyan, and Willis Walunga for help with written textual data. I am grateful to the University of Iowa Linguistics Department faculty, and to Shobhana Chelliah for comments on earlier versions of this paper, and to Jerry Sadock and Anthony Woodbury for valuable discussions related to the topic of this paper. De Reuse (1989) is a much abbreviated earlier version of this paper. Financial support for this research was provided by National Science Foundation Grant BNS–841826 to the University of Texas at Austin.

1. The following abbreviations are used in the morpheme analyses:

AB	absolute case	p	plural number
APO	appositional mood	PN	(independent) personal pronoun
d	dual number	PST	Past tense postbase
FUT	future tense postbase	PROG	progressive aspect postbase
IND	indicative mood	RL	relative (i.e., ergative or genitive) case
INP	intransitive participial mood		
INT	interrogative mood	s	singular number
MD	modalis case	TR	transitivizing postbase
N	noun	V	verb
NEG	negative postbase	VFO	volitive of fear mood

Examples of person and number abbreviations, following case and mood:

ABs	singular unpossessed, absolutive
RL(2s-s)	2nd person sg. possessor, sg. possessee, relative
APO(1s)	1st person sg. subject, intrans. appositional

IND-3s>1p 3rd person sg. subject, 1st person pl. object, trans. indicative
= marks an enclitic boundary

2. It can be noted at this point that the postbase *-vig-* in example [2] is actually the same RD affix, which can also be gathered from the fact that *yughaghvig-* has the somewhat unpredictable meaning 'church', rather than the fully predictable meaning '(any) place for prayer'.

3. Sometimes, reinterpretations are made. Example [i], another version of the same line, is problematic in that the person ending *-avnga,* appropriate with subordinate moods and not with the Indicative mood, immediately precedes *-yuke.* A formal interpretation as a VFO ending is thus necessary here, even though it is odd syntactically, since [i] does not occur in a subordinate clause.

[i] kumakighteknaaghyukavnga
kumakigh-te-ke-naagh-yuke-avnga
pick.lice-Ver-have.as.one's.N-eventually.V-VFO-2s>1s
'you think you will have me as your lice picker,' (lit. 'for fear that you might have me as your lice picker') [L. Badten personal communication, 1985]

I assume that, since the IS postbase *-yuke-* is not part of the speaker's competence, she misinterpreted it as a VFO mood marker, and replaced the original indicative mood and person ending *-agh-penga,* by the person ending appropriate for the VFO mood. There are also other versions of the same line where the problem has been solved by keeping the indicative mood and person endings, and not using the forms *-yuke-* or *-na+yuke-* at all, as in [ii], which comes from a St. Lawrence Island version:

[ii] kumakightekaghnaaghaghpenga
kumakigh-te-kagh-naagh-agh-penga
pick.lice-Ver-have.as.one's.N-eventually.V-IND-2s>1s
'you will have me as your lice picker' [Slwooko 1979, 7; fieldnotes, 43–19, 52–10]

This appears to be the only option used in the corresponding lines in Soviet Far East versions of this ungipaghaan [iii], even though the VFO endings are as common there as in the St. Lawrence Island variety.

[iii] a. itemunnaanghitamsi
iteme-ute-naagh+nghite-agh-msi
come.undone-TR-FUT.NEG-IND-1s>2p
'I will not release you' [Menovshchikov 1947, 33–34; Rubtsova 1954, 114]

b. qepghaghteknaaghaghpenga
qepghagh-te-ke-naagh-agh-penga

work-Ver-have.as.one's.N-eventually.V-IND-2s>1s
'you will have me as a worker' [Rubtsova 1954, 115]

Since these Soviet examples come from published texts, the postbase might have been edited out.

4. This amount of polysynthesis is, however, a typically Eskimo phenomenon, and can not be traced back to the Proto-Eskimo-Aleut stage, since Aleut has much less IS than any Eskimo language; Fortescue (1985, 219–20) gives a list of only thirty-nine Common Eskimo-Aleut postbases.

5. In all Eskimo languages, there are a few cases of inflectional endings occurring within the IS postbase system, and these could be considered counterexamples to the postulated tendency that inflectional endings never become postbases. A CSY example is:

[iv] ilutmiightuq
ilu-tmun-ighte-ugh-ø
inside-TM-go.N.ward-IND-3s
'
s/he went inward' [Badten et al. 1987, 76]

The only postbase that can follow the terminalis ending *-tmun* is *-ighte-*, and *-ighte-* can only occur preceded by *-tmun*. This is evidence that the inflectional ending became a lexicalized combination with the postbase, and that the resulting sequence *-tmiighte-* should be interpreted as a single denominal verbalizing postbase, rather than as a productive sequence of an inflectional ending and a postbase. Therefore, such sequences are not evidence that an inflectional ending has become a postbase, but rather that certain postbases can contain lexicalized inflectional material.

References

Angi, Fred, Mary Irrigoo, Lloyd Oovi, John Apangalok, Homer Apatiki, Beda Slwooko, Samuel Irrigoo, and Jimmy Otayahuk. 1975. *Pangeghtellghet: Visits to Siberia*. Fairbanks: Alaska Native Language Center, University of Alaska.

Apassingok, Anders, Willis Walunga, and Edward Tennant. 1985. *Sivuqam nangaghnegha: Siivanllemta Ungipaqellghat* [Lore of St. Lawrence Island: Echos of Our Eskimo Elders]. Vol. 1: Gambell. Unalakleet, Alaska: Bering Strait School District.

Aronoff, M. 1976. *Word Formation in Generative Grammar*. Cambridge, Mass.: M.I.T. Press.

Badten, Linda W., Vera Kaneshiro, Marie Oovi, and Steven A. Jacobson. 1987. *A Dictionary of the St. Lawrence Island/Siberian Yupik Eskimo Language*. 2d preliminary version. Fairbanks: Alaska Native Language Center, University of Alaska.

Chomsky, N. A. 1970. Remarks on Nominalization. In *Readings in English Transformational Grammar,* ed. R. A. Jacobs and P. S. Rosenbaum. Waltham, Mass.: Ginn.

Fabb, N. A. J. 1984. *Syntactic Affixation.* Ph.D. diss., M.I.T.

Fortescue, M. D. 1980. Affix Ordering in West Greenlandic Derivational Processes. *International Journal of American Linguistics* 46:259–78.

———. 1983. A Comparative Manual of Affixes for the Inuit Dialects of Greenland, Canada, and Alaska. *Meddelelser om Grønland, Man and Society* 4.

———. 1985. The Degree of Interrelatedness between Dialects as Reflected by Percentages of Shared Affixes. *International Journal of American Linguistics* 51:188–221.

Jacobson, S. A. 1983. *A Dictionary of the St. Lawrence Island (or Siberian) Yupik Eskimo Language.* Preliminary version. Fairbanks: Alaska Native Language Center, University of Alaska.

———. 1984. *Yup'ik Eskimo Dictionary.* Fairbanks: Alaska Native Language Center, University of Alaska.

Leer, J. 1985. Prosody in Alutiiq. In *Yupik Eskimo Prosodic Systems: Descriptive and Comparative Studies,* ed. M. E. Krauss. Alaska Native Language Center Research Papers no. 7. Fairbanks: Alaska Native Langage Center, University of Alaska.

Menovshchikov, G. A. 1947. *Nashi Skazki: Ungipaghaateput.* Leningrad: Gosudarstvennoye uchebno-pedagogicheskoye izdatel'stvo ministerstva prosveshcheniia RSFSR.

———. 1986. Ėskimossko-chukotskiiĭ bilingvizm i interferentsiia chukotskoĭ periferiĭnoĭ leksiki v Ėskimosskiĭ iazyk. In *Paleoaziatskie iazyki,* ed. P. la. Skorik. Leningrad: Izdatel'stvo Nauka.

Muysken, P. 1986. Approaches to Affix Order. *Linguistics* 24:629–43.

de Reuse, W. J. 1988. *Studies in Siberian Yupik Eskimo Morphology and Syntax,* Ph.D. diss., University of Texas, Austin.

———. 1989. Morphological Change and Internal Syntax in Eskimo. *Proceedings of the Chicago Linguistic Society* 25.

Rookok, R. n.d. Panekellemaa. In *Ayumiim Ungipaghaatangi V* [Stories of Long Ago V]. Unpublished ms., Alaska Native Language Center, University of Alaska, Fairbanks.

Rubtsova, Ė. S. 1954. *Materialy po iazyku i fol'kloru Ėskimosov* (*Chaplinskiĭ dialekt*). Vol. 1. Moscow: Izdatel'stvo Akademii Nauk SSSR.

Sadock, J. M. 1980. Noun Incorporation in Greenlandic: A Case of Syntactic Word Formation. *Language* 56:300–319.

———. 1985. Autolexical Syntax: A Proposal for the Treatment of noun Incorporation and Similar Phenomena. *Natural Language and Linguistic Theory* 3:379–439.

Sapir, E., and M. Swadesh. 1939. *Nootka Texts, Tales and Ethnographical Narratives, with Grammatical Notes and Lexical Materials*. Philadelphia: Linguistic Society of America.

Seppilu, M. 1985. Ungipaghaan entitled *Yuuggaaqa,* recorded for the Eskimo Heritage Program, in Savoonga. Ms. no. SV/HP-85-36-T1 in the Eskimo Heritage Program files, Bering Strait Native Corporation, Nome, Alaska.

Slwooko, G. 1979. *Sivuqam Ungipaghaatangi II* [St. Lawrence Island Legends II]. National Bilingual Materials Development Center, Rural Education Affairs, University of Alaska, Anchorage.

Smith, L. R. 1978. Some Properties of Labrador Inuttut Verbal derivation. *Etudes Inuit/Inuit Studies* 2:37–48.

Swadesh, M. 1939. Nootka Internal Syntax. *International Journal of American Linguistics* 9:77–102.

———. 1946. South Greenlandic (Eskimo). In *Linguistic Structures of Native America,* ed. H. Hoijer et al. Viking Fund Publications in Anthropology no. 6, New York.

Vdovin, I. S. 1961. Ėskimosskie ėlementy v kul'ture Chukcheĭ i Koriakov. In *Sibirskiĭ ėtnograficheskiĭ sbornik III. Trudy Instituta ėtnografii im. N. N. Miklukho-Maklaia* 64. Moscow: Izdatel'stvo Akademii Nauk SSSR.

INDEX

B

C

D

E

J

K

L

Q

R

S

T

U

V